HELPING THE BATTERED CHILD
AND HIS FAMILY

HELPING THE BATTERED CHILD AND HIS FAMILY

Edited by

C. HENRY KEMPE, M.D.
Professor and Chairman,
Department of Pediatrics,
University of Colorado Medical Center, Denver

AND

RAY E. HELFER, M.D.
Associate Professor, Department of Human Development,
College of Human Medicine,
Michigan State University, East Lansing

J. B. LIPPINCOTT COMPANY
Philadelphia and Toronto

Library of Congress Catalog Card No. 74-168861

Clothbound ISBN–0–397–59052–0

Paperbound ISBN–0–397–59054–7

PRINTED IN THE UNITED STATES OF AMERICA
SP-B

TO OUR WIVES AND CHILDREN

Contributors

HELEN ALEXANDER, M.S.W.
Social Worker, University of Colorado Medical Center, Denver

ROGER ALLOTT, LL.B.
*Executive Director, Colorado District Attorneys' Association,
Denver*

VINCENT DE FRANCIS, J.D.
*Director, Children's Division, The American Humane
Association, Denver*

THE HONORABLE JAMES DELANEY
*Juvenile Judge, 17th Judicial District Court, Brighton,
Colorado*

HARRIET DELNERO, M.S.W.
*Social Worker, Children's Memorial Hospital, Chicago,
Illinois*

KAY DREWS
*Former Child Abuse Coordinator, University of Colorado
Medical Center, Denver*

STANFORD B. FRIEDMAN, M.D.
*Associate Professor, Department of Psychiatry and Pediatrics,
University of Rochester School of Medicine, New York*

RAY E. HELFER, M.D.
*Associate Professor, Department of Human Development,
College of Human Medicine,
Michigan State University, East Lansing*

JOAN HOPKINS, R.N.
Child Abuse Coordinator,
University of Colorado Medical Center, Denver

JACOB ISAACS, LL.B.
Attorney-At-Law, New York City

C. HENRY KEMPE, M.D.
Professor and Chairman, Department of Pediatrics,
University of Colorado Medical Center, Denver

KAY MCDONALD, LL.B.
Attorney-At-Law, New York City

HAROLD MARTIN, M.D.
Assistant Professor, Department of Pediatrics,
University of Colorado Medical Center, Denver

BOYD OVIATT, D.S.W.
Professor, Graduate School of Social Work,
The University of Utah, Salt Lake City

RUDOLPH A. PITCHER, JR.
Major, U.S. Army, Military Police Corps

THE HONORABLE JUSTINE POLIER
Family Court, New York City

CARL POLLOCK, M.D.
Assistant Professor, Department of Psychiatry,
University of Colorado Medical Center, Denver

CAROL SCHNEIDER, PH.D.
Consultant Psychologist, University of Colorado, Boulder

BRANDT STEELE, M.D.
Professor, Department of Psychiatry, University of Colorado
Medical Center, Denver

Introduction

ONE HUNDRED YEARS ago Mary Ellen, a little girl, was unchained from her bed and provided safety, away from her home and adoptive parents.[1] Her rescue came only after the intense and persistent efforts of an incensed group of church workers who pressed the Society for the Protection of Cruelty to *Animals* into action on Mary Ellen's behalf. Thus began the Society for the Protection of Cruelty to *Children*, in New York City in 1875. The relentless efforts of the SPCC and other committed individuals resulted in the gradual recognition of the rights of children.[2]

Although the gains were significant they seemed to have reached a plateau some 90 years later when another group of incensed individuals embarked on a rather intensive study of physical abuse to small children at the hands of the very persons responsible for their care and safety. This study resulted in an understanding of some of the problems relating to child abuse and the psychodynamics of the abusive parents. This work, together with valuable contributions of other workers in the field of child abuse, was summarized in the publication, *The Battered Child* (University of Chicago Press, 1968).

The Battered Child presented most of the theoretical and empirical studies of child abuse available in 1968. The medical, social, pathological, psychiatric and legal contributions began to bring into perspective the multidisciplinary aspects of this serious problem.

This publication left the editors with a certain feeling of frustration since many more gains had to be made if we were to make this knowledge both practical and feasible for the day-to-day care of the battered child and his family. The transition from a research study to a service oriented program was difficult, especially for the pediatricians and social workers who were continually confronted with the ongoing problems of caring for these families. It became unquestionably clear that, if the work of the last few years was to be utilized and effective, an efficient therapeutic program had to be developed which was not dependent upon long-term psychiatric treatment for the parents.

PURPOSE OF THE BOOK

Helping the Battered Child and His Family has three primary objectives:

1. To suggest a child abuse treatment program which, if implemented, should prove helpful in either the large or small community.

2. To demonstrate that many people of a variety of backgrounds and experiences can be helpful both to the abused child and his family.

3. To provide these individuals with a practical "how-to" and "what-to-do" approach to the many problems that arise when one attempts to provide this help.

The many suggestions made by the contributors are not intended to be all-inclusive. There is certainly no *single* therapeutic approach that will be effective in all cases of child abuse. We would, however, hope that new workers in this field will be able to start by building on the experiences of others and by avoiding some of the mistakes which we have made.

DEFINING THE "BATTERED CHILD"

The use of the term "the battered child" has had both advantages and disadvantages. Its origin came at a seminar sponsored by the American Academy of Pediatrics in 1961. Knowing that pediatricians had for years been complacent about the problem of child abuse, it was felt that something had to be done to gain their attention and increase their desire to do something about the problem.[8] The term "battered child" was adopted to make an impact upon pediatricians and to shake society loose from its complacent attitude. The fact that this objective has been partially achieved is documented by the existence of reporting laws in all 50 states and the increasing general understanding of the problems of child abuse. The phrase caught on and proved to be effective.

While the positive aspects are apparent, certain disadvantages stemming from the use of the term "the battered child" must be fully recognized. For some, this term means only the child who has been the victim of the most severe form of physical punishment, i.e., that child who represents the far end of a child abuse spectrum. For others, the term implies the total spectrum of abuse, beginning with the parents (or future parents) who have the potential to abuse their small children and ending with the severely beaten or killed child. This lack of clarity has led to moderate confusion, both in the literature and in the minds of those wishing to help these children and their families.

Our view of "the battered child" is one that encompasses the total spectrum of abuse. As will be brought out in the section on "prediction" (Appendix A), this spectrum has now extended beyond the early and mild case of physical abuse to the point of early recognition of those parents who have the potential to abuse their small children. The confusion and lack of definition have limited communication between those working in the field and often are the primary sources of misunderstanding among those who wish to define the problem more clearly.[8]

Our definition of the battered child is:

Any child who received nonaccidental physical injury (or injuries) as a result of acts (or omissions) on the part of his parents or guardians.

This brings us to the obvious consideration of whether or not the term "the battered child" should be abandoned. Has the impact been of sufficient degree to warrant a more clearly understood and all-inclusive term, which will move us more completely into physical abuse and neglect? The editors seriously considered dropping the phrase from the title of this book, thereby broadening the scope of the book. We decided that this would be premature for two specific reasons. First, our total understanding of the problems of abnormal rearing is still inadequate and, second, the need to provide a continuous impact on the problems of physical abuse to small children remains. This latter point is brought home more intensely by consideration of the fact that state legislatures, even though they have passed reporting laws, have rarely provided any significant increase in funds to implement these laws or to develop programs to assist these children and their families.

LIMITED GOALS OF THERAPY

Most workers in this field recognize that a small number (less than 10 percent) of seriously abused children have parents who are seriously mentally ill, i.e., psychotics or aggressive psychopaths. These parents must be recognized early in the treatment program and have need of a much more intensive psychiatric approach than will be described by the contributors to this book.

On the other hand, the large majority of abusive families present with problems that will respond to the approaches described herein. A reasonable goal of therapy could be stated as follows:

That at least 75 percent of the children reported as a result of state reporting laws to have been nonaccidentally injured by their parents or guardians should be residing safely in their homes within one year after the report of abuse has been made.

With this as a stated goal of therapy one immediately recognizes the need to involve many different types of people to help these children and their families. Certainly large numbers of the children will be able to return to their parents in considerably less time than one year. On the other hand, it may, on occasion, take several months to establish a meaningful therapeutic relationship with some parents. During this initial period temporary removal of the child from his home is often indicated. If the home cannot be made safe (i.e., to maintain the child free from repeated physical injury) during this year of intensive effort, a therapeutic failure must be admitted and, in all fairness to the child and his parents, parental rights may have to be severed.

The separation of child and parents should *not* be considered an end in itself, although this is ofttimes necessary in the early phases of the therapeutic program. We would agree with those who maintain that the protection of the child is of primary importance and certainly takes precedence. The editors, however, would hasten to add that the establishment of a positive therapeutic relationship with the therapist is often *the* most important step in protecting the child.

COMMENTS ON INCIDENCE

Although the true incidence of child abuse will likely never be known, a realistic assessment can now be made from the current reporting rates in the cities of Denver and New York. They now range between 250 to 300 cases reported per million population per year. Both of these cities have achieved this level of reporting after a rather intensive effort, an effort which has been focused in completely different directions, however. Denver used a method of community education, which consisted of ongoing consultations with community members, documentaries in the mass media, and providing services to families and professional workers within the city. New York, on the other hand, experienced a sudden surge of increased numbers of reports (700 to 800 cases reported in 1968, as compared with 1,700 cases reported in 1969 and over 2,700 in 1970), after a rather sensational series of articles in one of the daily newspapers (see Chapter 14). Even though both cities have almost identical reporting rates, the former method resulted in a community that was prepared to provide the services to these children and their families, and the latter in a community unprepared for the tremendous increase in the demands for service (see Chapters 9 and 14).

THE ABUSIVE PATTERN

In order for a child to be physically injured by his parents or guardian several pieces of a complex puzzle must come together in a very special way. To date, we can identify at least three major criteria.

First, a parent (or parents) must have the *potential to abuse*. This potential is acquired over the years and is made up of at least four factors:

1. The way the parents themselves were reared, i.e., did they receive the "mothering imprint?"

2. Have they become very isolated individuals who cannot trust or use others?

3. Do they have a spouse that is so passive he or she cannot *give*?

4. Do they have very unrealistic expectations from their child (or children)?

Second, there must be a *child*. As obvious as that might sound we point it out because this is not just *any* child, but a very special child. One who is seen differently by his parents; one who fails to respond in the expected manner; or possibly one who really is different (retarded, too smart, hyperactive, or has a birth defect). Most families, in which there are several children, can readily point out which child would have "gotten it" if the parents had the potential to abuse. Often the perfectly normal child is "seen" as bad, willful, stubborn, demanding, spoiled or slow.

Finally, there must be some form of *crisis*, or a series of crises, that sets the abusive act into motion. These can be minor or major crises—a washing machine breaking down, a lost job, a husband being drafted, no heat, no food, a mother-in-law's visit and the like. It would seem most unlikely for the crisis to be *the* cause for the abuse, as some would like to believe[3]; rather it is the precipitating factor. The simplistic lay view that child abuse is caused by parents who "don't know their strength" while disciplining their child has been shown to be false.

It is this combination of events that, when they occur in the right order and at the right point in time, lead to physical abuse.

DEGREES OF INVOLVEMENT

The "involvement" continuum diagrammed below is based on a 5 point degree-of-involvement scale. These points are very arbitrary and they are not necessarily equal. The "0" level of involvement is defined as no involvement at all. The child is at home and abuse continues. The 1+ level of involvement provides little meaningful intervention: The child is at home and the social worker, probation officer or nurse visits on occasion and essentially says to the parent, "Be a good mother and I'll see you next month."

The 2+ level of involvement is little more as far as the parents are concerned but does provide a rather significant degree of protection for the child. This level assumes that the child is separated from the family on a voluntary basis or by the court. No other meaningful therapeutic intervention is made and the hopes of having the child returned and *remain safe* upon his return are minimal. Separation fails to solve the basic problem and should not be considered as an end in itself unless there truly is no other "solution."

The 3+ level of involvement is based on the belief that the home can be made safe (in the large majority of instances) by the *early* initiation of a practical and feasible community-hospital based treatment program. *This book is based upon this premise.*

The 4+ level of involvement is probably an unrealistic general goal. Not only is the home made safe and the child returned, but the psychiatric problems of the parents are largely resolved. Although this is not impossible it is an impractical goal in most situations. There are certainly not enough psychiatrists available to undertake the overwhelming task of establishing a meaningful one-to-one therapeutic relationship with parents who abuse their small children.

The Degree of Involvement Continuum

0	1+	2+	3+	4+
No involvement; child home.	Little meaningful intervention; child home.	Child and parents separated.	Home made safe; child home.	Psychiatric problem resolved; home safe; child home.

The worker in the hospital or social agency is often caught up in the trap of not knowing if a particular child has been physically abused, i.e., does the child meet the criteria for "battering?" All too often, children and their families find themselves without *any* meaningful treatment program because of the disagreement over whether or not abuse has occurred. The definitive diagnostic study usually is not available, and confessions rarely occur. Our recommendation in this situation is to get off the "did-it-occur" or "who-done-it" kick, and get on with helping the child and his troubled family. The implementation of a meaningful therapeutic program must often occur well before any firm determination of child abuse has been made. We are rapidly moving toward the point when, by early recognition of the potential to abuse small children, a treatment program can begin even before the child is born— and possibly even before the child is conceived.

Helping the Battered Child and His Family consists of a series of essays written by experienced professionals. Individual style and point of view have been left largely undisturbed by the editors. Where duplications exist they either illustrate two different valid points of view or are included for emphasis. The book is divided in four separate but interrelated parts. Part One discusses the parents and their desire and need for help. Several therapeutic approaches are presented which we feel have either been effective or shown considerable promise. Part Two brings us closer to the world of the battered child (which unfortunately is still quite obscure in all of our minds). Where the help can best be given is discussed in Part Three. Neither the community nor the hospital can handle these multiple problems without the help of the other. The courts and the law can take on a very positive role if we are willing to make and accept certain changes in our current thinking and practices. Part Four deals with this concept in some detail.

The editors hope that this book will be the transition point between *The Battered Child* and some future treatise which will consider a more complete study of abnormal child rearing, including physical injury, child neglect, failure to thrive and emotional abuse. We are not as yet at that point, but have moved much closer to it during the last decade.

R. E. H.
C. H. K.

REFERENCES

1. Allen, A., and Morton, A.: This Is Your Child: The Story of the National Society for the Prevention of Cruelty to Children. London (Eng.), Routledge and Keegan Paul, Ltd., 1967, p. 16.

2. Radbill, S. X.: A history of child abuse and infanticide, *in* Helfer, R. E., and Kempe, C. H., eds.: The Battered Child, chap. 1, Chicago, Univ of Chicago Press, 1968.

3. Gil, D.: Violence Against Children, Physical Child Abuse in the United States, Cambridge (Mass.), Harvard Univ Press, 1970.

Contents

Part One

THE PARENTS: *THEIR NEED AND DESIRE FOR HELP*

Part Two

THE CHILD: *HIS NEED FOR HELP*

Part Three

THE SETTING: *WHERE CAN HELP BEST BE GIVEN?*

Part Four

THE COURT AND THE LAW: *A POSITIVE ROLE*

Appendices

Part One

THE PARENTS

Their Need and Desire for Help

EDITORIAL NOTE

For many, seeing the parents of an abused child as people in need of help is not too difficult; seeing them *wanting* this help does, at times, tax the imagination. Many of us fail to spend the required time with these desperate people to fully appreciate their basic desire for help. Understanding the parents, their needs and desires, is an essential part of any therapeutic endeavor. The reader is encouraged to review the writings of Steele, Pollock and Davoren, in Chapters 6 and 8 of *The Battered Child* (see Introduction), for further insight into the approaches described in this section.

1

A Therapeutic Approach
to the Parents

CARL POLLOCK, M.D. and BRANDT STEELE, M.D.

FAMILIES IN WHICH a child has been abused or there is potential for such behavior require particular kinds of support and help if the goal of preservation of the family is to be reached. People from several disciplines become involved in the care of these families and all can be of great use. Social workers and case aides, functioning within departments of child welfare or protective services, constitute a major reservoir of help, especially for long-term contact. Their counterparts in hospitals and clinics may often be involved for shorter but critical periods when problems of abuse are first discovered. Public health nurses bring a variety of skills to aid these families and, in some situations, constitute the main therapeutic contact. Inevitably, because of the nature of the problem, pediatricians, psychiatrists and other hospital physicians play important roles. Sensitive, devoted persons without specific professional training can be extremely valuable, adjunctive "lay therapists." Often, representatives of two or more agencies or disciplines combine their skills in a process of cooperative care of members of a family in which abuse has occurred.

Determining whether a child has been abused, and the handling of the case, are difficult problems. Many workers feel that these families present almost unsurmountable difficulties because of poor motivation, evasion, denial of problems and breaking of contacts. However, what appears to be a baffling or even hopeless situation may often develop into a rewarding experience through the use of principles derived from knowledge of the dynamics leading to physical abuse of small children.

A SUMMARY OF THE PSYCHODYNAMICS OF CHILD ABUSE

Parents who physically abuse their babies and children come from all walks of life and all socioeconomic levels. There is no specific psychiatric diagnosis which encompasses the personalities and behavior of all of them. They share, however, a common pattern of parent-child relationships or style of child rearing characterized by a high demand for the child to perform so as to gratify the parents, and by the use of severe physical punishment to ensure the child's proper behavior. Abusive parents also show an unusually high vulnerability to criticism, disinterest or abandonment by the spouse or other important person, or to anything that lowers their already inadequate self-esteem. Such events create a crisis of unmet needs in the parent, who then turns to the child with exaggerated demands for gratification. The child is often unable to meet such parental expectation and is punished excessively.

Both this pattern of a demanding, aggressive behavior toward the child, and the crises of emotional deprivation which trigger the pattern of abuse, stem directly from the parents' own childhood experience and learning. Abusive parents were raised in a similar system, i.e., were expected to perform well, to gratify parental needs very early in life, and then were criticized, punished and often abused for failure to do so. They felt their own needs were neither met nor adequately considered; rather, they had to orient toward parental expectation and develop an almost intuitive understanding of what would satisfy the parents and prevent severe punishment. (It should be emphasized that while these factors are not abnormal or unusual in themselves, the degree to which they are expressed is distinctly excessive.)

These childhood experiences are profound and provide lasting imprints which are revealed in the way the adults feel about themselves and their children. Abusive parents have no basic, firm cushion of self-esteem or awareness of being loved and valuable to carry them through periods of stress. Instead, they are in constant need of reassurance. They are inwardly shattered by anything that indicates poor performance resulting in disapproval from their spouse, relatives, employer, or any other person significant in their lives. In such a crisis of insecurity, they repeat what they learned in childhood about how parents behave and they turn to their own infant or child for the nurturing and reassurance they so sorely need to restore this sense of self-esteem.

EVALUATION OF THE FAMILY
(Early Management)

From this brief description of the dynamics of the abusive parent, it is easy to see that there will be problems which make evaluation difficult. Parents will be reluctant to talk about their lives to those authoritative figures who will be checking up on their performance and seeing their failures. All workers are likely to be seen as such critical authorities. True, conscientious offers of help may mean little or nothing to these parents. Early life experiences led them to believe that the people looked to for help are the very ones who criticize and hit.

PATTERNS OF RESPONSE

Lifelong patterns of being very acutely aware of what is expected of them will lead some abusive parents to be very submissively cooperative and try to say the things that the worker wants to hear, even though this may not be a very accurate description of what has been going on. On the other hand, some parents, feeling cornered and expecting great criticism, may respond by being quite belligerent, uncooperative and resistant. In an effort to protect themselves, they may resort to criticizing others and are especially prone to find flaws in those who have been taking care of the injured child or investigating the family.

Interrogation of the parent to discover his misdeeds almost invariably leads to denial, withdrawal or an increased loss of self-esteem and depression. This makes cooperation difficult; on rare occasions, even suicide is a possibility. Some parents will respond fairly quickly to an expression of real interest in themselves, while others will begin by distrusting the worker, becoming more open only after several evasive tactics and rebuffs. Sometimes after many frustrating weeks of uncooperative experiences the parents will reveal how desperately they have wanted the relationship to continue and grow, but have been absolutely terrified about feeling close to the worker. Abusive parents have often had a life style of trying to do well and make things look good to please authorities. To deny that there are any further troubles is part of this pattern.

CRISES

In the early stages of dealing with these parents, it is always safe for the worker to assume that some sort of a crisis has occurred in the family. Early recognition of this fact is a most important aspect of establishing a working alliance with the parent. Even though the facts are not yet known, it is both safe and helpful to express a sympathetic understanding that the parent has been trying very hard to do well in the face of unusual difficulties and that the circumstances have created overwhelming problems. The crux of this technique is the focusing of the worker's attention on the parents' problem and the parents' needs. This avoids centering attention on the child and his injuries, which will only highlight the parental failures and increase their sense of being criticized.

If the worker can accept and approve of any improvement that may have taken place in the family, but still maintain contact, much more important material about family interactions will soon be forthcoming. It may soon become apparent that what appeared to be a unique and unusual crisis is only one of a long series of crises. A recurrence of the same or another type of difficult situation is probable unless time is given for the development of greater strengths in the parents or for more significant environmental changes to be accomplished.

As an integral part of the establishment of this therapeutic alliance, the crisis which has triggered the trouble in the family will often be identified. Two elements in the family crisis are sometimes detected. One most easily described by the parents is what has happened in relation to their child. The child did something that taxed their patience and tolerance to the breaking point. He has not eaten right, has soiled his bed, broken something, been disobedient or in some way improperly responsive to the parental wish and need.

More subtle, more important, and more difficult for the parents to describe is the second element of the crisis—the events which have led to their unbearably low sense of self-value, resulting in a desperate need of reassurance and nurturing from the environment. A common precipitant of such feelings is the withdrawal or alienation of a spouse. This may range all the way from simple emotional coolness or lack of conversation on the part of the spouse, to actual separations such as a husband in the Army being transferred overseas. As we have pointed out, criticism from anyone important to them can produce the same desperate emotional state.

For some women, pregnancy is a long lasting, crisis producing state. The mother may feel overburdened by the tasks of caring for her children, and the prospect of an additional child becomes overwhelming. The pregnancy may represent an unwanted addition to the family because it comes too soon or is the product of an unhappy sexual relationship with a man who is unloved and unloving.

Although some crises are clearly recognizable as significant, such as the serious illness or death of an important person, others appear quite trivial, such as a dented fender, or a hair tint that did not turn out exactly right. It must be borne in mind that what might appear trivial to the casual observer may not be insignificant to abusive parents. They live with a very precarious sense of stability; the slightest untoward event in the environment may topple the balance, resulting in a feeling of worthlessness and anger.

During this early evaluative phase, it may become quite clear to both parents and worker what kind of a crisis occurred in the family and what precipitated it. Frequently the parent will seem to understand the crisis situation quite well, will picture it as an unusual circumstance, and give assurance that such things will not happen again. And so the worker may feel that the problem has been adequately clarified and the trouble is not likely to recur.

Rarely would it seem wise to terminate at this point, even assuming the situation were as clear and simple as it appears. If any degree of positive relationship has developed between the worker and parents, breaking of contact at this point, even at the parents' request, may be felt as abandonment or rejection.

In some families it seems as if there are no well-developed techniques of preventive planning or anticipation of trouble that can be handled. Rather they live from crisis to crisis as a normal way of life, as if the only time to think about a problem and to try to deal with it is when it becomes acute.

In addition to these warnings about recurring crises, it must be remembered that for some individuals life can be so chronically stressful that a single crisis may precipitate child abuse.

The following case illustrates several aspects of an abusive parent's life which can be carefully explored during the period of evaluation.

A young Indian woman had adopted a one-year-old child. She showed evidence of having adequately coped with and solved many problems concerning the rearing of this child, but her life pattern was suddenly changed when she left the supporting culture in which she had lived and came to an area where she had no contact with relatives or friends. At the same time, her mother died and this precipitated a rather severe reactive depression. Under the stress of her mother's death, the depression, loneliness and lack of adequate support from the environment, this woman felt pushed beyond her strength. On one occasion she became impatient with her child and abused her, causing minor injury.

She reacted to this episode as if it were a quite surprising event in her life. This woman's history indicated that the particular pattern of child rearing involving abuse was not an overriding factor, but rather that major stressful situations had been sufficiently intense for a very mild, latent tendency toward abuse to become manifest. She soon responded to therapy and with the resolution of her depression and her reintegration into her own community, it was possible for her to resume a very adequate parental role, modeled after her own mother's ability to meet her needs.

ABILITY TO SEEK HELP

One must carefully assess the parents' past experience of having reasonably good figures in their environment to whom they could turn for help. Of equal importance is the determination of those supportive elements available in their environment. In general, the greater amount of aggression and abuse to which the parents were exposed in childhood, the more likely they are to have a pattern of abuse toward their own children, and the more difficult it will be for them to seek help. Conversely, the more the parents, in their own childhood, have been exposed to considerate, gentle, loving care, the less severe will be their tendency toward abusive behavior, and the easier it will be for them to seek and use support in their environment.

The helpful, kind person of early childhood could have been a parent, grandparent, relative, housekeeper, school teacher or family friend, and such a person may have been the only model of mothering. Memories of good times with this person can provide the groundwork for further development of the parents' own caretaking abilities. Talking about such an important person in the past, the worker can determine what type of person is felt to be good and what behaviors were comforting and useful to the parents as children. These are clues to what can be done to help as well as what should be avoided.

The degree of confidence these parents have in the availability of help inevitably affects both their marital relationship and their ability to cope with the children. The parent who is unable to turn to the spouse with confidence and expect to get help in times of trouble, is inevitably frustrated and will often turn to the child for emotional support. The parent-child relationship is then out of balance and abuse is more likely to occur.

ATTITUDE TOWARD CHILDREN

In addition to observing how the parents tend to look to their children for emotional satisfaction, the worker will need to explore the more intricate details of their attitudes towards each of the children. Usually each child has a special meaning to the parents. One child may be perceived as entirely comforting, gratifying and satisfactory. This is usually the child who has learned very early in life just what to do to please the parents and how to avoid displeasing them; he has become quite sensitive to his parents' emotional state. Compared to the "average" such a child appears overly controlled, submissive and cooperative, without initiative of his own. Even though this child may be deprived of what might be considered an optimum amount of empathic, loving consideration, he is rarely physically abused.

At the other end of the spectrum is the child who is perceived as a complete failure, rarely performing those things which the parents want for their own satisfaction. Even worse, he may do things which thwart the parents' desires. Such a child may be the product of a difficult pregnancy and starts life under the handicap of being seen as an unsatisfying troublemaker. This child is likely to be the recipient of abuse.

Abusive parents view infants and children as if they were much older than their chronological age and as possessing much greater intellectual development and physical ability than they actually have. There is the corresponding disregard of the infant's physical immaturity and limited intellectual development. These parental misperceptions mistakenly endow the child with the ability to understand and meet parental expectations which are inappropriate. This means that when the child fails to perform properly, the parents attribute this behavior to deliberate stubbornness, willful disobedience or a malicious desire to thwart their wishes. In the parents' style of child rearing, such behavior, of course, calls for severe punishment.

Between the extremes of parental perceptions of the child as being very good or very bad, there are innumerable varieties of parental estimates of what is satisfying or disappointing in their children. Often children are seen as being fairly satisfactory much of the time, but at intervals having deficits which make them inadequate. This is reflected in such statements as, "Johnny is generally fine, but I can't stand him when he is sick," or, "He is usually pretty well-behaved, but I find him unbearable when he is in one of his moods."

Some parents, because of the idiosyncrasies of their own personalities, focus on particular phases of the child's growth and development and become distressed by the child's failure to perform adequately at such periods. For some, the earliest months of life are the hardest to cope with because the child is so much more demanding and much less rewarding. For others, it may be only during the stage of toilet training when the most difficulties will arise. And for still other parents, it may be after the child has learned to walk and talk and has some degree of motor skill that he is expected to perform beyond his ability and disappoints his parents. At this age the child may strive for an independence and self-assertion which the parents cannot tolerate. The child may initiate parental verbal and physical aggression, which the parents interpret as rebellion and promptly punish even more severely.

One of the most common precipitants of abuse is the persistent crying of an infant, despite parental efforts to comfort or care for the child's needs. Such behavior is interpreted by the parents as criticism of their efforts and evidence of their inadequacy. This is the opposite of the self-esteem enhancing response wanted from the child. The parents feel attacked and may release abusive punishment.

The worker can often obtain important data about parental perception of the child by asking who in the family the child resembles, and then finding out what the parent thinks of that person. If the family prototype of the child is seen by the parent as an unloving troublemaker or an otherwise deficient person, it is obvious the child is in some danger. The child is probably in even more danger if he is seen as having the bad qualities of one of the parents. This is particularly evident in such statements as, "Johnny has a mean streak in him, just like his no-good father," or "Johnny is just as stubborn and useless to me as my mother said I was." Punishment was received for this type of behavior in the parent's own childhood and, hence, the parent is likely to punish the child for similar behavior.

Considerable emphasis has been placed, for a very good reason, on the process of evaluating the parental perceptions of the children. One of the first difficult problems faced by workers caring for a family where abuse has occurred is to answer the question whether this child should be allowed to remain at home, kept in the hospital or be placed in foster care for a while. Can the home be made safe? Valuable data for making this difficult decision come from the worker's estimate of the degree of distortion and rigidity of the parents' perceptions of the children, plus the estimate of how much exaggeration there is in the parental wish for the child to perform well. Information of this type can be gained through somewhat informal conversation with the parents, as well as by more structured questioning. Several home visits to see interaction between parents and children should be considered an essential part of this evaluation.

ESTABLISHING A THERAPEUTIC RELATIONSHIP

The success or failure of the attempts to form a therapeutic alliance can often be measured by the degree of testing to which the therapists are subjected. A sense of basic distrust versus a sense of wanting to have the worker be all things to the patient is reflected in questions such as, "Why would anyone like me?" or "What is there about me that is valuable enough to have anyone really help me?" Some parents comment, "You only see me because you are paid to do so. You don't really like me." Such an attitude, however, may herald the real beginning of the parents' ability to use therapy and to receive what is more useful from the worker.

ALTERNATE THERAPISTS

Ideally, the therapeutic relationship will begin during the evaluation process. If the parents have been approached with gentleness and understanding, the alliance that is so necessary for a treatment program will have begun. The worker not only needs to establish a relationship with the mother, but will also need to begin to develop the alliance with the spouse and other family members. This is best accomplished by providing the parents with an alternate therapist who can be one of several people who have been involved with the family during the evaluation process, or who might be someone the primary therapist has selected during the early phase of the relationship.

Although the alternate worker may not be as intensely involved with the family as is the primary therapist, there will be times when this secondary person is of extreme value. During the early phases of treatment, parents often become defensive and confused and develop feelings of being rejected and frustrated. At this time they are often convinced that the worker who has been a helpful person has now abandoned them. Yet, despite feeling misunderstood and criticized, they have a genuine desire to reestablish the relationship with the worker. Providing an alternate person to whom the parents can complain and vent their frustrations often ensures the reestablishment of the original alliance. The primary worker must remain available and maintain a reassuring and supportive role to assist the parents over this difficult period.

Patients who break away from therapy most often do so because of an imagined or exaggerated feeling of being rejected by the worker. These misunderstandings must be discussed openly. The parents will gradually develop an awareness that the relationship between them and the worker is not one that demands continuous perfection and immediate understanding of the other person's problems. The worker who is open about her own failings and is comfortable in discussing them will enhance the development of a relationship that is not built on a constant requirement for the parents to meet the worker's needs.

Having someone who is sincerely interested in listening, and who is not critical of what is heard, can be of extreme importance in the development of a therapeutic relationship. Once the parents realize that the worker will be considerate of whatever complaint they have about this relationship, often passed on via the intermediary secondary worker, they will eventually feel more comfortable about expressing these feelings directly to the worker. This give-and-take is important in correcting the many fears of authoritative figures that have existed and grown since the parents' early childhood. The parents nagging sense of inferiority is diminished by knowing that they are accepted by the worker, even though they have certain limitations.

Frequently after the primary and secondary workers have interviewed both parents, there begins a series of communications to each of the therapists. These are often exaggerations or questions which really represent attempts on the part of the husband and wife to communicate with each other. This should be understood and the therapists must realize that their own constant communication is indirectly a way of integrating the family. As the workers compare notes they often will find that there are messages relating to the spouse's unmet needs. Threats of divorce and expressions of disgust can be translated into the message of one spouse to another, which is "shape-up, pay attention to me, and relate to me as if you were a good parent relating to a child."

THE GROWTH PROCESS

The goal of treatment is to help the parents grow out of their isolated, trapped, hopeless pattern of living into a sense of self-esteem and to develop an ability to find enough gratification in the adult world so that they can become loving and giving to their children. It is the task of the worker to be the catalyst in this process and to be a person with whom the abusive parents try out new ways of relating to adults as they change their style of living.

DEVELOPING A SENSE OF SELF-ESTEEM

In general, this process falls into sequential phases as the therapeutic relationship develops as described above. At first, due to basic lack of trust, the parents maintain distance from the therapist and evade significant self-revelation. This is true in spite of superficial cooperation and evidences of underlying wishes for help. Through repeated experiences of the therapist listening and responding without belittling criticisms and judgments, the parents develop a trusting dependence on the worker. This is quite different from their previous compulsory submission to the authority of their own parents.

In some cases this dependency and wish for help may seem almost overwhelming to the therapist, as if the total responsibility for family action, child rearing and troubles in general had been turned over to the worker for solution. This can be best understood as a good omen, a sign that the parents feel safe enough to acknowledge their deep sense of helplessness and inferiority, their deep needs for aid, and the relinquishment of their defenses of fearful isolation and righteous sureness. The worker's recognition of the parents' needs, the willingness to help find ways to satisfy such needs, and the acceptance of less-than-perfect performance, enable the parents to develop new techniques of coping and a greater sense of self-esteem.

The intensity of the dependency needs expressed by parents can sometimes be almost frightening to the worker, as well as being something which many workers and agencies consider "bad," and feel should not be allowed, let alone encouraged. We believe the experience of a dependent relationship is an essential ingredient in the optimal growth of the abusive parents. It reworks an unsatisfactory experience of their own

early development and provides a new, emotionally understood standard or ideal of parent-child relationship.

Furthermore, such dependency is not total, nor is it permanent. Abusive parents have many unfulfilled strivings
toward maturation and independence which the worker can
gently and skillfully encourage without coercion or rigid
control. The growth out of dependency is facilitated by open
discussions of possible alternative ways of problem solving,
relieving frustration and coping with children. The more the
parents' own ideas, which have special value and meaning for
them, can be brought into discussion, the more it promotes
growth. Praise must be given freely, although judiciously, to
parents for their efforts, even when results are less than ideal
and less than hoped for. Growth involves the development of
a sense of value and self esteem, even though one is not perfect.

CRITERIA OF GROWTH AND IMPROVEMENT

Not all parents involved in abusive behavior toward their
children can be successfully treated. A few parents are too
emotionally disturbed, either psychotic, mentally retarded or
severely sociopathic, to be able to resume the tasks of caring
for their children within a reasonable length of time before
the children are grown. On rare occasions parents will bring
an abused, neglected or injured child to the hospital, talk to
the physicians and social worker, then disappear into limbo,
never to be seen again, abandoning the child.

Occasionally, when legal proceedings for protective custody
of an abused child have been instituted, the court may decide
there is insufficient evidence to warrant temporary suspension
of parental rights; the parents feel exonerated and immediately
terminate any therapeutic relationship that has been started.
In metropolitan areas where it is easy to move from one welfare
district to another by merely changing residence to across the
street, parents of lower socioeconomic levels can get lost in
"jurisdictional disputes" and administrative delays in trans-
ferring responsibility for care from one agency to another.
Such unfortunate events reinforce the abusive parents' belief

that no one really cares about them or wants to help them, and they become more resistant, more negative and more difficult to treat. Under the pressure of very high work loads, agency workers find such parents "unmotivated" and "untreatable," and after brief attempts at therapy the case is closed and the parents join the group of treatment failures.

In some cases treatment fails despite our best efforts. Sometimes this seems to be due to the existence of so many problems in the family, emotional, marital, financial, social, medical, etc., for such a long time that no real improvement can be accomplished. In other instances it is our own ineptness or lack of sensitivity that has led us to make mistakes despite our good intentions. Under the best of conditions we would estimate that at least 80 percent of cases can be treated with reasonably satisfactory results.

The response of parents to therapeutic intervention may be rapid or slow. In some cases marked improvement in parental attitudes and child caring ability can occur within three months. As a rule, such rapid change occurs in those parents who have had the least amount of difficulty in their own childhood and whose reality situation is reasonably good. It must be borne in mind, however, that in some cases of rapid improvement no real basic change has occurred in the parents and that they are only using their lifelong ability to be sensitive to what is expected of them and perform accordingly. Such pseudo-improvement can be easily detected by an experienced worker, as it does not hold up under stress.

A clear indicator of real growth and improvement is the way parents report and handle crises. Early in therapy, parents tend to report numerous crises with a sense of being overwhelmed and helplessly unable to cope. Quite often the "crises" seem blown up out of all proportion to reality. The parents need a great deal of reassurance, patient support, and sometime a direct, realistic help from some source. Later the frequency and intensity of crises diminish and the parents need less support or advice, although they still need a good deal of open discussion of problems. Then the parents begin to figure out their own ways to deal with crises, and need only some sense of approval or permission from the therapist to go ahead. Finally, they are able to report with a sense of pride and achievement how a crisis has already been handled reasonably well without the therapist's help, or how it was successfully managed by finding appropriate help from some other source. By this time the parents are also aware of their own sensitivity to particular events and people, and have learned some techniques of how to handle stresses in life before they become critical.

It is obvious from the way the parents are handling crises that they have come to some degree out of isolation. They have increased the ability to find helpful contacts and are more trusting of others, as well as confident in themselves. These changes are usually accompanied by improvement in the marital relationship.

An important sign of significant improvement in the parent-child relationship is the change from viewing the child as an object for parental satisfaction to seeing the child as an interesting individual in his own right. The parents get a sense of pleasure and satisfaction from seeing the child develop and behave in age-appropriate fashion, and take pride in the child's accomplishment for his own sake. The child is also allowed to have his own pleasures. A most satisfactory result of therapy is pictured when a parent says something like, "I am listening to my children the way you have listened to me. They are fascinating kids and lots of fun."

THE CHILD'S RETURN TO HIS HOME

In some situations it will be necessary for a child to be removed from his home and put into foster care as a protective measure. There is usually a second court hearing in three or six months to determine if the child can be returned to the parents. It is the task of the workers who have been in contact with the parents to provide the court with information which will permit the judge to make a sensible decision about the safety of returning the child to his parents (see Chapter 12). If there are other children in the family, home visits to see if there has been improvement in parent-child interaction are a valuable source of data, although this cannot be used as an absolute criterion of how the parents will get along with the child who has been in custody. A child should not be returned home until there have been several visits between parents and child observed by the workers.

Sometimes visiting privileges are demanded by the parents to prove that they are good parents by demonstrating an interest in the child and also to test the worker's willingness to believe in and cooperate with them. Under such circumstances the visits are usually not very rewarding for either the parents or child. Later in the treatment program, after a period of growth, the parental desire to see the child demonstrates a more genuine interest in his welfare and the interaction between parents and child can be observed as rewarding to both parties.

In general, it is not safe to return a child until there is good evidence that the parents have found more ways of getting satisfaction and pleasure in their lives and no longer need to turn so strongly to the child to satisfy emotional needs. If the parents have developed a pattern of getting in contact with one or another worker when they are in trouble, and are actively seeking help, this is a further indicator of safety in the home. If the parents have had significant misperceptions of the child and significant rigid distortions of what the child's behavior should be, the worker should find clear evidence that these are much diminished before feeling safe in returning the child.

Parents will often pressure the worker and court to return the child because the child's removal exposes them to public or family disapproval. Similarly, one parent may be pressuring the other to get the child back for the same reason, or the parents' parents may be pressuring them to get the family together again to "make things look better." Significant pressures of this type for the return of the child are strong indications against permitting such return. It is rare for a child to do well back in a home where there is this pressure from grandparents or other individuals to have the child returned prematurely.

When all has gone very well, the parents have improved and the child has returned home, there is often a tendency for either parents or worker or both to consider that everything is now all right and treatment should be discontinued. This should *never* be done. The continuation of treatment is crucially important at this time. Not only is there a need to consolidate gains which have already been made, but it is necessary to follow through and see that the inevitable shifts in emotion and changes in living patterns caused by the return of the child can be managed without regression to previous unhealthy patterns. The purpose of treatment was not just to get the child back, but to improve the total living pattern of the family and significantly change the parent-child interactions. This necessitates considerable follow-up after the child comes home.

A child who has been abused and placed in a foster home may have received a great deal of attention and love, to which he responds by developing into a very happy, healthy, cheerful, outgoing youngster. On being returned home, this child has a great reservoir of affection and the parents are delighted and pleased with him. However, unless the parents can continue this empathic giving to the child, the child will run out of his store of affection and the parents may see him again as unrewarding and unsatisfying. Such a happening indicates to the worker that the child was probably returned prematurely and that the parents will need an extra amount of help to tide them over this period.

Not all children should be returned to their parents. Sometimes workers find that the parents do not change in their patterns despite all the effort towards treatment that can be mustered from all available sources. It is probably unwise to return a child to the custody of parents in such situations, although it is true that sometimes a child is reasonably safe, at least for a time, because of the parents' fear of further prosecution by the law. Unfortunately, such families often move from one jurisdiction to another and are lost sight of until some time later when the child is seriously injured again or possibly dies from injuries.

Sometimes parents, even though expressing a strong desire to have their child returned, are also giving the more subtle message that they do not want the child back at all or do not feel ready to have him back at this time. This is particularly likely to occur if one parent is pressing for the child back because of prestige reasons, while the other parent realizes that the return of the child would result in impossible stress. At other times, parents openly request that the child never be returned. They have such a deep conviction that he is a "bad" child that they are quite willing to relinquish him and never see him again. Under such circumstances, it is a mistake to try to urge the parents to try to change their attitude and take the child back again.

LONG-TERM AVAILABILITY

It is clear that we consider the worker's empathy and availability to be the most essential elements in the therapy of abusive parents. Even though therapy terminates through mutual consent of worker and parents it seems advisable for the worker, or at least the agency, to be available at any time for reinstitution of contact. The parents are not automatically protected from future trouble. Loss of significant relatives or friends by death or separation, economic stress, future pregnancies or illness can occur and lead to temporary upsets in the parents' lives. They will need to know there will always be a place where help can be found and where there are people who will be aware of their problems and appreciate their accomplishments.

2

The Social Worker
and the Family

HELEN ALEXANDER, M.S.W.

BEGINNING TO ESTABLISH A therapeutic relationship with these families is often the most difficult phase. Our own intense feelings about abuse, and more specifically the feelings about particular parents and what they have done to their child, must be openly recognized. Our own children come before our eyes and disbelief and fury play havoc with the attempts to be helpful and understanding. In attempts to cloak the anger we may hide behind our authority and need to protect the child. Anger is a natural reaction and protection of the children essential but when mixed together they can be explosive and lethal to the development of any therapeutic attempt with the family. These are extremely difficult situations and the families require so much of our support that we need understanding colleagues with whom we can share our feelings and who can offer support and help.

Another essential point at the outset, especially for social workers, is to clarify for ourselves and others who would press us into the role, that we do not "play detective" or try to determine "who did it." It is difficult to overcome our own curiosity and the desire to know exactly what happened and identify our patient. Frequently we are asked to see a family to determine what occurred or who was responsible for the injury. If we can recognize abuse as a symptom rather than the core of the problem we may find this less difficult. An unexplained injury of a child is adequate information to determine that involvement with the total family is needed. In situations where the history is questionable and further evaluative material desirable, it is most important to find out what stresses this family has been facing. These parents are extremely vulnerable to criticism, often feeling rejected or spurned, and are tremendously isolated from sources of comfort or help. We should be extremely sensitive to these areas and explore them with care. We seldom will hear a confession or adequate explanation of what transpired in reference to the injury and if we seek this information we will alienate the family and still not accomplish our goal.

When the parent is feeling bereft, unloved and/or personally attacked, he turns to the child as a source of comfort to meet his overwhelming needs. From the onset the response must be to the parents' needs. Although the family comes to our attention usually because of the child, it is the parents on whom we must focus our attention.

HOW THE PARENTS SEEK HELP

Parents who abuse their small children present themselves in many different ways. Most often the child is brought as the problem and the parents may sincerely believe the difficulty rests with the child. Some parents are openly hostile and antagonistic to everyone. Others, though pleasant, are very uncommunicative. Only a few are direct in their request for help and acknowledge the need for it.

> Carol first came to the attention of the welfare department because of a neighbor's complaint regarding the screaming of her 3-month-old baby. The child was temporarily placed in a foster home because of concern expressed by relatives, and Carol was referred to the local mental health clinic for evaluation. She describes her contacts there as "a series of lies" as she had learned long before to cover her feelings and tell people what she determined they wished to hear. Consequently, she stated "they de-

cided I was no crazier than most people and told me I did not need their help." The baby was returned to her custody and no continuing contact with the family maintained. Fortunately, while Carol was visiting the medical clinic, a social worker offered help and focused on the severe financial difficulties and the father's lack of employment. Abuse, although still a consideration in the worker's mind, was not the focus of interest or concern. Carol, much less threatened about her role as a mother, could share some of her worries about her little girl and how troubled she was about herself.

No matter how the parents appear or present themselves, their expectations are that they will be used, attacked and accused of being "bad" parents. One's immediate and continuing response must be to this underlying fear, hurt and frustration that the parents are feeling. It may just be the simple statement, "It really seems like you have been having a rugged time." If we can help them express how difficult it has been for them to care for this child or the frustration they are experiencing with the child, therapy has begun. Whatever the words, the message must come across clearly, unclouded by our own unresolved feelings, that we are indeed interested in what the parents are feeling and have been experiencing. Any hint that they are doing an inadequate job can jeopardize the relationship. Concrete action may be needed to demonstrate our interest, extending ourselves far beyond our usual professional expectations. In essence we will "put ourselves out," as Elizabeth Davoren[1] described so well of patients who flee:

> If one is offering help in a hospital setting to those who use flight as a defense, the availability of the prospective patient diminishes with each new move to make an appointment, even though the appointment is offered entirely at the patient's convenience. Therapy deteriorates into a footrace down the corridor as the therapist tries to prove to the potential patient that he only wants to help, not hurt him, and furthermore that he is quite capable of helping. If home visiting is *modus operandi*, make an appoint-

ment with the patient who uses flight as defense and you guarantee his absence. Fail to let him know you are coming, and he somehow discovers you and does not let you know he's there. I have traveled seventy miles to find a woman "who never leaves the house"—gone. I have visited twice weekly for six months at a stretch to leave notes to the parent absenting himself. This sounds pretty tedious I know, but I should like to add that once those who are fleeing from you stop doing so and are willing to meet with you, you have someone you can really work with. If you do not pursue with persistence, you have no one at all.

If the worker can learn to see beyond the subterfuge to the truly troubled parents, she still will find them "highly unmotivated clients." Even those who ask for help thwart it at every turn. When we understand that these parents have always found that those to whom they have turned for help usually hurt or disappoint them, it is not difficult to understand their distrust. This distrust is not quickly resolved; to develop trust is something we must work on throughout the relationship. Some parents have so difficult a time allowing anyone close that, just when we feel we are beginning to reach them, they reject us. The ability to trust is so underdeveloped, and yet the longing for closeness is so intense, that once begun the dependency can be consuming. It requires that we be quite comfortable with this dependency and respond in a nurturing and supportive way, not by controlling or thwarting. The opportunity to advise and manipulate is great. Advice is often sought by the parents whose pattern is to determine the other's expectations and then, by attempting to meet these expectations, gain a sense of worth. This is, of course, a self-defeating pattern which we are attempting to change. Because it may seem flattering it is a tempting pattern which we may share with the patient unless we recognize it. Sometimes straightforward advice on matters of reality should be given, provided it is offered as a reasonable suggestion of a good friend. It should be understood that the advice can be rejected and that we expect the parents will find their own solution. The difficult task is to determine the parent's needs and aspirations and then try to meet and support them. Our belief in them and their unique abilities becomes the basis for a new way to develop their sense of personal worth.

ESTABLISHING THE RELATIONSHIP

Fear of abandonment is a deterrent to the development of trust. The parents are so sensitive to being deserted that often our actions of inadvertent slip-ups are misinterpreted. If they begin to trust, the fear grows that we will decide they are hopeless or worthless and will stop seeing them.

As the relationship is developed we encourage them — by providing them with an alternative to the old pattern of using the child — to look to the worker as a source of help in a crisis. Crises are the life style for these families, particularly because they have so few resources on which to draw, both within themselves and in their relationships. What would seem to be a minor incident to us becomes a major catastrophe for the parents. Therefore, in order to provide the parents with an "escape" at the time of these crises, it is helpful if the worker can be available by phone on a 24-hour basis.* If the parents receive a warm and interested response at the other end of the phone, the crisis may be bearable. Whatever precipitates the crisis, it is the feeling of failure, worthlessness and being abandoned to which we are responding.

Early in the relationship the child is often seen as the source of irritation and one of the causes for the parents' difficulties. When a parent calls, she often begins telling how impossible or misbehaving the child has been. Parents' misperceptions and unrealistic expectations of the child are, at times, so flagrant that it is tempting to say "Oh, come now." More helpful than confronting them with these misperceptions, is to ask how *they* have been feeling and what has happened

---

*This can often be exhausting—or impossible—for the social worker. For this reason this responsibility can often be shared between workers or team members. The parents usually understand and accept this "on call" system.

in *their* lives. Sometimes we can determine very quickly the source of their distress. More often it is very confused and may not be resolved for some time. Finally we piece together what is causing the parent to feel unloved, criticized or deserted. The phone call may be from a weeping, hysterical mother, with a crying child in the background, who can only blurt out that the child has been impossible and nobody will help her. The phone is then slammed down and repeated attempts to call her only result in a busy signal indicating she has taken the phone off the hook. Often the message received is so confused, and the patient so upset or angry, that an appropriate response can be given only because the pattern and the principles for helping are understood. Slowly one can help them begin to understand their feelings until they learn themselves to look for what has precipitated their anger and frustration with their child.

> Judy, who has had much help over a long period of time, now calls and explains: "I was pretty upset today. I was even yelling at Ann (the seven-month-old baby). She is so crabby and I have to hold her constantly. I have things to do and I cannot fuss with her all day. I guess it is not that though. Jack stayed home today and all he did was sleep, again. I am so angry with him and then when Ann fusses, I feel myself getting so upset with her until I am angry if she bothers me at all."

She recognized basically what has transpired: Jack's staying home from work indicates to her that he did not care enough for her to hold a job and provide adequately. When he stayed home he would not help her or even talk to her, completely cutting her off. She was then angry with the baby when she fussed or needed anything. She needed to call for reassurance that she was still a good mother and that her frustrations with Jack were legitimate. The added ingredients needed were praise for her ability to reach out and use somebody, encouragement and approval for doing something for herself. These were initially almost impossible concepts for the mother to accept, and they needed reinforcement.

MOTHERING

What has been described is much more an experiential change than developing insight. It is a kind of repetitive patterning in which the worker assumes the "good mother" role which the parents so desperately need and which is such a crucial element to the healing process. For so many years their own needs have been unmet, and their worthlessness and failure so constantly reinforced, that the reversal of this pattern is a long and arduous task. It requires much greater flexibility, openness and time than social workers are used to giving.

Home visits are invaluable, particularly in the beginning. They offer an opportunity to gain a tremendous insight into the family's life and struggles. They provide a more relaxed, giving climate than the behind-the-desk "professional" approach. We offer friendship and love, someone who is unreservedly on their side and who is pleased to see them grow and thrive. The skill and knowledge we bring should not be minimized since they will be desperately needed. Many social workers feel that it is unprofessional to permit this degree of dependency to develop. They may feel uncomfortable with it. Without a free giving of ourselves, however, our efforts will be limited, if not useless. The closeness also may be so frightening to the parents that they may run from the contact and need to be pursued.

The parents' fear of "spoiling" their children by coddling or meeting their normal needs is one of the things we are trying to remedy by our treatment. A common statement made by parents who seriously injure their children is, "You can't give into kids and do what they want or they'll be spoiled rotten. They have to learn respect. My folks taught me respect with a belt and I'll teach mine the same way." This disregard of the normal needs of the child for fear of spoiling, and the infliction of physical punishment to insure good behavior, are common factors in the childhood of these parents and continue in their relation to their own children. As the parents are allowed to be dependent and have their own needs met, they are able in time to respond more appropriately to their children. There is no great risk of harm in allowing these parents to be dependent; in fact there is much greater risk in expecting them to "stand on their own feet" and be responsible. This is what they have experienced all their lives with no recognition of their legitimate dependency needs.

A fair amount of time may be spent "just visiting," listening to the mother (or father) and sharing whatever is of interest to her. The feeling that she is a person of importance must be imparted. It is such a unique experience for many of them to be truly listened to, that at times the worker feels like a tape recorder. After one such session with one mother, she told me later: "I was so lonely and blue before you came, and then after you left I felt good and wanted to do something, so I did my ironing." This had been a formidable task for her and one which seemed to represent failure most clearly.

Abusive parents are especially sensitive to the feeling of failure and have difficulty in saying they want relief. They also find it almost impossible to enjoy getting away from the home and children because they feel criticized for not doing their duty well enough.

When parents feel overwhelmed and exhausted by child care they are most easily frustrated and likely to abuse their children. Therefore the therapist needs to be sensitive to such states and do everything possible to encourage the parents to get help and "get away from it all" for a while. There is an urgent need for day care centers or other facilities where parents can have children cared for while they have some chance for relief.

Temporary foster care can also be a means to provide relief, particularly in a time of family crisis, and can be an "enabling" process for the parents as well as a safety factor for the children. Frequently I have heard the statements that "foster care is not a babysitting service," and "this mother just wants to get away from her children and dump her responsibility." Indeed, any parent who requests that a child be removed from the home should be seriously heeded. There are too many histories of permanently injured and dead children whose parents previously requested placement and were refused. One welfare worker attempted a very unique but helpful plan of utilizing a foster home as a "grandmother" arrangement for a family. When stress mounted and the mother indicated a need for relief, the children would go to "grandmother's" for a weekend or a brief stay. The family was supplemented, not disrupted, making better child care possible. At times it would be most desirable to have a foster home for mother and child, particularly for a very young mother or one who is having difficulty establishing a comfortable relationship with her newborn.

ANGER AND COMMUNICATION

There are problems in establishing a relationship of trust. It is nearly impossible for these patients to express anger or disappointment directly, especially with anyone of significance in their lives. It is inevitable that we will cause anger or disappointment, sometimes inadvertently and unknowingly, sometimes with full awareness. Not being home to answer a phone call, having to cancel an appointment or simply not being able to respond adequately to all their needs—all may lead to anger on the part of the parents. They are afraid to express their anger for fear of punishment or abandonment. Often they feel responsible for our behavior and may respond by increased attempts either to please or to avoid.

By having more than one person involved with the family— a pediatrician, social worker, nurse, psychiatrist or lay worker— these feelings of rejection and anger are better handled. Usually the patients can share with someone else how angry they are with the social worker. It may be a rather guarded message but it is imperative that these messages be relayed to the worker. The patient must also be aware from the beginning that this kind of communication between the members of the team will occur. Then the worker can come back to the patient and say, "I hear you really were upset with me; I do not blame you," or "Could you tell me what it was about?" For them to learn that we can accept their anger, legitimize it and work something out together because of it, is of tremendous importance. This is not just an initial phase or temporary malaise but a recurring theme.

Most communication occurs in this indirect way. For this reason, a situation can be very puzzling or unclear until everyone involved gets together and the full picture unfolds. If only one person is involved with a family it may not be possible to see what is transpiring or to deal adequately with certain areas.

> To the psychiatric resident, Molly seemed consistently able to cope in a reality oriented way, although her use of an unusual pattern of child rearing was obvious. To a home visitor, a very different picture of a totally overwhelmed woman emerged, a woman whose fantasies were interwoven in her accounts of her life as a constant whirlwind of confusion over which she seemed to have no control or direction. The worker and psychiatrist each were truly amazed to hear the other's views and observations. Neither could have known the totality without the other.

FINDING JOY

There are several important areas where we may be of some help to these parents. Even though the many neurotic problems and marital difficulties are as varied as in any random sample of clinic patients, there are several common denominators in all the families who abuse their small children. One of these is the need for some meaningful, enjoyable outlets and the ability to find some joy in life. Obviously what may appeal to one mother might be loathed by another. It takes tremendous sensitivity to perceive what might truly be desired. Often we simply encourage whatever the parents attempt to do but sometimes we must actually assist in the initial tries at new and meaningful experiences. Such activities as taking a housebound mother out to coffee, working alongside her on a difficult household task or taking her to a job interview can be some of the ways. We may need to comfort when the attempt fails or enthusiastically applaud if it succeeds in some measure; we must always show our approval and support.

> On one regular visit to Gail's home she ran out to my car to greet me. She was looking particularly nice, hair curled, make-up fresh and face aglow, as she explained she was having a party and had invited a few neighbors. For her this was an unbelievable feat. She frankly acknowledged she had planned it at the time of my visit so I would be there for "moral support." This was her first attempt, ever, at having a party.

Because there has been so little recognition of the accomplishments in their lives, abusive parents need to know very frequently when something has been well done. Constant recognition and praise are essential. One mother was an excellent cook. She prepared special treats for me and waited patiently but eagerly for my approval, which was certainly well deserved. After showing me how to make flour tortillas, she was obviously pleased when I asked for the recipe. Though this process seemed simple my attempt was a complete failure. When I reported this to the mother she was truly smug. It reminded me of a young child's pride when she can do something an adult cannot.

When I admired a Christmas ornament that one parent had made, she prepared all the materials for the following visit and showed me how to make it. Not only was she deriving a sense of having some value, she also was *giving to me,* a very important step.

Sometimes friends are introduced with eagerness—and with a desire for approval. Their own parents have so often discouraged any close contacts with friends that they need much approval and praise both for reaching out and for their selection. Spouses also tend to perpetuate this disapproval of friends and outside activities, including the relationship with the social worker.

> Judy can now laugh when Jack accuses her of "being in love" with her psychiatrist. She, however, admits that at

times she is jealous of Jack's contacts with his social worker. She can also relate how the baby fits into this pattern. "Wherever I go everyone notices Ann first, they start playing with her or talking to her. It reminds me of when I was a child when everyone noticed my mother and I felt no one noticed me or cared about me. I get some of that same feeling sometimes with Ann. I get angry with her and feel she's taking everyone away from me."

It is imperative that we do not focus on the children. In like manner it also makes working simultaneously with both parents very difficult. Sometimes, however, a wife is willing for her husband to share in the help (or vice versa) when she has had some measure of fulfillment. In some situations it is advisable to have different therapists available to each spouse so that one does not feel left out or that too much time is spent vying over whose needs will be met. Many fathers, however, cannot admit needing or wanting this contact and we have to be satisfied with helping the wife, who in turn can begin to respond more adequately to her husband's needs. Obviously our aim is to enable the parents to meet each other's needs, rather than using the children for this purpose.

REACTION TO DEMANDS

It may be tempting to push or pressure, particularly when a patient constantly states how bored, lonely and unhappy she is, while making no apparent attempt to move out or try anything. This pressure is usually met with superficial compliance but may lead to further depression, sudden withdrawal or actual avoidance, such as not being at home or by missing appointments. Seldom is pressure met head-on. Sometimes excuses are offered but most often an attempt will be made to comply, as this is the life pattern. Instead, we need to help them learn to please themselves.

After a brief hospitalization in a psychiatric hospital, Gail was visited by one of the nurses who wanted to help bridge the gap between hospital and home. Because Gail talked frequently of her wish for activities and friends outside the home, the nurse suggested she contact several nursing homes to inquire about volunteering some time. Gail immediately called and made an appointment. I saw her several days later and she was visibly agitated, more severe with her daughter and unsure about what was bothering her. Finally, she was able to trace it to her wish to please the nurse, fearful she would be angry if she had not followed through. She panicked at the prospect of the appointment and the involvement this type of volunteering would require and knew she could not do what she felt was expected of her.

Expectations and demands are often felt by the patient when they have not been intended. This is frequently the clue to a depression or irritation with the child. At times members of the team or a person from one of the agencies involved may make demands, particularly in attempts to teach child care. This will be felt by the parent as criticism as well as pressure.

Judy was seen by a public health nurse following the birth of her second child. Very soon a struggle developed over how to sterilize the baby's bottles. Judy was using an unsterile technique. The nurse repeatedly attempted to explain and demonstrate the sterile methods. She was utterly frustrated by Judy's superficial compliance but flagrant disregard of her directions. I heard the story from both sides. Judy was determined no one would tell her how to care for her child as that implied she wasn't a capable mother. The nurse was bound by agency policy, which was to "teach sterile technique." Fortunately the nurse was most eager to help and when she understood what was happening, immediately dropped her "instructor's role" and began to focus on Judy. Out of this grew a very warm and close relationship in which Judy could ask, when she wanted, about child care. The baby at one year is a healthy, alert and appealing child.

Demands are made by family and friends. Even when the patient recognizes what is occurring she may feel impotent to deal with it.

Jan became seriously depressed, once again attacking her daughter and slowly recognized that it was due to her mother-in-law's impending visit. The mother-in-law had assumed that she could come for a long visit, even implying a permanent stay. The woman was nearly blind, and a severe diabetic. Jan had a long history of fights with her, but because of her mother-in-law's poor health she felt she must accept the visit. She also feared her husband's reaction if she said she did not want his mother to come. She felt trapped and unable to do anything about it. She became so depressed and abusive with her child that both she and her husband requested psychiatric hospitalization to protect both Jan and her little girl. In this protective setting, with much support and help she was able to tell her husband of her fears and concerns regarding his mother's visit. He was exceptionally understanding, quickly reassured Jan that she was his first concern and that he would tell his mother she could not come. Not all spouses have been so helpful!

The parents need reassurance that they do not have to meet every demand. The worker must help them, when possible, to refuse the role of "everyone's caretaker." Frequently, some family members assume that the patient should help out in any situation. They are errand runners, babysitters, etc., and if they refuse are bitterly attacked. Friends are also usually "users." This pattern must be understood by the patient. Caution is needed as attempts to clarify what is occurring are easily misinterpreted as criticism. The support and encouragement must be massive to counteract both the patient's feelings about refusing and the actual attack made by others. The worker may need to intervene directly with a parent or spouse but only with the patient's knowledge and approval.

PARENTAL TIES

Abusive parents may be in very close contact with their own parents, which may play an important part in what transpires within the family. Family relationships have not only been unsatisfying but have resulted in the pattern which demanded the children take care of the parents. A letter or phone call can precipitate a crisis. A visit from the grandparents may be eagerly awaited but leave the parent either upset, angry with her child or completely withdrawn. Frequently patients can relate how unhappy and frustrating their relationships with their parents have been but nonetheless find themselves running to them whenever called. They become devastated when they are criticized or used and yet they find themselves unable to break away.

The ability of the patient to deal with this problem varies greatly. For some it is impossible to be critical of their parents. Even for those who can acknowledge how hurt and attacked they have been, the longing for parental love and approval is so strong that they cannot chance breaking the tie. Our first intervention in this area may be to sympathize with the hurt and disappointment they feel. This is a very delicate area in that their self-esteem and often their very existence have been built around pleasing their parents. Even if they have consistently failed, this remains the only way they know to develop a sense of personal worth. There is great guilt and fear in expressing anger with their mothers, just as they tolerate "no backtalk" from their own children. When one sees the severity with which their own child's normal behavior is met one can understand the fear and guilt that has been instilled in them in the same manner. This "bottled up" anger can be frightening to them, spilling out in violent episodes. Joyce chased her husband with a butcher knife when he returned home late from work after she had a particularly trying day. Judy recently described wanting to smash her fist into the wall and verbally exploded when a nurse asked her what she was feeding her baby. These kinds of aggressive attacks have been focused on the children. As progress is made and the parent becomes more aware of the real sources of her frustration and hurt it may seem to aggravate her behavior with her spouse or other members of the family.

Jack's mother, who had been extremely brutal to him as a boy, was now a critical, nagging woman who ordered him about constantly and belittled him for being a failure. When it seemed likely his parents might move to the same city, he decided to write his mother a letter telling her to "stay off his back" and if she wanted any contact with them it would have to be on his terms. He needed much assurance that it was permissible for him to do this and finally after the letter was sent he became very angry with his wife for "making" him do it.

His mother refused to answer his letter for some time but sent word via his sister that they were very unhappy and angry with him. She finally wrote. Her letter was short but void of the usual criticism and advice. The fear of loss of his parents' love, as well as his fear of their ability to destroy him, continued. The dilemma was so intolerable that he chose to withdraw completely, sleeping most of the time. Although there were other factors involving his present family, this parental crisis seemed to be the precipitating factor.

If there is enough "input" coming from others, Jack may be able to tolerate some rupture of the relationship with his parents so that something can be altered. Not only is the ability to say no with some degree of comfort essential but a more realistic appraisal of what he can expect from them is required. This may be difficult to accept but much less frustrating than constantly seeking what can never be. Often this is mellowed and softened by a growing self-awareness that recognizes his plight as being very similar to that of his parents.

MARITAL PATTERNS

The marital difficulties are usually hidden in the cycle between parents and child. As one helps the parents understand what precipitates their difficulties with their child, one often unearths an almost nonexistent marriage. The parents' communication and ability to perceive and deal with each other are so limited that the child often seems to be their only link. Frequently the abusive parent is abetted in this pattern by the nonabusive spouse. Being left alone with the children when other pressures have been mounting can provoke an attack. Criticism of the way the children are handled or how the wife performs as a homemaker or the husband on the job, may be the precipitating factor.

Particular sensitivity must be maintained as to what is transpiring between the parents. Often they describe the relationship as good, denying any problems. When they are distressed and angry with the child, describing how frustrating and terrible his behavior is, we can respond by questioning what has been happening in the parents' life that day. At this point they may be able to relate the events that have led up to their outburst with the child. Sometimes feelings are denied and the worker may then offer subtle suggestions of what the feelings might be. If we are alert to anything that can be construed as criticism, desertion (a husband's going to sleep when the wife wanted companionship) or failure (the iron breaks and the ironing cannot be finished), we may be able to understand what has happened and help the parent to understand this as well. Just the process of clarification can alleviate considerable anxiety for the parent. Determining what is happening and translating it to the parent often must be done over and over again. Slowly some ways must be built for the husband and wife to communicate to each other what they want from each other and how they feel. Both partners are usually feeling the criticism from their own parents. Occasionally, this is an area in which some empathy can first be felt and shared.

Sometimes they need concrete suggestions of ways to express things to each other. A certain amount of family education can be helpful if offered as alternatives not directives. The pattern for family and marriage is so poor that they may need some models. The primary one, of course, will be the relationship between the parent and the worker, which offers a prototype of the parent-child relationship as well as a model for adult relationships, most especially the opportunity to turn to someone and derive help when needed.

Their attempts at communicating and seeking help from each other may be fraught with disappointment and anger. They will need to come back to tell us how such attempts have failed, but be praised for trying. Again, offering praise and encouragement is one of our major functions, as each tiny step needs much reinforcement.

PREGNANCY

Pregnancy is a difficult time for these parents. The mother's needs are heightened (as are all pregnant women's), and the added stress may cause the father to retreat. The parents' views of the pregnancy and unborn child can give many clues as to what they are feeling and what to expect when the baby arrives. Fantasies may be about the expectation of how rewarding and loving the baby will be, or in the form of fear of a deformed or rejecting child. Often the sex is highly significant, one considered very desirable and the other dreaded or feared as impossible to manage.

The most significantly detrimental thing during pregnancy is the feeling by the mother that she is deserted or rejected. The worker may need to redouble her efforts and involvement during pregnancy. If contacts have lessened they may need to be increased again. Attempting to involve other persons, such as a public health nurse, homemaker, or friend, is helpful. This makes more resources available to the family and should be continued after the baby comes.

The husband's reaction to the pregnancy may be jealousy, particularly if he has already felt that the children have taken his wife's time and attention from him. He may view her moodiness and added needs as undue demands on himself, consequently becoming angry and less responsive. He may, on the other hand, be delighted, eager for the baby to meet his needs. The wife may feel that this indicates a loss of interest in her. The possibilities are many and the worker needs to assess what the parental expectations are and how these are affecting their relationship. The parents need help in understanding each other, as well as themselves.

PARENT-CHILD RELATIONSHIPS

When the parent is really trusting of the relationship with the worker, help will be sought in relation to the children. This is the area in which they feel most vulnerable and the sense of failure is so acute. The wish is to be "good" parents and, ironic as it may seem, the parents are making a real effort to do what is right by their child. With this desire we can readily align ourselves. Although any improvements in the other areas will make their relationships with their children better, eventually most will ask our help in understanding their children and being better parents. It is a very guilt-laden area and, many times, fears and concerns can be allayed or be adequately dealt with by helping them get a good, thorough medical and psychological evaluation of the child or children. Knowing the truth is easier than the vague or nagging doubts that have been pushed back for so long. Plans may have to be made for children who have special needs. Educating the parent about the child's development program and capacities is helpful, but often the mother is more concerned with how she can cope or deal with certain behavior or situations. She is eager to know that others make mistakes, including the worker.

Realistic limited goals both for the worker and the parent are essential. If our expectations and hopes are too high we will feel frustrated and certainly cause the parent to feel she has failed, the very process we have worked so hard to change. If the child can live in safety, be accepted as an independent being in his own right, with needs and desires of his own to which the parents can usually respond comfortably, both we and they have succeeded admirably. Their style of child rearing will probably still be rigid and their ability to tolerate stress and demands limited, but now they have learned to use others in times of crises.

REFERENCE

1. Davoren, Elizabeth: The role of the social worker, *in* Helfer, R. E., and Kempe, C. H., eds.: The Battered Child, Chicago, Univ of Chic Press, 1968.

3

Innovative Therapeutic Approaches

C. Henry Kempe, M.D. and Ray E. Helfer, M.D.

The obvious limitation in availability of skilled psychiatrists and social workers demands that other therapeutic approaches must be sought if we hope to help the battered child and his family. Our experience has been that in the great majority of cases, the problem of "insufficient mothering" can be handled by someone other than a highly skilled professional therapist.

Extensive experience has shown that it is absolutely essential to have a highly skilled and accurate evaluation of the psychopathology within the family structure when the battered child syndrome is first suspected or diagnosed. In less than 10 percent of the cases, the diagnosis is that one of the parents is suffering from a major psychosis or the attacking parent may be an aggressive psychopath. In these cases it is unrealistic to expect a therapist other than a skilled psychiatrist, psychologist or psychiatric social worker to be involved. Clearly, such mentally ill parents deserve excellent psychiatric care.

If, after the initial psychiatric evaluation, the diagnosis of the family pathology is that of "insufficient mothering"* then, in our experience, an individual with considerably less training can also be most effective. Fortunately, the great majority of parents who abuse small children are not paranoid or psycho-

---

*The term "insufficient mothering" is used in general terms to describe the problem seen in the large majority of families who come to our attention.

paths and can benefit significantly from an intense relationship with a nonprofessional therapist.

Although excellent results can be obtained in most families by having the therapist be a psychiatrist, psychologist, social worker, general physician, pediatrician, or public health nurse, the qualities that a therapeutic person must possess are not necessarily related to a particular professional identification, course work or training. We have had excellent results with lay workers (Parent Aides) who receive their training "on the job." The ideal therapist is one who is prepared to become meaningfully involved over a period of eight to 12 months in the lives of these very deprived parents in a very major way. This is accomplished through weekly or twice-weekly visits, often in the parents' home. This relationship is characterized by a listening, approving and noncritical point of view. A great deal of dependency is encouraged early, and the therapist often shows special affection and concern with a birthday card or small present. He or she must be available, often by telephone, in the evenings and on weekends, and a substitute made available when this is not feasible. In other words, a lifeline or rescue operation is firmly established for moments of crises.

The goals of therapy by the Parent Aides are limited since it is not realistic to expect a substantive maturation to occur which will undo the severe deprivation experience by these parents. They are:

1. That the child eventually be returned to his home.

2. That the child not be reinjured.

3. That the child is seen as an individual and somewhat enjoyed.

4. That the family is now well enough to recognize impending crises.

5. That the parents reach out to others in the community for help and friendship and are able to give as well as receive.

6. That they can mature and gradually relinquish their marked dependency on the primary therapist.

FOSTER GRANDPARENTS (PARENT AIDES)

For the past four years the Pediatric Service at Colorado General Hospital has utilized the services of a group of "foster grandparents" whose job is simply to cuddle hospitalized children. They are paid a modest wage to supplement their pension. Each "grandparent" is assigned one child for the duration of his hospitalization if the mother is not able to remain for long periods of time. The foster grandparents are all over 65 years of age because of rules of the funding agency.

In the early course of this work a few of the foster grandparents were assigned battered children. Some were totally unable to form any relationship with the parents of these children because of their understandable great anger. Approximately one third uniquely began to fill the mothering needs of some of these parents. This relationship occasionally was extended beyond the hospital with good results. It seemed quite feasible that a larger lay treatment program, therapeutically directed toward the parents, could be developed that would utilize these elderly men and women as Parent Aides.

The program was begun on a small scale, using a group of lay therapists in a similar therapeutic role and in the absence of any formal training. These men and women come from all walks of life and social classes. They are paid a small hourly wage. To date, our Parent Aides, whose age range is from 24 to 60 (use of individuals over 65 also would be most advantageous), have had the good fortune of being raised by loving mothers and fathers. They themselves are parents and are quite ready to take on the care of a deprived adult.

The selection of therapeutic foster grandparents or Parent Aides was done with some care. We try to match up our therapists and patients by social and economic class. It is often important to have a working class therapist for a working class family. Flexibility, patience and compassion, a willingness to listen and be nondirective and noncritical, are the basic requirements for a successful Parent Aide. The qualities are those of a mild and loving individual who is not easily upset by an ungrateful, suspicious and often initially unwilling client.

We introduce the lay therapists to the parents by saying that we would like to have someone visit who is interested in them and their problems. We urge our therapists to ask for a cup of coffee or tea and sit in the kitchen, to pay little attention to the children and to listen with interest to the problems of the *parents.* Sometimes they see both parents together and other times the mother alone. They must be available in moments of crisis; their phone number and that of an alternate lay therapist is in the client's hands.

Every two weeks a group therapy session of the Parent Aides is held with a pediatrician, psychiatrist and/or social worker. The lay therapists are allowed, indeed encouraged, to ventilate some of their frustrations, anxieties and anger at their clients. They often require encouragement because progress is slow; they may be feeling that they are wasting time and money. Ongoing supervision by a highly skilled social worker is also extremely important. One social worker can work with several Parent Aides in addition to having a small caseload of her own.

Provided the goals are limited and an initially correct diagnosis is made of the family pathology as being deficient mothering, clinical results have been outstandingly good at a fraction of the cost of employing psychiatrists or social workers as therapists. By and large the training of these lay therapists is not difficult. Essentially they already have had the basic course—the experience of having been raised by a good mother or father themselves. With the shortage of skilled psychiatrists and other professional mental health workers, it is clear to us that a broad part of therapy must involve what amounts to substitution of intense therapy for the parents who are in need of mothering by those in the population who have the interest, time and talent to provide such help.

The emotional wear and tear on the therapists precludes their having more than two or three families on a part-time basis, with one or two visits each per week. Parent Aides are encouraged to take the clients out for tea or a meal, and to begin to function as a mature and reliable friend. Much more needs to be learned about the selection of these lay workers, but one must not be afraid to try someone who looks promising and then discontinue after a trial period if necessary. Simply the desire to help or the feeling of compassion for battered *children* is not enough to be a successful Parent Aide. The focus is on the *parents* and not the children. Our premise is that if the parents are all right, the children will be protected.

The job would seem clearly to require a kind of empathy, gentleness and patience which comes with time to all those who have the basic capacity to love and mother other adults in need. Those who have had some of the difficult experiences which come with marriage and parenthood, who have a few "scars of battle," are most successful. To date we have found that many very pretty, young unmarried girls who have all the desired qualities to be successful therapists, somehow have considerable difficulty getting started. To the abusive mother these girls represent everything she has herself failed to achieve. It is important to regard the therapist as something other than ladies bountiful. They should, if possible, be well matched in terms of educational achievements as well as economics, class and race.

Since Parent Aides need ongoing careful supervision it seems best if they are hired by an agency or hospital that has these backup professionals available. Any group, be it state or private, wishing to provide help to abusive parents could well use the services of the skilled and motivated lay worker.

THE VISITING NURSES

By training and experience public health nurses are comfortable in calling on clients in their homes, having coffee in the kitchen and providing many needed health services. Such nurses are often readily admitted to family homes and they are a potential resource for advice in many aspects of health care. Some, but not all, public health nurses have great talents in caring for parents who batter their children. As described above, a helpful person is one who is not critical or judgmental and who is prepared to use himself or herself as a therapeutic agent.

This very deep involvement with the life of another person does not come readily to everyone. The very crisp and efficient nurse, or one who is critical of a slovenly home or an inadequate mother, simply becomes another condemning figure to the abusive mother, reminding her of her serious experience with her own critical mother. Nurses are often trained to give "how-to" advice and to direct attention toward the child. In her role as a therapeutic person, the public health nurse must not give very much advice. She does a great deal more sympathetic listening than talking. She is patient, takes time and does not obviously seem to teach. When possible, a weekly or twice-weekly visit to the home in an informal friendly way, with ready willingness to listen, is often an acceptable way to provide treatment. In parts of the country where highly trained social workers, psychologists or psychiatrists are not readily available, or where the patient is only willing to deal with a nonthreatening health professional, the visiting nurse becomes an invaluable person.

It must be stressed that the job of the visiting nurse is *not* that of an "inspector" and is *not* to provide "supervision." Treatment of the battering family involves an experience in "mothering," the development of trust of another adult and the gradual improvement of the parents' self-image. Helping these parents to obtain a reasonable understanding of their child and to enjoy his presence are two very important goals. Many public health nurses function in such a role quite spontaneously and with considerable success. One has to be certain, however, that they do not discontinue their visiting too soon. The plan should be to continue a relationship on a regular basis, first twice a week and then weekly for approximately a year, but never less than eight or nine months. In time, spacing between visits can be increased but it must not be discontinued and contacts should be maintained essentially until the child is clearly no longer at risk. This decision must be made jointly by the nurse, physician and social worker, if one is involved.

HOMEMAKER SERVICES

Many mothers simply do not have the strength to cope with all the demands of several children. In some situations a part-time homemaker may be an essential part of treatment and support in order to keep the family together or to return the child to the family at an early date. Clearly the homemaker who is too brisk or efficient would simply make the mother feel worse, more inadequate; but one who is willing to work along in a gentle way, by actually helping in the house and with the children, and also providing some of the support which we have described above, can be most helpful. The homemaker is also a part of the therapeutic team. She must not be considered either as *the* therapist or the spy within the household who checks up on the childrens' welfare. She will have problems in dealing with her anger at the mother. This must be recognized. Often the homemaker needs to be part of the group therapy which is established for the Parent Aides. An urgent need for the development of these special home-maker services in communities will, if met, undoubtedly bene-fit such families who can then be kept together at a much less cost to the community.

One word of caution must be interjected. When a homemaker is sent into a home that clearly does not need the services of someone to cook, clean, help with the children, buy groceries, etc., then the roles of the homemaker and the mother become confused. The very tidy woman who keeps an immaculate home with one or two children does not need a homemaker in the usual sense of the word. She may, on the other hand, be in great need of a Parent Aide or foster grandparent.

CRISIS NURSERIES

While it is readily possible to park a car for a modest fee in all parts of the United States, it is extremely difficult to have, without much explanation or preparation, a place where a mother might leave her child for a few hours, in moments of great stress. This service should be available either on an intermittent or even regular basis each day. We have known many mothers who would be quite able to cope with their two or three children if they had some relief, even if it were only for two or three hours a day. At some economic levels this is readily arranged for by employment of babysitters or by the mothers seeking employment outside the home on a part-time basis. This is often done not for the financial reward but, in fact, to get away from their child and thereby prevent battering. At the other end of the economic scale, and particularly when mothers have no special working skills, it becomes very difficult to find a place where a child can be safely placed for no other reason than that the mother wants relief.

SRS pays for this service

The attitude of many welfare agencies appears to be, "you have had your fun now take care of it." The fear expressed by many departments is that once the word got around that a child could be placed for a time, the welfare departments would be confronted with thousands of children, many of whom would never be picked up again. In our modest experience thus far, it would seem clear that when given a free choice mothers do not abuse this kind of liberal facility. Clearly, in housing developments or by arrangements between groups of mothers and under the supervision of welfare departments or the schools, it should be possible to provide drop-in nurseries. Justification for use of this service is a positive rather than a negative action on the part of the parents who have come to recognize their limitations and are willing to contribute as much as they can for this type of relief.

MOTHER'S ANONYMOUS

Mother's Anonymous is one of the brighter lights that has recently appeared upon the horizon of therapeutic innovations for parents who abuse or may abuse their children. This self-help group was founded by a striking, dynamic woman whose enormous energies were, for 29 of her 30 years, directed toward the destruction of herself and the "little slut I brought into this world." This woman's educational experiences and preparation for motherhood included approximately 100 foster homes, 32 institutions, rape at age 11 (which she enjoyed, for this was the first time she had personally "meant anything" to an adult), exotic dancing, prostitution, five years of grade school, a disastrous first and second marriage, and innumerable negative experiences with men in general. Her background, coupled with her basic innate intelligence, driving personality, seemingly unlimited stamina and a fortuitous third marriage, provided the leadership for this new and exciting therapeutic adventure.

Her "credentials" and cries for help turned off at least nine established agency "professionals" who found it difficult to accept this form of "field work" as suitable criterion for motherhood, much less leadership. Fortunately for many women and their children, one social worker, who had worked with her for several months, recognized the potential and seized upon the opportunity. The "conversion" came after one particular harassing session of complaints about the dearth of services available to abusive mothers, when finally the suggestion was made by the social worker that she should "do something about it."

Something *was* done about it and, in early 1970, M.A. was founded. The organization's basic tenets and guidelines are expressed in its brochure:

> A crisis intervention group, whose primary objective is to help and prevent severely damaging relationships between a mother and her children.
>
> A long or short term of "DO IT NOW" therapy to help establish, strengthen, and maintain a healthy emotional and physical coexistence for mothers and their children.
>
> Our goal is to rechannel destructive attitudes and actions into constructive ones. If we, *Mother's Anonymous,* attain our goals with the group members, this can produce a lifetime of

more meaningful experiences for the child and family involved.

We all know that the parent/child relationship is the most important a child forms. A destructive, disturbed mother can, and often does, produce through her actions a physically or emotionally abused, or battered child.

Present available help is limited and/or expensive, usually with a long waiting list before the person requesting help can actually receive treatment. Often, because of that very reason just stated, the uncared for immediate crisis goes unchecked and severe damage results. The present solution of out-of-home placement (foster home) for the child and much too infrequently, possible counseling for the mother is antiquated, inadequate and downright unfair when the total situation *could* have been dealt with in the earlier stages prior to severe crisis.

Our organization asks no fee of its members. We offer positive behavior alternatives in a "DO IT NOW" approach to alleviate critical problems. We, M.A., believe that this method can curb the slow, but painful, day by day deterioration found in many family relationships.

Guidelines for Achievement

1.

WE will recognize and admit to ourselves and to other *M.A. MEMBERS* the child abuse problem in our home as it exists today and set about an immediate course of constructive actions to stop any further abusive actions in our homes.

2.

WE want and accept help for ourselves and will follow any constructive guidance to get the strength, the courage and the control that we must have in order that our children will grow up in a loving, healthy home.

3.

WE will take one step, one day, at a time to achieve our goals.

4.

WE may remain anonymous if we desire, but we may identify ourselves and at *anytime* call upon other *M.A.* members or seek constructive help *before, during or after, OUR PROB-LEM* of child abuse occurs.

5.
WE must understand that a problem as involved as this cannot be cured immediately and takes constant acceptance of the *M.A.* program or other constructive guidance.

6.
WE admit that our children are defenseless and that the problem is within us as a parent.

7.
WE believe our children are not to be blamed or subjected to our abusive actions regardless what the cause is.

8.
WE promise to ourselves and our family that we will use, to the fullest extent, the *M.A.* program.

9.
WE admit that we are alienating ourselves from our children and our family and through the *M.A.* program we will make ourselves the center of reuniting our family as a loving, healthy *FAMILY UNIT.*

10.
WE admit we must learn to control ourselves and we do these things in order to achieve harmony in our home and to earn the love and respect of ourselves, our family and our society.

Talking with the mothers of M.A. is truly an exciting experience. Without exception they responded to the many queries with the comment, "Do you mean before or after I joined M.A.?" By no means has everything suddenly turned right for their chaotic lives but "at least I don't beat my kids anymore." M.A. is a bootstrap, here-and-now operation that deals with the mother's problem at her level. One mother admits she can now tell her son to go take his bath, whereas she use to scream "Get your bath, you bastard, before I drive your ass right up the wall." These are not uneducated, crude women. They are real mothers who are frankly expressing their innermost feelings about someone they cannot tolerate.

M.A. members use each other for support and guidance. Since they all aren't "up tight" at the same time, they can rescue each other during their more stressful moments. They share each other's first names and phone numbers and call day or night. The look of anticipation and satisfaction is really visible upon their faces when they state how much they look forward to the time when they will be called by another member. "I'd like to feel that I was helpful to someone." They constantly try to redirect the destructive forces of their daily lives to produce more meaningful lives for their children.

There appears to be no difference in the psychodynamics of these women and those described elsewhere in this book. M.A. members have never had a mothering imprint, are extremely isolated people, have disastrous unsupporting marriages, have unrealistic expectations of their children and, above all, reveal an immeasurably low self-image. In contrast to most abusive parents, these women talk about it, sometimes kid about it, but above all help each other by taking "one step at a time."

M.A. is a youthful movement. And, as with most young self-help groups, has a few rough edges that need to be smoothed down to permit it to flourish and spread as it should. The members are understandably turned off by professionalism. They have been beat on so frequently by our unhelpful social system that no love is lost by the attempts to keep the "establishment" ties with M.A. from developing. Some way must be found to maintain this necessary autonomy and yet profit by the guidance and help of certain special "professionals."

First, the weekly group meetings are such an important and integral part of the M.A. program that the recognized leader(s) must be guided in developing the skills of running small groups and understanding their dynamics. Second, any M.A. program would do well to loosely but specifically identify themselves with a recognized hospital or community-based child abuse consultation team (see Chapter 11). The professionals on this team could provide the necessary backup for those mothers and children who occasionally need the special care and treatment that M.A. cannot provide.

Third, these mothers need and are ready for some ongoing counseling in usual child rearing practices and the normal growth and development pattern of children. Rarely do their individual or collective backgrounds provide enough experience for the M.A. members to be helpful to each other in this area.

Fourth, an active follow-through program for the "drop-outs" or "no shows" is mandatory. The present M.A. program represents only those mothers (and fathers) who, on their own, could make it to the first or second meeting. The scores of parents who could not get that far are unaccounted for.

Finally, there is the problem of love. "I don't beat him any more, but I cannot really say I have any feeling or love for him." M.A. rightfully has the initial limited goal of decreasing or eliminating the abuse (physical and emotional) of the children. But then there is the next step—"How can I love that little bitch?" Somehow a mothering model must be injected into the M.A. concept. Possibly this would be the "graduate" program, the *second step*.

M.A. is exciting, it is beginning to meet its limited but critically important goals. With the proper support and nurturing, this youthful program could have as significant an impact on child abuse as A.A. has had on alcoholism.

SUMMARY

Regardless of who is involved in the care of battering parents it seems clear to us that a lifeline must be provided which is available seven days a week, 24 hours a day. All clients should know at least two telephone numbers to call: That of their primary "friend" (Parent Aide) and a backup number. In times of crisis it is essential that if one therapist is not available some other knowledgeable person is. In the city this can be the pediatric emergency room in a local hospital, assuming the staff is trained and understanding. In time, answering services will have to be provided by all social agencies handling these cases. The use of a telephone lifeline has worked well in the prevention of suicide in the United States and Great Britain. Clearly, the battered child syndrome deserves a similar approach for those crises which do not occur between 9:00 A.M. and 5:00 P.M., Monday through Friday. Finally, available therapeutic manpower in the population at large is not limited to the skilled professional therapist in the fields of psychiatry and social work for the specific needs of the battering parents. There is an immense reservoir of capable potential Parent Aides, paid or unpaid, who are ready to be brought into the therapeutic picture provided they are given encouragement and adequate consultation and supervision.

We view this as the next important step in the field of child abuse. The major role of the social worker, psychologist and psychiatrist should probably be limited to making an accurate diagnosis of family pathology early in the treatment program and then to the supervising of the Parent Aides, visiting nurses, therapeutic homemakers and the staff of drop-in nurseries. All of these individuals will be regarded as multipliers of the primary skills of the more highly trained professionals.

4

Interviewing the Parents

CAROL SCHNEIDER, PH.D., CARL POLLOCK, M.D.,
and RAY E. HELFER, M.D.

AN UNDERSTANDING of the psychodynamics of child abuse can be put to practical use in developing an interview in which the parents are provided with an opportunity to have their own feelings and concerns understood. Many children might be spared if the appropriate people were able to question parents and listen for answers which indicate a setting in which a child might be abused. Each of the professionals involved with the problems of the abused child and his family must develop the ability to gather appropriate data if they truly wish to begin a meaningful therapeutic program. The interviewer must, at all costs, resist the desire to find out who actually hurt the child. This approach is much too threatening and unrewarding.

As was pointed out in the Introduction, there are three separate and distinct areas that must be covered if we hope to gain an understanding of a particular family in which a small child may have been physically abused. In the interview, we first must determine if the parents have the *potential* to abuse a small child. Second, there must be a *particular* child—not just any child, but a very special child. Finally we must determine the crisis(es) that precipitated the abuse. It is unlikely that the battering situation will occur unless each of these factors plays some role. Gathering this information is most rewarding in helping the therapist to determine the type and degree of help that is required.

It is imperative that the questions asked during the interview elicit responses which are predictably different for known

55

abusers and nonabusers. Otherwise, when these questions are used to identify potential abusers, many false identifications will surely be made. Differences in child rearing attitudes and practices of the various socioeconomic classes and cultures must be well understood so that cultural attitude differences between examiner and patient are not taken as indicators of potential battering. Certain abusive parents try very hard to please interviewers by giving them what they want. Some answers are so well-defended that only a highly trained professional could hope to spot signs of trouble. Thus, no set of questions or particular technique will give completely error-free results.* However, we will present here an approach which hopefully will aid skilled interviewers as they try to separate parents who physically abuse their small children from parents who do not.

Probably the most important factors that assist in developing rapport with the parents are:

1. Keep the interview parent-centered; e.g., begin by saying, "How are *you* doing?" or "You must have been through a lot today." Avoid extensive discussion about the injured child.

2. See the parents in a relaxed setting. The social worker's or doctor's office is ideal. The bedside or the emergency room (see Chapter 5) is unacceptable.

3. Avoid prolonged interviews. Several short sessions are more rewarding.

4. Be honest at all times, *but* do not give the parents more than they want to hear or are able to handle at any one setting.

5. See the parents separately and then together, but do not withhold information from one that you give the other.

6. Be available to see them at once when they arrive, even if only to explain that because they are two hours (or days) late you have to ask them to wait a little while to see you.

*The attempts to develop a reliable and valid questionnaire to assist in the early identification of those who may injure their small children are discussed further in Appendix A.

7. Go out of your way to keep them informed about *everything* that is going on. Don't be concerned if they disagree with you on some issue. The important thing is that they know what is happening.

8. Structure the interviews in such a way that at least one person who talks with them gathers data in each of the three major areas, i.e., The Potential to Abuse, The Child, and The Crisis(es).

THE POTENTIAL

There appear to be at least four major categories in which assessment needs to be made in order to evaluate the potential to injure a small child. Each of these will be discussed in detail to enable the interviewer to develop an approach in his attempt to gather this very important data.

CATEGORY I: HOW THE PARENTS THEMSELVES WERE REARED

Parents who physically abuse their small children have, almost invariably, been reared in a similar manner. At least the relationship they had as small children with their own parents left a great deal to be desired. They truly were never or poorly "imprinted" with that highly important and essential ability to "mother" a small child.

Some of the questions that can be helpful in gathering this type of information are:

1. How did your parents punish you when you misbehaved or displeased them as a child?

2. Do you feel the way your parents punished you is the best way to get children to behave?

3. Did you feel your parents were pleased with you?

4. Do you feel you've let your parents down?

5. What kind of things did you try to do to please your parents?

6. What kind of relationship did you have with your mother when you were younger?

7. How would you describe your relationship with your mother now?

There is a general trend in the answers to these questions. In the battering parents what one obtains is a feeling that their own parents did not regard them as worthwhile people, and yet they believe that their parents were justified in this viewpoint. They have the feeling that they were never able to relate to, or please, their parents in such a way as to be seen as worthwhile individuals. Many statements will be forthcoming which indicate how their parents made few, if any, attempts to understand the needs of the children.

Abusive parents will complain that everything their parents gave them seemed to be wrong or seemed to have more to do with the parents' needs than the child's. They will describe a lack of having been cherished as individuals with their own wants, and continually having to please their parents by meeting the parents' needs and wants. They will alternate between a kind of glowing account of what they did that pleased their parents and a vacant account of their failures to please. All these are indications of how their self-esteem had been built around meeting the needs of their parents, coupled with pride as well as with discouragement. One sometimes gets the feeling that there was little else in the interaction between these abusive parents and their own parents. Very often one notes that if their ability to be gratifying seemed to be working, then the abusers' description of their own parents is that of an over-idealized person and not a person with failings and deficiencies.

CATEGORY II: THE PATTERN OF ISOLATION

In taking the history, the second step necessary to determine whether or not a particular family has a potential to abuse small children is to inquire about the wall of isolation which could keep a family from turning to others for help. It is very important to look at this carefully. The wall of isolation can be explored from many vantage points. Particular attention should be placed in the area of how the parents are dealing with the problems relating to their children.

Ask the mother, "What do you do when the baby cries?" She will often say, "Oh, I pick him up." Then ask, "What do you do if he doesn't stop crying?" "Well I walk him." "If he doesn't stop crying, what do you do then?" Keep pushing this until she convinces you that she has both the understanding of the necessity and the capability of acting to get someone else to help her. Just because she says someone helps her out doesn't mean she really uses this person. You must be convinced in your own mind that when this mother gets upset about her baby she calls somebody, such as her neighbor or her mother, to help her. Some realistic way of getting out of difficulty when she's "up tight" with her children must be demonstrated. If this mother has no realistic way of handling the usual problems that small children present, such as with eating, crying or accidents, or of handling defiance and disobedience on the part of her older children, her frustration and anger may lead to physical abuse as the only untried "solution." A past history of having coped successfully with a series of problems normally encountered with children makes most experienced clinicians rule out abusing in a parent, or at least assign abusing a very low probability of occurrence.

Some possible questions for assessing whether the parents have reasonable ways of getting out of difficulty when problems arise are:

1. What kind of things make you feel really nervous and upset?

2. Are you having any problems with your child's behavior? (If yes, what kind of things have you tried to solve these problems? How have these worked?)

3. How do you feel inside when the baby cries?

4. Does it ever make you feel like crying yourself?

5. How do you handle the problem of a baby messing when he eats?

6. What is a good method of toilet training a child?

7. How do you handle accidents when they happen to your child?

8. Do you ever feel "at the end of your rope" or helpless to deal with problems like crying, disobedience or misbehavior?

9. Whom do you have to turn to at such times?

10. How do you reach this person(s) at 10 P.M. on Saturday night?

11. Who has been helpful?

12. Do you use a babysitter? How often? Who?

13. What do you do when you have concern about your children?

Significant answers relate to feelings of anxiety, anger or despair in dealing with problems. Note especially an outpouring of anxiety arousing problems and a lack of available coping techniques for handling them. It is rare that batterers can discuss actual problem situations for which they found solutions which made them feel satisfied.

If the parents cannot clearly demonstrate that they have a way to use others, not only that they know how, but that they actually use others meaningfully, then you have added information to assist in determining the *risk* within a particular family. This wall of isolation is of significant importance not only in the gathering of evidence but also in developing a therapeutic plan.

CATEGORY III: THE INTERRELATIONSHIP BETWEEN THE PARENTS

The third area of inquiry is to look within the family structure itself. The relationship between the husband and wife and the support (or lack of it) they provide each other is of extreme importance in trying to determine the likelihood that a given child might have been abused.

After following a large number of abusive parents one begins to realize that whether or not a small child is battered is somewhat similar to a genetic inheritance pattern of dominance, sex linked or recessive. It appears that:

1. If an adult with a weak potential to abuse children marries a normally reared individual then physical abuse will probably not occur.

2. If, on the other hand, the potential in one adult is very strong and the spouse is a rather passive individual then abuse does indeed occur.

3. If two adults, both with weak or moderate potential marry, then abuse is likely.

This documents the very real role that interrelationships between husband and wife play in determining whether or not abuse occurs. Such interrelationships must be carefully looked at if we hope to develop an understanding of the problems within a specific family structure.

Questions that may prove helpful in this area are:

1. Can you rely on your spouse?
2. What happens when you and your husband (wife) disagree on how to handle the children?
3. Does your husband (wife) recognize when you are "up tight"?
4. Is he (she) helpful at these times?
5. To whom do you turn in times like this?
6. Is your spouse helpful with the children?
7. What is there about your marriage that could be better?

If both the father and mother are living together with their children as a family unit then child abuse appears to be a *Family Affair.*

CATEGORY IV: HOW THE PARENTS SEE THE CHILD?

The fourth step to assist in determining the potential for abuse is to explore the expectations parents have of their children (or a particular child). Most parents who abuse their small children are completely turned around in this area. They have very unrealistic expectations of their children, often one particular child.

There is a feeling that children must provide them with emotional support when they are upset. Children are expected to perform certain developmental tasks based more on the demand of the parent than on the readiness or ability of the child.

Questions which might help in assessing such attitudes are:

1. When should parents start toilet training a child? At what age should the child be fully trained?

2. How well do your children understand your feelings?

3. How have your children been of help to you?

4. Can they tell when you're upset and do they help you then?

5. Do any of your children seem to have problems being warm and loving enough?

6. Do all your children live up to your expectations? .

7. When you're upset do your children comfort you?

Listen for the feeling that their children are failing to live up to their ideal of how good children should behave. Also listen for feelings that the child should do better than he does. Unrealistic expectations that the child provide parental comfort and respond to parental needs may be present, along with the feelings that the child is deficient in meeting these demands. A very rigid, righteous attitude in response to these questions should be noted.

In summary, the potential, as described, to physically abuse small children can be demonstrated in most abusive parents. The degree of risk to which a particular child is subjected is dependent upon the strength of this potential within the parents. It is unlikely that the potential to abuse a small child *alone* will be enough for the abuse to occur. To this potential we must add *the child* and *the crises.* The three together, in the right combination, are often deadly.

THE CHILD

To accurately assess the likelihood that abuse will (or has) occurred, the interviewer must gather data about the child, both by questions and careful observation.

As we've emphasized, it takes a very special kind of child for battering to occur. Usually not every child in a family will be beaten, especially if the potential is low to moderate. If, on the other hand, the potential is very great, then every child may be beaten, first one then the next.

How do parents with the potential for abuse determine which child? Many things have to fall into place in order to determine this. Into these complex, confused and isolated lives is born a child. If this new child happens, by chance, to come at a period when the family situation is reasonably stable, when there are no particular crises, and the child happens to be a "good" baby who doesn't cry much, sleeps all night, eats well, sucks well, goes to bed early, is awake only three or four hours a day, doesn't have colic or get sick, has no birth defects, and doesn't remind the father or mother of someone he or she doesn't like (including themselves), then all will probably go well. This baby "lucked out," and will probably not be beaten.

If, on the other hand, you place the parents with a moderate potential up against a baby who has colic, is fussy, has his days and nights turned around, has a stool every time he eats, and is just an ornery little kid who has a few illnesses, this child finds himself in a family structure where he is in severe trouble.

Any physician who recognizes a mother with the potential must be constantly alert when a baby is placed under his care. Watch that baby! If he's a "good" baby and lives up to all the mother's expectations he may do very well. If something goes wrong in the newborn period, even if it's nothing serious but makes the mother begin to think of the baby as a little different, then he may be in deep trouble. Someone must look very carefully and determine what can be done to "bail him out," quickly.

If the child is older, he can be looked at from a different vantage point. Once he reaches 18 months and more we must begin to observe what he is doing in his household to deal with the particular demands and expectations of his parents. Is he beginning to take care of some of their needs? A good example, and a true one, is that of a little 20-month-old girl who, whenever she realized her mother was upset, immediately went to her side and comforted her. This child, in her 20 short months, had learned that when her mother became upset she had better respond by beginning to take care of her needs. She herself was doing for her mother what most mothers would do for their child.

When the social worker or the public health nurse visits a home, she must observe how the child deals with periods of stress in her mother. The judge, social worker, nurse or doctor may be completely confused when the child goes over to his mother to cuddle her. They might even conclude that the child could not possibly have been beaten *unless* they are fully aware of the dynamics involved.

In summary, there are two particular areas that must be taken into account in considering the child.* First, the little baby is of concern if he is difficult and fussy and is in a family with a moderate or high potential. Second, the older child must be observed to determine what role he or she is taking within the family. These may be very significant aspects of the total picture as one tries to determine how vulnerable certain children are in a given family. The child who is seen as *different* in some way may be most vulnerable.

THE CRISIS

The actual act of abuse usually occurs during a crisis within the family unit. If the injury has already occurred then we must try to discover what set it off: Was there a single crisis or a series of crises? What was the crisis about? If the child has not yet been beaten then we must do everything possible to know the family well enough to avoid the crisis. Unfortunately, one of the things that obscures our ability to discover the crisis and its meaning is that it may not have been a crisis in most families, but in that particular family it was a very significant one. The television set broke down, the husband went out, or the mother-in-law was critical of the mother's child rear-

---

*There is obviously a third area which is of extreme importance. This is the actual degree and type of physical injury a child may have received. These are discussed in detail in *The Battered Child.*

ing ability. The crisis may often take the form of losing someone (temporarily or permanently) who is important to one of the parents, someone who is able to rescue them when they are "up tight" with their children. (The concept of the crisis and its importance was discussed in much more detail by Drs. Pollack and Steele in Chapter 1.)

SUMMARY

Regardless of the professional background of the individual interested in gathering pertinent information, he or she will find it useful to develop a good rapport with the parents and then consider the three areas discussed, i.e., an evaluation of *the potential* for child abuse to occur within a given family unit, a determination of how vulnerable *the child* is in this particular setting, and understanding of the *crisis*(es) that occurred or may occur to place the child in jeopardy.

The institution of an appropriate and meaningful therapeutic program is most dependent upon an accurate assessment of the total situation. With this evaluation one can usually determine, with a fair degree of accuracy, where the therapy should be directed, what type of treatment is indicated, and how urgent the problem really is.

Part Two

THE CHILD

His Need for Help

EDITORIAL NOTE

Woefully little is known about the battered child and his world. From retrospective studies it is clear that he is likely to rear his children as he was reared. He also may be prone to violent actions against others. We know little about his thoughts and feelings or how he learns the art of caring for his parents' needs so early in life (sometimes as early as one year). We also recognize that children have certain basic rights, the most important of which is the right to be a child. When children are deprived of this normal developmental growth, as are most abused children, unusual and strange things happen to their ability to make decisions, use others, trust and become dependent on someone else. The material presented in this section represents only the beginning of our attempts to better understand these children and help them — now and as they become adults and parents.

5

The Child's Need for Early Recognition, Immediate Care and Protection*

RAY E. HELFER, M.D. and C. HENRY KEMPE, M.D.

THE GREAT MAJORITY of child abuse cases are first seen either in a physician's office or in the emergency room. The children usually arrive without warning, often at a time when the doctor can ill-afford the time and emotional commitment required to make an appropriate diagnosis, begin treatment and arrange for a disposition. And yet, these children present as an emergency if not a medical/surgical emergency, then one where the children are in urgent need of immediate care and protection.

The manner in which this emergency care of the suspected case of child abuse is handled will set the stage either for a smooth flowing therapeutic relationship for the child and his family or an ineffectual treatment program which often leads to repeated abuse or even death. With few exceptions emergency rooms are staffed by young physicians who are too inexperienced and busy to handle adequately these emotionally charged situations. For this reason the emergency care for these children and their parents must be kept simple and straight forward. In our experience the following guidelines for the emergency room physician have proved helpful:

*Helfer, Ray E.: Guidelines for the emergency care of the battered child, reprinted in part. In Spitzer, Stanley, and Oaks, Wilbur, eds.: Emergency Medical Management, Grune & Stratton, 1971.

1. The diagnosis of child abuse must be considered in all cases involving traumatic injury to small children.

2. *All* pre-school children (and most older children), in whom the diagnosis of child abuse is suspected, must be admitted to the hospital.

3. The parents should rarely, if ever, be accused or confronted by the emergency room physician with the possibility that their child may have been physically abused.

4. A pediatrician and/or social worker who has had considerable experience in dealing with the multifaced problems of child abuse should be consulted by the ER and/or admitting physician.

The final diagnosis of child abuse can rarely be made in the emergency room. The physicians are busy and inexperienced, the parents are usually upset, specialized social workers are rarely available, diagnostic studies are often time consuming, and the child can rarely be protected in this setting. Only hospital admission will afford the time, atmosphere and expertise for an adequate evaluation of the child and his family. The extent of the physical injuries must never influence the decision of whether or not these children require admission. The decision for admission rests entirely on the degree of suspicion of child abuse.

CONFRONTING THE PARENTS

The parents of the abused child are very suspicious, defensive and helpless people. Even though they are difficult people to like, the emergency room physicians must make every effort to control their own feelings toward the parents in their dealings with them. It is best, if at all possible, not to bring up the issue of child abuse. A routine emergency room history and physical examination should be completed. If nonaccidental injuries are seriously suspected then admission to the hospital must be arranged.

This admission is explained to the parents by *truthfully* stating that the child has an injury and needs further study and observation in the hospital for diagnosis and treatment. Parents will usually agree to the admission if they have not been accused, threatened or otherwise upset by ER personnel. The staff members must go out of their way, often acting contrary to their own feelings, to handle these parents with extreme care if they hope to begin, and not hinder, the development of a positive therapeutic relationship.

Telling the parents more than the physician actually knows, or more than the parents can handle at any one time, usually results in a disastrous sequence of events which detracts significantly from the overall goal of developing a positive therapeutic program for the family. Telling parents in the emergency room that they are suspected of causing the injury *before* a definitive diagnostic evaluation is made is comparable only to informing parents, before studies are complete, that their anemic child needs to be in the hospital because he might have leukemia.

If, however, the parents ask about the possibility of abuse the ER physician should *truthfully* state that he is uncertain about the cause of the injuries and strongly recommends hospitalization for further study. The great majority of parents who injure their children are anxious to be helped. They will cooperate if not threatened and antagonized. Only rarely should it prove necessary to use legal means, such as a "hold order," to confine a child to the hospital. The "child abuse consultation team" (see Chapter 11) must be consulted by the ER staff if this form of intervention is contemplated.

CONSIDERING THE DIAGNOSIS*

An analysis of emergency room patients made at the Rochester (N.Y.) Medical Center and at the University of Colorado Medical Center revealed that 10 percent of the children who entered with a traumatic injury had been physically abused (see Chapter 6). Data from our Colorado experience indicate

*The reader is referred to related chapters in *The Battered Child* for further assistance in making the diagnosis of child abuse.

that a high proportion of unrecognized cases of child abuse was uncovered by reviewing all x-rays ordered by the emergency room staff for the purpose of evaluating a traumatic injury in small children.

The diagnosis of child abuse must be seriously considered in every child who presents with an injury. The physician should carefully explore the explanation for the injury provided by the parents and make absolutely certain that the degree and type of injury can be adequately explained, and any inconsistency between the history and physical findings must be diagnosed as a suspected case of child abuse.

The practicing physician, house officer, nurse and social worker are frequently confronted with the problem of whether or not a particular child has been (or might be) physically abused. Recognizing the severely beaten child usually does not present any significant difficulty. We would, however, much prefer to be able to identify the abused child at an earlier point in time which would permit a meaningful therapeutic program to be instituted.

Table 1 lists certain signs and symptoms which, when present, warrant the consideration of child abuse. Like many problems in medicine there is no *one* diagnostic study that can be considered pathognomonic. One should feel quite comfortable, however, in considering the diagnosis of child abuse when some of the signs and symptoms outlined in Table I are present. Any physician or social worker who recognizes the presence of some of these findings in any given case should *quickly* proceed with a further and more definitive evaluation. This can *only* (except in the most unusual situation) be accomplished in the hospital setting. Even though many of these signs and symptoms are not specific, when found in various combinations, they indicate the presence of a very serious problem. Most diagnoses in medicine are approached in exactly the same manner, i.e., putting together a combination of signs, symptoms and laboratory findings and developing the most logical diagnostic pattern.

All too frequently we are unwilling to recognize cases of child abuse because of our extreme distaste for the subsequent events (reporting, implications, legal action, need for personal

TABLE 1. *The Diagnosis of Physical Abuse Should Be Considered When*
Some *of the Following Are Present*

WHEN THE PARENT:

1. Shows evidence of loss of control, or fear of losing control.
2. Presents contradictory history.
3. Projects cause of injury onto a sibling or third party.
4. Has delayed unduly in bringing child in for care.
5. Shows detachment.
6. Reveals inappropriate awareness of seriousness of situation (either overreaction or underreaction).
7. Continues to complain about irrelevant problems unrelated to the injury.
8. Personally is misusing drugs or alcohol.
9. Is disliked, for unknown reasons, by the physician.
10. Presents a history that cannot or does not explain the injury.
11. Gives specific "eye witness" history of abuse.
12. Gives a history of repeated injury.
13. Has no one to "bail" her (him) out when "up tight" with the child.
14. Is reluctant to give information.
15. Refuses consent for further diagnostic studies.
16. Hospital "shops."
17. Cannot be located.
18. Is psychotic or psychopathic.
19. Has been reared in a "motherless" atmosphere.
20. Has unrealistic expectations of the child.

WHEN THE CHILD:

1. Has an unexplained injury.
2. Shows evidence of dehydration and/or malnutrition without obvious cause.
3. Has been given inappropriate food, drink and/or drugs.
4. Shows evidence of overall poor care.
5. Is unusually fearful.
6. Shows evidence of repeated injury.
7. "Takes over" and begins to care for parents' needs.
8. Is seen as "different" or "bad" by the parents.
9. Is indeed different in physical or emotional makeup.
10. Is dressed inappropriately for degree or type of injury.
11. Shows evidence of sexual abuse.
12. Shows evidence of repeated skin injuries.
13. Shows evidence of repeated fractures.
14. Shows evidence of "characteristic" x-ray changes to long bones.
15. Has injuries that are not mentioned in history.

commitment, and inadequate treatment programs). As with most illnesses the *early* recognition of the problem permits the implementation of a much more acceptable and effective therapeutic program. If the problem is recognized early (hopefully even before the injury occurs) then our efforts can be directed toward prevention, a much more palatable method of helping the family.

Physicians, nurses and social workers alike must make every effort to appreciate the significance of the presence of those findings listed in Table 1, so that the diagnosis of child abuse can be considered soon enough to facilitate early treatment and prevention.

PRE- AND POSTNATAL OBSERVATIONS

In the prenatal setting, the general practitioner or the obstetrician and their nurses and receptionists can often recognize mothers-to-be who are likely to have difficulty with their babies. Among these are women who for one reason or another have strong desires not to bear the child and may have tried to induce or obtain an abortion. Some high risk mothers-to-be are not only extremely young but have unrealistic views of motherhood. Often, expectations of perfect motherly bliss are so completely unrealistic that they can alert the physician to possible trouble ahead. Other women at risk are those who are unduly concerned about the baby's sex and appearance being "just right." Such mothers-to-be often spontaneously ask the obstetrical nurse or the doctor about child rearing practices with great concern about "control of bad behavior" and express fears of "spoiling the baby."

The very first contact between a new baby and its mother often yields important clues to future relationships. Some mothers will spontaneously express pity, but no love or tenderness, for their new baby. Others will make very disparaging remarks on first seeing the new baby and may express extreme distaste or profound rejection. While in the hospital some mothers either fail to name the baby or select a highly impossible name. It is common practice on the part of the physicians and nurses, in this situation, to assume that the mother will come to love the baby "in time." This may happen. A particularly rewarding "good" baby may enhance minimal mothering capabilities, just as a very warm and giving husband may be able to increase mothering capabilities on the part of borderline mothers. Careful observations in the very first few minutes of mother-newborn reaction can often be extremely helpful in identifying a mother who might be at risk in terms of her mothering capabilities.

The routine six-week or 10-week well-child visit to a pediatrician or well-baby clinic often allows both nurse and physician to see mother and baby interaction at a time when the mother has already come to know the baby and to form definite attachments. At this time some mothers may feel quite depressed. In the past, we have assumed that mild postpartum depression ("the blues") is a physiologic and probably universal event which, rarely, may be of serious impact (postpartum psychosis). We have now come to realize that while some mothers cannot love their babies because they are depressed, many more are depressed because they cannot love their babies. The opportunity to express negative or aggressive feelings toward a new baby rarely exists for most mothers unless the pediatric nurse or physician is able to sympathetically allow her to express such feelings of disappointment or, at times, frank rage. Such an event is most commonly observed when the baby has been expected with too much hope of repairing the mother's past emotional deprivation; the mother then looks to the child for total comfort and tends to interpret the child's crying, or difficulties with feeding, or other ordinary infant problems as if the baby were rejecting her. Such mothers tend to describe the baby almost from the start in negative terms—for example, the baby described as "spoiled" or "bad" or "slow" or "miserable" when, in fact, he is quite a normal baby. The impression by the physician that the mother is describing a baby quite different from the one he sees is his most useful subjective point of warning. At this time, not infre-

quently, the child fails to thrive and is not following his predicted growth curve. This, to the mother, simply proves that the
child is "not right." A period of early encouragement followed
by diagnostic hospital evaluation often reveals that the baby
thrives in the hospital, where normally a baby should not
thrive. The diagnosis of maternal deprivation as the cause of
"failure to thrive" can then be made and therapy instituted.

The subjective warnings of abnormal parent-child interaction
require on the part of the physician and his associates an open
mind and a careful eye toward clues which indicate that all is
not well between parent and baby. Clearly, to wait for marked
expression of the "failure to thrive" syndrome or frank child
abuse simply fails to focus on the importance of preventive
medicine in this important field. Every baby needs a giving
mother figure. When mothering of sufficient quality is not forthcoming on the part of his own mother or mother substitute,
serious and predictable long-term damage, which may not be
repairable, will result. Early clinical diagnosis of insufficient
mothering is, therefore, an essential part of the care of the newborn and his mother.

MILD BATTERING

In moments of rage or hopelessness parents may cause mild
injuries. These include bruises, particularly of the cheek, abrasions on the mucosa of the inner portion of the upper and lower
lips—usually in connection with forced feeding, or slapping the
mouth of the crying baby—and unexplained small burns and
bites. In some instances retinal hemorrhages will be seen in
children who may have no skull fracture or any evidence of
subdural hematoma following severe shaking or blows to the
head. It must be stressed that all injuries to small babies are
highly significant and they must be investigated in terms of the
psychodynamics of the parent-child relationship on the one
hand and the parent-expectations in early child raising experiences on the other. It is rare to have true accidents occur in
infancy. Any injury at that age period is highly suspect. The

institution of a treatment program at this stage will ofttimes prevent reinjury which may well be severe or fatal.

Early bone trauma in small infants is seen frequently as periosteal bleeding in the long bone of the arms and legs, often associated with traumatic episodes related to diapering — rough handling of the baby, a twisting and pulling of the extremities. Clearly, at the time of injury, when the child is still in distress and pain, no positive x-ray findings can be expected since no overt fractures have occurred. This bleeding in the sub-periosteum will calcify in three to six weeks *after* the injury. The new bone formation, which appears like an internal cast, will be seen in the injured areas. It is, therefore, most important in children who have bruises or pain, but no frank fractures, to repeat the x-ray of the long bones approximately three to six weeks after the injury to demonstrate the healing process found by the skeletal survey (see Bibliography, under *Radiology*).

It is in these situations that excellent rapport with parents is mandatory if the child is to be adequately followed and protected. When the child is at home, therapy becomes mandatory. Someone must set up a positive relationship with the parents who in turn must feel comfortable with this individual and be able to contact her at any time. An experienced social worker, public health nurse or lay therapist can be life saving during these critical times.

If the child has been placed under the temporary care of a child welfare agency by the courts, the case is not over. Welfare agencies rarely request opinions of the referring physician when the case returns to court for a rehearing, but they should do so (see Table 2). Children whom the physician thinks are safe in a foster home occasionally reappear in the emergency room severely injured or dead, the case having been heard by the judge and the patient returned home without the knowledge of the physician. It is a good policy to follow up each case of temporary dependency with a letter to the welfare agency and court, stating that this child should not be returned to the home under any circumstances unless the referring physician is consulted and his testimony heard at the rehearing.

Unless this is done, it is surprising how often children are returned home without the knowledge of the doctor, hospital
social worker, or psychiatrist who initially referred the case.

TABLE 2. *Is the Home Safe?**

USING OTHERS

1. Have parents *demonstrated* both a willingness and an ability to
use others in time of need?

2. Are helpful people available to the parents on a 24-hour basis?

3. Are parents developing out-of-home interests?

4. Do the parents have an improved self-image?

THE SPOUSE

1. Is the husband and/or wife able to realize when the partner needs
help?

2. Do they do something about it when recognized?

THE CRISES

1. Does someone know the family well enough to have sufficient contact and knowledge to recognize both immediate and pending crises?

2. Can that person(s) intervene to help when problem(s) is recognized?

3. Are obvious crises resolved: Housing, food, in-laws, job, illness, etc.?

4. Are obstacles to getting help minimal, such as is the phone working, carfare available?

THE CHILD

1. Do the parents see the child as someone "*different?*" (Is the child
different?)

2. Are their expectations of the child realistic?

3. Is the child pleasing to the parents?

4. Can the child be giving? (Can he meet these expectations?)

5. How big is the child?

6. Do they see the child as an individual?

*These guideline questions are not all-inclusive or "fool proof."
They hopefully will be helpful in determining if a child should be at
home.

6

The Need for Intensive
Follow-Up of Abused Children*

STANFORD B. FRIEDMAN, M.D.

THE EARLY IDENTIFICATION of a child already the victim of abuse is obviously not optimal prevention. Yet it would appear from our investigations that the severe permanent damage associated with the "battered child syndrome" usually does not occur with the initial incident.[1, 2] Identification of abuse at this time thus offers an opportunity for intervention with the goal of preventing subsequent trauma and irreversible injury to the child. Unfortunately, as will be discussed later, actual implementation of this preventive approach is often difficult, and this may seriously limit the practical usefulness of the early detection of the battered child.

At our own institution, a deliberate effort was made in 1963 to coordinate our approach in the detection and management of the abused child.[1] This endeavor was initiated and headed by a social worker in the Department of Pediatrics, and from 1963 to 1965, 19 cases of child abuse were identified by our staff. This represented a dramatic increase in the identified incidence of this problem at our hospital. However, these cases still represented less than 1 percent of the children under six years of age seen in our emergency department for trauma,

*Studies by the author and co-workers referred to in this review were supported by Grants No. 148 awarded by the Children's Bureau of the Department of HEW and U.S. Public Health Service K3-MH-18, 542 awarded by the NIMH.

though it was of the same order of magnitude as the 0.2 percent of childhood injuries, due to abuse, reported in a recent epidemiological study.[3] A low incidence of abuse also has been suggested on the basis of a nationwide survey by Gil, who states that "the magnitude of the phenomenon (child abuse) has been exaggerated."[4] Recent work by ourselves[2] and others[5] has, unfortunately, led us to believe that these previous impressions grossly underestimated the true frequency of child abuse (see Introduction). Of more import, we have come to realize that merely having a skilled professional person assigned to the problem of child abuse, even when this individual works in close collaboration with the pediatric staff, does not in itself assure an adequate detection program.

Sixteen of the children mentioned above, plus nine other cases of abuse seen during 1965 to 1966, were reevaluated approximately three years following the episodes of abuse. Even though not all of these children were returned to their homes following hospitalization for their injuries, a third of the total number were judged to have suffered from repeated abuse or gross neglect during the ensuing three years.[6] This clearly demonstrates that early identification of abuse is only the first step in preventing further injury, and that methods of professional intervention still need to be perfected.

CHARACTERISTICS OF CHILD ABUSE

A systematic review of what currently is known about families involved in child abuse is well beyond the scope of this chapter, and several general texts on the subject are now available.[7,8] However, the early diagnosis of abuse, as with other clinical entities, obviously is enhanced by an awareness of etiologic considerations and knowledge of the common manifestations of the problem. An attempt will be made, therefore, to summarize those studies which have been performed at this institution that pertain to the identification of early child abuse cases.

The concept that the abused child is merely the convenient target of parental conflict and frustration, has been questioned in recent work by Morse, et al.[6] In this study, abused children were recontacted 2 to 4¼ years (median: 2 11/12 years) following an identified episode of abuse or gross neglect. From a total of 26 cases, the investigators were able to locate and study, with varying degrees of completeness, 25 children. Though the study was admittedly limited by the retrospective approach, review of the previously obtained data and interviews of family members strongly suggested that many of these children had been perceived as being different by their mothers *prior to* the episode of abuse. In nine instances, the children were thought to be "slow" in development or mentally retarded, and six additional children were described as having been "bad," "selfish," "defiant" or "hard to discipline." It has been our clinical impression that within the latter group may be children who are, relative to their siblings, hyperactive or intellectually precocious. We also have seen several instances where the intellectual endowment of the child appears to so exceed that of one or both parents that his inquisitive behavior makes him vulnerable to parental abuse. Thus, there appears to be a group of children whose behavior makes them particularly vulnerable to abuse, a phenomenon also described by others.[4,9]

It is difficult to characterize by use of psychiatric diagnoses parents who physically abuse or neglect their children. As Steele and Pollock have stated, attempts to do so invariably reflect the use of skewed samples.[10] When suggesting etiologic implications, one must always compare the incidence of psychosocial problems in abusive parents to the occurrence of similar problems in other groups of parents. This latter consideration was highlighted in our attempt to relate psychological and social stresses to child abuse in our survey of emergency room admissions of children.[2] The parents of abused children had a high incidence of physical and psychiatric health problems, marital discord, financial difficulties, inadequate housing and social isolation. However, neither these factors, nor others examined, clearly differentiated these parents from those of children who were judged to have experienced true accidents. One conclusion, and it may be correct, is that the parents of children involved in accidents (as well as abusive parents) have a high incidence of psychosocial problems, but it may also be true that we were merely recording a seemingly high frequency of these problems in the general population. However, in our survey, we observed that the type of injury has predictive value in the early detection of child abuse.

Figure 1 shows the distribution of injuries in 156 children under six years of age seen during two two-week periods.[2] In the first of these periods, 69 children were admitted to the emergency department. Through a review of each child's medi-

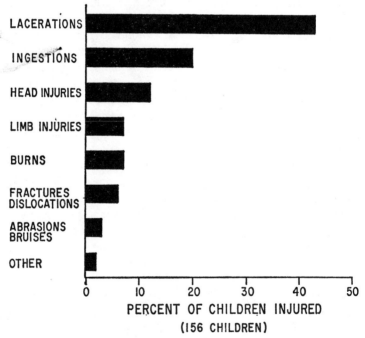

Fig. 1. Types of injury presenting to the hospital emergency department with a history of an accident. (*From*: Holter, J. C., and Friedman, S. B.: Pediatrics 42:128, 1968.)

cal record and contact with the appropriate emergency room physician, a judgment was made as to whether the injury could be categorized as representing: (1) an accident, (2) a repeated accident, or (3) suspected abuse. In the second survey of 87 children, this procedure was augmented by data collected independently by a nurse making a home visit. As emphasized in the more detailed description of the method of study, a case was classified as "suspected abuse only when the situation would have warranted reporting to a protective agency." In this manner, approximately 10 percent of the 156 children were judged to have experienced physical abuse.

The 17 cases of suspected abuse were not, however, equally distributed among the type of injuries seen. Though the most common types of injury were classified as lacerations or ingestions, only one case of suspected abuse presented in this way. (This single exception was a three-year-old child seen for multiple lacerations on the soles of his feet received when he "stepped on broken glass outside of the bathtub." The child had a past history of unexplained injuries and neglect. Children presenting with lacerations or ingestions were therefore empirically labeled as a "low risk" group. Children experiencing any other type of trauma (head injuries, burns, fractures and dislocations, abrasions and bruises) were defined as a "high risk" group. In this latter group were, of course, 16 out of the total of 17 cases of abuse; this was one out of every three children in the "high risk" group.

There was no *a priori* reason to believe that lacerations, as a form of injury, would be underrepresented by cases of child abuse. Perhaps it reflects the impulsiveness of most cases of abuse, and that rarely does a parent approach the child with a knife or other instrument that would produce a laceration-type injury. Rather, abusive parents appear to lose control while actually engaged in interacting with the child, and the injury results from direct bodily contact. Physical abuse is often an extension of "more or less acceptable disciplinary measures."[4] If our results are confirmed, the primary focus of an early detection program of child abuse should be upon children presenting with injuries other than lacerations and ingestions.

GUIDELINES FOR THE EARLY DETECTION OF
ABUSED CHILDREN

The foundation for the early identification of child abuse is the education of those who have contact with injured children. The first step is a general awareness of child abuse as a clinical identity. However, those directly involved in the medical and surgical care of children must be familiar with the common clinical manifestations of the problem, have some skill and experience in the initial management of abusive parents, and know how best to mobilize those agencies and individuals particularly versed in the long-term management of these families. Though multiple professional groups have been exposed to specific aspects of child abuse, an emphasis upon the need for a longitudinal approach and carefully planned intervention is often lacking. Further, it is especially important to include physicians in the various surgical fields in such educational efforts, for they are often the only physicians involved in the care of injured children. Thus, the presentation of child abuse as a medical problem is most effective in settings that are apt to attract surgeons, as well as those physicians more medically oriented. Meetings of local medical societies, hospital staff meetings, and joint pediatric-surgical grand rounds are particularly well suited for discussions in this area.

The injured child generally is brought first to the attention of a physician, who by treating the injury assumes the primary responsibility for the child's care. However, child abuse demands that the overall responsibility for the child's welfare be shared. No matter how well motivated, a physician who attempts to manage the problem by himself may actually be doing his patient a disservice. Child abuse cases are often so complex that the perspective and talents of other professionals are crucial. The following vignette will illustrate the value of involving allied health professionals.

A female child was hospitalized at three months of age with pneumonia and fractured ribs. Abuse was suspected, but not thought to be willful. The mother, judged by the hospital staff to be intellectually limited, showed overconcern regarding bodily functions and gave a history of often inappropriately responding to her infant"s normal functioning and behavior. However, she appeared warm and affectionate toward all of her children, and the case was not reported to a protective agency. A public health nurse was requested to visit the family for purposes of guidance and supervision of child care. The nurse followed the family, after the child's hospital discharge, with regular home visits and observed continuous physical neglect of all children. The mother also described alleged instances of the father sexually abusing an older female child. One year after the infant's hospital discharge, the public health nurse reported the family to the child protective agency.

This multidisciplinary approach typically is difficult for the physician in private practice, who may, for instance, only have infrequent contact with hospital or agency-based social workers. It is therefore highly desirable that every locality have available to the medical community an individual or office that can give immediate guidance and help to a physician involved in managing a battered child. Establishing such a service logically may fall within the operations of a county department of welfare or medical center. Many areas have programs of this sort, but often several agencies are involved and no single office takes the total responsibility for a coordinated effort of education and service in the area of child abuse. If multiple agencies are to be involved, obviously good communication should exist between them, and among themselves they must agree upon a central source of help for the medical profession.

The establishment of a registry of suspected child abuse cases may significantly promote early detections, especially in metropolitan areas. It has been recognized that abusive parents often seek medical care from multiple sources, which may be to conceal repetitive acts of abuse or may represent the parents' unrecognized "cry for help." With their needs not satisfied in one setting they are thus forced to look further for assistance. No single physician or hospital facility may be aware of previous incidences of "accidents" or neglect within a family, and a community registry of all childhood accidents would allow the treating physician to ascertain easily whether there is a past history of unexplained trauma. A cumulative record of injuries would help the physician in some difficult situations in diagnosing suspected abuse and the hospital administration in reporting these cases to the proper authorities.

It has been suggested by some that not all accidents be recorded, but only those where the physician "suspects" abuse or neglect. This plan seems questionable to this author for three reasons. First, our own experience strongly suggests that under such a scheme most cases of suspected abuse would not be detected, for, as yet, physcians (often residents) working in the hospital setting do not often consider this diagnosis. Second, the physician who does indeed suspect abuse is already under an obligation to report his suspicion to the appropriate agency, and further reporting of this kind would appear redundant. Lastly, reporting one's suspicion of abuse *without* communicating this clinical judgment to the parents raises an ethical issue for the physician. These objections would be by-passed if *all* childhood accidents were automatically recorded in a central registry, and if this fact was generally known in the community. In any event, the actual value of a child injury registry must await further research as data currently are not available to show that this preventive approach will aid in the identification of child abuse cases. It is clear however that abuse is diagnosed only after repeated visits even to the same emergency facility, as illustrated in the following vignette.

> A 19-month-old girl was hospitalized by way of the emergency department with the diagnosis of dehydration and severe diaper rash. It was learned that four months prior to this current problem, the child had been seen in the emergency department for a fractured left leg. During the hospitalization, gross neglect was suspected by the pediatric staff to be a major contributing factor to the child's medical condition. The neglect was not believed to be willful, however,

and the case was not reported to the child protective agency. Instead, a public health nurse was assigned to visit the family. One month after discharge, the child was brought back to the emergency department for the third time with a fracture of the right leg. Overt physical abuse was now suspected, and it was only at this time that the case was reported to the child protective agency for further investigation.

THE EMERGENCY DEPARTMENT

Though an unknown number of child abuse cases present to physicians in private practice, it would appear reasonable to focus one's attempt at early detection on those children seen in hospital emergency departments for injuries. Increasingly such facilities are being utilized by families from all socioeconomic levels, and there is a tendency for even those families who normally use private physicians to bring their children to emergency departments in cases of abuse. The early detection of child abuse *and* the initiation of a program of early intervention are somewhat contrary to the traditional role of an emergency department which is usually perceived as existing in order to solve an immediate medical problem. In the area of child abuse, the function of an emergency department must encompass preventive services and a recognition of the social and psychologic needs of its users. As stated by Bergman and Haggerty:[11]

> A basic premise in pediatric medicine is that regular health supervision helps to prevent illness and accidents, minimizes their complications, or prepares families to deal effectively with such crises. It is generally accepted that a physician who has a continuing relation with his patient is usually better equipped to deal with these acute illness problems by being familiar with the patient's personality and previous medical history. . . . The usual emergency room, organized to care only for the acute problems presented, offers none of these advantages.

Changes are taking place in many emergency departments. The addition of full-time professional personnel—physicians, social workers, specially trained nurses—can improve both the teaching and service functions of an emergency facility. Specific to the needs of the battered child is the availability of a social worker or nurse skilled in identification and management of abusive parents. Though it is generally assumed that such individuals might only be available during the usual working hours, it is conceivable that nighttime and weekend coverage might be provided at the larger facilities. Such a person might assume the primary responsibility for the educational and service activities of the emergency department in the area of child abuse. This need not imply a full-time commitment of such a professional person, who might well be responsible for coordinating other preventive functions of the emergency unit. The administrative organization must vary among institutions, but it is the assignment of responsibility which is critical. In addition, the existence of an established policy for managing child abuse encourages some consistency within the institution, and such policies have been outlined.[1] (See Chapter 12.)

The professional worker responsible for child abuse cases seen in the emergency department may function in many ways. For smaller services, being available on an "on-call" basis may be adequate, or the individual responsible for the early detection of child abuse cases might briefly interview the parents thought to represent a "high risk" group (such as described earlier in this chapter.) Even the systematic retrospective review of all emergency department records is helpful, as illustrated by the following case vignette.

A three-year-old boy was seen in the emergency department for second-degree burns involving the right deltoid area. The attending intern alluded to the curious crisscross nature of the burn, and included a sketch of the lesion. Later that day another child, four years of age, was seen for an identically described burn involving the left shoulder area. The second child was treated by a different intern, who, though not aware of the previous admission, also commented on the strange nature of the burn. Both children were treated and given appointments for a return visit to the clinic. Review of the emergency department records disclosed that the children were cousins and had previously been seen at this hospital. However, follow-up was not possible as the address, the same for both children, was found to be fictitious, and neither clinic appointment was kept.

This vignette also demonstrates the typical lack of communication within the staff of a large emergency department. This problem is compounded by the fact that large emergency departments are staffed by multiple clinical departments, and there is often a primary division between "surgical" and "medical" problems. In regard to child abuse, it would appear imperative to coordinate the efforts of the pediatric and surgical personnel involved in the care of children.

Abusive parents bringing children to an emergency department are often quite vague in their description of the "accident" and this in itself should alert the physician to the possibility of abuse. If parental neglect also has been a contributory factor to the child's injury, we have noted that there is often a delay in seeking medical attention. Parents frequently attribute the injury to what they perceive as a common type of accident resulting in injury, such as falling off the bed, twisting a limb between the slats of a crib, or falling down the stairs. Often the injury appears suspiciously severe in terms of the explanation given, such as fractured femur occuring as the result of a fall from a sofa. As previously noted, the parents may have used other medical facilities in the past and therefore the presenting injury is the first contact the hospital may have had with the family. The parents may or may not be belligerent; more commonly, they are seen as frightened and confused. Typically, there is no mention of the parents being "uncooperative."

The type of injury itself may raise the question of abuse. Fractures, bruises, dislocations, burns and head injuries are especially common in abused children. Bizarre injuries, such as described in the last vignette, may be manifestations of abuse. Such bizarre lesions may have been inflicted not only by parents or their surrogates, but by older siblings or children in their "play".

Unfortunately, there are no pathognomonic findings in cases of abuse, and the diagnoses, even to some degree in cases of admitted guilt, are clinical judgments on the part of the physician. When the emergency department physician suspects abuse, it has been suggested (see previous chapter) that he not confront the parents with his suspicion within the setting of the emergency department. It is argued that by so doing the parents may be antagonized, perhaps unncessarily, and that the primary role of the emergency department physician is to suspect the diagnosis and admit the child to an in-patient unit. After hospitalization, the issues of child abuse may be explored more systematically, and personnel with expertise in the problems of child abuse can be made available. This author would take some exception to delay telling the parents of his suspicions. It is not uncommon that the injury itself does not necessitate hospitalization, and that the overriding reason to admit the child is suspected abuse. With rigid adherence to this advice, the physician may be placed in the position of explaining, or defending, his plan to hospitalize a child on illogical medical grounds. This skirting of the issue of abuse, in parents aware of their own behavior, may detract from subsequent doctor-parent communication and trust. In our experience, bringing this issue "out in the open" often is a relief to the parents, and the abuse may be viewed as a "cry for help." This is consistent with the observation that the very physician who initiates the discussion of possible abuse with the parents often can continue in a therapeutic role.* There are, of course, few situations in which the physician's compassion and interview skills are more important.

The role of the physician in the emergency department and the decision regarding admission for children not seriously in-

*It would seem that the major reasons for differences of opinion expressed here may be in the capabilities of the physicians who may see the child. In the emergency *department* in Rochester, Friedman's plan may well be acceptable. In the emergency *room* in New York City it would not (eds).

jured depend upon many factors, including the physical facilities of the emergency department, feasibility of consultation and follow-up, and the skill and sophistication of the particular physician seeing the child. As emergency departments increase their ability to investigate and manage social and psychological problems, hospitalization of some of these children may be unnecessary.

It should be emphasized that the physician is mandated by law to report only his *suspicion* of child abuse, and should not limit his reporting to only those cases where he believes there is conclusive evidence. It is the responsibility of the protective agency to obtain the data necessary to document the existence of physical abuse. Final "diagnosis" is the result of a judicial process, which relies to varying degrees upon the findings of the physician. We have noted repeated examples of physicians being reluctant to report cases of suspected abuse because they did not believe they could "prove it," and did not see the act of reporting as potentially helping not only the child but also the parents.

REFERENCES

1. Holter, J. C., and Friedman, S. B.: Principles of management in child abuse cases. Amer J Orthopsychiat 38:127, 1968.
2. _____: Child Abuse: Early case finding in the emergency department. Pediatrics 42:128, 1968.
3. Zollinger, R. W., Creedon, P. J., and Sanguily, J.: Trauma in children in general hospital. Amer J Surg 104:855, 1962.
4. Gil, D. G.: Physical abuse of children: Findings and implications of a nationwide survey. Pediatrics (Suppl.) 44:857, 1969.
5. Gregg, G. S., and Elmer, E.: Infant injuries: Accident or abuse? Pediatrics 44:434, 1969.
6. Morse, C. W., Sahler, O. J. Z., and Friedman, S. B.: A three-year follow-up study of child abuse and neglect. Amer J Dis Child 120:439, 1970.
7. Elmer, E.: Children in Jeopardy: A Study of Abused Minors and Their Families. Pittsburgh, Univ of Pittsburgh Press, 1967.

8. Helfer, R. E., and Kempe, C. H., eds.: The Battered Child, Chicago, Univ of Chic Press, 1968.

9. Court, J.: The battered child: Part I: Historical and diagnostic reflections. Med Soc Work 22:11, 1969.

10. Steele, B. F., and Pollock, C. B.: A psychiatric study of parents who abuse infants and small children, *in* Helfer, R. E., and Kempe, C.H., eds.: The Battered Child, Chicago, Univ of Chic Press, 1968.

11. Bergman, A., and Haggerty, R. J.: The emergency clinic: A study of its role in a teaching hospital. Amer J Dis Child *104*: 36, 1962.

7

The Child and His Development

HAROLD MARTIN, M.D.

ALTHOUGH THERE ARE no long-term prospective follow-up studies on the consequences and sequelae of abuse to the child, data from several short follow-up studies are available.[1-9] The John F. Kennedy Child Development Center at the University of Colorado has followed 42 abused children during a three-year period. Even though all of the children have not been followed the full three years, the study reveals significant findings about the abused children and their development.

SUMMARY OF STUDY

Population studies of the subsequent development of abused children demand careful assessment of the nature of the study population, including the use of selected criteria in applying the term abuse. The definition of abuse varies in different reports and may include physical abuse, neglect, nutritional deprivation and affective deprivation. Abuse in our study group includes children with significant physical trauma unexplained by history or admitted to by parents; repeated unexplained physical trauma; and neglected children who are seriously suspected of being physically abused and who have siblings with documented abuse. Excluded from the study are children who presented with the single diagnosis of neglect, failure to thrive, or affective deprivation.

A relevant factor affecting our study population is the type of children served by this Center. As a public institution, this

Center does not serve a large number of middle- or upper-class people. Also, the child abuse team has been very active in case finding so that more children with less dramatic physical trauma are identified than in some institutions. Through education, the threshold of suspicion of housestaff has been lowered. Due to this effort, patients admitted to the Orthopedic Services or Neurosurgical Service or children seen in the Pediatric Outpatient Department are less likely to be attended to for their medical needs alone, without awareness of the family's contribution to ostensible "accidents."

A critical factor affecting the subsequent development of the abused child is the type and quality of intervention, once the diagnosis is made. Intervention in psychosocial pathology varies considerably and it is difficult to know the exact nature of some treatment plans. Terms such as "support" or "following the family" are frequently heard and may reflect active support and therapy, or may mean a casual administrative concern as to the whereabouts and welfare of the family. If the development of the abused child is a reflection of the effectiveness of post abuse management, then the type and quality of intervention must be closely scrutinized.

Finally, the effectiveness of a follow-up study must affect the reported outcome of these children. It has been the experience of this Center that it is very difficult to follow abusive families. They tend to be very mobile and frequently are not receptive to repeated evaluation from the institution which first involved them in legal, family and personal intervention. One study of abused children[5] reports that five years after hospitalization, 33 percent of the children and families could not be found. It cannot be assumed that the families we are able to locate and motivate to cooperate in long-term follow-up are the same type of children and families as those who cannot be found or refuse to cooperate.

METHOD

The developmental evaluation of abused children included anthropometric measurements, a neurologic examination and developmental testing. The test instrument used for children under six years of age was the Revised Yale Developmental Schedules. This test consists of selected items from several standardized tests, primarily the Gesell Developmental Schedules, the Stanford-Binet Form L-M, and the Merrill-Palmer Scale of Mental Tests. The evaluation of older children included the Stanford-Binet or the Wechsler Intelligence Scale for Children. While most children were seen at the time of hospitalization, formal test scores could not be obtained routinely due to the child's behavior or medical problems. Clinical judgments were made on the basis of the examiner's observations, reports of nurses and foster grandparents, and history. Subsequent evaluations were scheduled four to six months after treatment was instituted and every six to 12 months thereafter. This schedule was often interrupted by requests for development evaluation when court action or changes in the child's home were being considered.

RESULTS

Data from this follow-up study are listed in Table 1. Children with retarded function are arbitrarily defined as those children who have a developmental or intelligence quotient

TABLE 1. *Follow-up of 42 Abused Children*

	TOTAL GROUP	RETARDED FUNCTION	NOT RETARDED
A. Number and Percentage	42	14 (33%)	28 (66%)
B. IQ or DQ Mean and Range	88 (19-118)	69 (19-79)	98 (81-118)
C. Skull Fracture or Subdurals	13 (31%)	9 (64%)	4 (14%)
D. Neurologic Sequelae	18 (43%)	11 (79%)	7 (25%)
E. C and/or D	22 (52%)	13 (95%)	9 (32%)
F. Failure to thrive on admission	14 (33%)	7 (50%)	7 (25%)
G. Language Delay	16 (38%)	4 (29%)	12 (43%)

below 80. Failure to thrive includes those children whose height or weight fell more than two standard deviations below the mean at the time of the injury. Language delay is a term used to describe children whose language abilities are considerably poorer than their general performance. Children in this group have language scores 15 or more points lower than their full-scale or performance scores on formal testing.

Other clinical findings and observations of these children are included in the following discussion of the developmental consequences of child abuse.

DISCUSSION

TYPE OF CHILD ABUSED

To evaluate the consequences of abuse, one must first consider the kind of child who is battered. Milowe and Louire[10] and others[9] have suspected that some children may be "at risk" who, indeed, may unwittingly invite physical abuse. In our follow-up, only three (7 percent) of the children were probably difficult children from birth. None were small prematures. Two were probably retarded prior to the physical assault, and a third child was very difficult to care for because of numerous medical problems, including pyloric stenosis. These three children presented special problems making them difficult to care for and less able to give positive emotional feedback to their parents. They obviously are not a large contribution to this study population. While Birrell and Birrell[5] state that 26 percent of the 42 maltreated children they report had congenital anomalies, they do not state the severity of these anomalies. Gregg and Elmer[1] report that none of their 30 abused children had physical defects which should affect the quality of mothering. Further, they compared these 30 children with 83 children who were thought to have accidental injuries. Consideration of the personality of these children included assessment of mood, activity level and distractability, using the model described by Chess.[11] No differences in mood or activity level were found. In fact, it was thought that the abused children had been easier babies to care for. Los Angeles County General Hospital recently reported 50 abused children.[4] Only 12 percent were thought to be retarded before admission to the hospital. It is important to note that 50 percent of their study group had a history of previous injury, suggesting that of the 12 percent who were retarded when hospitalized, the basis for the retardation may very well have been previous abuse. Similarly, the temperament or personality of the child prior to hospitalization need not be thought of as inherent. But, rather, one must remember that the abusive environment, frequently accompanied by neglect and deprivation, has helped shape that personality from birth to the time of hospitalization.

Credence may be given to parents' reports of the child's personality prior to abuse. However, these data must be suspect as they often reflect the parents' perception of the child with little relationship to objective reality. Two families described will highlight this point.

> Mrs. S. recently relinquished her three-year-old daughter. A younger sibling had been beaten six months previously with resultant skull fractures. Mrs. S.'s relinquishment of her daughter was accompanied by strident anger at having had this retarded, ugly child. She described the daughter's behavior as extremely unpleasant, unrewarding and obnoxious. After seeing this child, it was clear that the mother's perceptions were quite distorted. The girl has an intelligence quotient of 118, is an unusually attractive girl, and has encaptured the hearts of her foster parents who want to adopt her.

> Mrs. M. recently brought her son to the hospital indicating she would kill the child if someone did not take him. She described the boy as a monster and declared he looked at her with murder in his eye. Interestingly enough, the boy, now 29 months of age, was named after a television soap opera vampire, Barnabas. It seems clear that even at a few days of life, as demonstrated by the mother's name for the boy, she had a negative fantasy about the kind of a child her baby was going to become and certainly gave him messages to match her distorted perception.

CENTRAL NERVOUS SYSTEM DEVELOPMENT

Neurologic Dysfunction. Permanent damage to the brain is a frequent sequela of physical abuse. Forty-three percent of our study group have abnormality on follow-up neurologic examination. Two thirds of these children have obvious findings as hemiparesis, focal signs, optic atrophy and pathological primitive reflexes. The other one third have more subtle signs, including the various "soft" neurologic findings of the child with minimal brain dysfunction. Of these 18 children with neurologic dysfunction, only 50 percent had a history of skull fracture or subdural hematoma, suggesting that in many instances brain damage is related to less dramatic trauma. Almost one half of these brain damaged children have normal intelligence, but special schooling will probably be needed for all of them as it is anticipated that their handicaps will preclude success in learning in a traditional classroom and curriculum.

Retardation. A definition of retardation was arbitrarily established to include children having an intelligence or developmental quotient below 80. Thirty-three percent of our study group continue to function retarded to this point. Table 1 gives some data on these children. It is clear that there is an intimate relationship between central nervous system insult and residual retardation. Ninety-three percent of the retarded children had a history of severe head trauma and/or continue to show abnormality on neurologic examination.

A very pertinent question arises: Does an abusive environment cause retardation, or is the retardation seen in battered children always secondary to central nervous system damage? The literature abounds in data to indicate that environmental deprivation can result in retardation.[12-16] While the data in Table 1 clearly relates central nervous system insult to retardation, it is extremely important to point out that this can lead to erroneous interpretation. When abused children are admitted to the hospital with trauma, most of them appear and function retarded. It must be stressed that the data presented are after intervention has taken place. Objective data on children at the time of abuse are difficult to obtain. Most of these children are initially untestable, being quite withdrawn, oppositional and fearful. Many are very weak and apathetic and are engaged in recovery from serious trauma and often associated undernutrition. However, histories and the earliest observations of nursing and medical staff indicate a high degree of retarded development. This suggests then that retardation might well be a permanent sequala if identification and intervention had not taken place.

Some children have not shown significant improvement in their development, both clinically and by an increase of at least 10 points in formal test results. Fifteen children have thus far shown little or no improvement in their development. Seven of these children had significant brain insult with serious neurologic sequelae. Their minimal subsequent developmental progress seems related to static brain defect. One child's developmental progress has been impossible to detail due to a serious emotional disturbance. In seven other children, intervention was minimal or inappropriate. In three children, no intervention was possible. In one instance the parents, who still have their child, have persistently refused supportive care, psychotherapy, speech therapy or appropriate schooling for their boy. Removal of the child to a different home was legally unsuccessful. Three children, while removed from their homes, were victims of poor foster home placement. One of these children, at 27 months of age, had had three different foster homes, while a second girl at 21 months of age had lived in four different homes. It is important to note that, with effective intervention, eight children with damage to the central nervous system are functioning in the normal range of intelligence. Further, even in those children who are still retarded, considerable improvement in motor abilities, language and mental function has been possible, although not complete, with intervention. However, this improvement may be impossible because of structural damage to the brain.

FAILURE TO THRIVE

Maltreatment of children is a spectrum. Physical assault, neglect and nutritional or emotional deprivation are points on that spectrum and overlap considerably. The relationship between abuse and undernutrition is critically important to the subsequent development of the child. Chase and Martin[17] have pointed out that permanent retardation can result from undernutrition in the first year of life. This is particularly pertinent as this critically important first year of life is the time during which the child is most susceptible to battering.

Fourteen (33 percent) of our study children (Table 1), in addition to physical abuse, demonstrated failure to thrive as indicated by height and/or weight below the third percentile. Failure to thrive occurred twice as frequently in the children who are still functioning retarded as in those with subsequent normal mental function. Birrell's report of 42 children with maltreatment[5] included 35 children with serious physical trauma, 10 of whom (29 percent) also had undernutrition to the point of marasmus. In Elmer's follow-up study of 20 abused children,[2] 10 children were living in substitute homes and 10 were still living in their original homes at the time of reevaluation. In those 10 children living in substitute homes, seven had had symptoms of growth failure at the time of hospitalization and all seven had fully recovered physically. In contrast, of the 10 children living in their original homes six either remained or had fallen below the third percentile for height and/or weight. It is also important to note the significantly superior mental abilities in the former group.

Some reports have suggested that impaired growth can be a psychosomatic disorder[16,18] or secondary to deprivation of appropriate maternal affect.[19] Other studies[20,21] indicate that sensory or affective deprivation alone does not impair physical growth, and that the dwarfism or undernutrition in these children is due to lack of caloric intake. Undernutrition in the physically abused child may be considered a form of "passive" abuse coincident with "active" abuse. We see, then, at least two different types of abused children. Some children upon hospitalization are neglected, undernourished and poorly cared for. Other children have had adequate physical and medical care. The former group of children are at higher risk of serious permanent sequelae and will need more active intervention.

PATTERNS OF SUBSEQUENT DEVELOPMENT

Deficits in motor abilities have been referred to by pointing out that 43 percent of our study group have permanent neurologic impairment. While all of this group have some deficit in gross or fine motor abilities, only two thirds have severe motor deficits. Several of these children have normal intelligence so that the motor deficit is not part of a generalized central nervous system insult.

A second striking observation is the large number of children with absent, minimal, or impaired speech and language. Even after intervention, there remain 16 children (38 percent) with developmental delays in language (Table 1). On intelligence or developmental testing, their language scores are 15 or more points lower than their full scale scores or their performance scores. Seventy-five percent of these children with language delays are of normal intelligence, the remainder having a full scale score below 80. An even greater number of children had impaired language before treatment and have since shown accelerated development in speech and language skills and abilities. Whether more of these children will "catch up" is, of course, unknown, but with many children there has been little indication of beginning acceleration in language development several years after treatment.

The basis for delay in language is conjectural at best. It is clear that language is an extremely vulnerable nervous system process. Phylogenetically, it is one of the human being's most advanced cognitive processes. Perhaps that partially explains why it is so often selectively impaired regardless of etiology. For example, it is well known that in the neurologic-cognitive repertoire of the child with Down's syndrome, language is typically the most severely affected process. Severe language deficit in emotional disturbance is well known, with childhood autism as an extreme example. Language is a prime target of deprivation. The paucity and concreteness of language in the socially disadvantaged child has recently been studied.[22-25] However, to acknowledge the sensitivity of language and the propensity for delays in its development from various causes does not explain the basis for this occurrence.

It is a common practice in some communities for an abused child to be put in a foster home as a diagnostic procedure. Consider a child who is hospitalized for abuse and neglect. He is tested and found to be functioning as a mildly retarded child. However, he is very apathetic, difficult to test, and the clinical hunch is that he has more ability. Knowing that neglect or an abusive environment may result in "pseudo-retardation," the plan is to put the child in a good foster home and in three to six months to repeat the developmental testing. It is assumed that if the child has normal inherent potential, the later test scores will reflect a tremendous growth in development. This is *not always* a valid assumption. Indeed, some children will show no significant changes in developmental or intelligence quotient after this period of environmental therapy.

It appears that there are personality precursors to a gain in acquisition of developmental milestones. The common pattern of development is seen in the greater availability for learning after three to six months in a good home. Changes that are apparent include: Increased attention span; willingness to imitate; interest and drive in solving problems; response to praise; more appropriate use of toys; the child is easier to motivate; disappearance of apathy; investigative behavior; interest in people. These behaviors are precursors, essential prerequisites to learning. If one is only interested in test scores, the erroneous impression may be reached that the child has not improved and that he is organically retarded, in that he has apparently not responded significantly to environmental therapy. *Not true.* This child has made tremendous improvement. Now, armed with the essentials he stands on the threshold of accelerated development. Another three to six months may be needed to define developmental acceleration as measured by test scores.

Certainly some children show rapid progress and the developmental precursors of learning have gone overlooked. Why some children show slower developmental rehabilitation is not clear. It would be helpful if the dynamics of varying rates of development were better understood.

At this point in our knowledge, it is important to underscore that behavior may reflect the earliest changes in a child's development, rather than developmental or intelligence test scores. Changes in behavior seem to be necessary reagents to acquisition of new information and skills. It is only after the child is available for learning that we can see whether an increased rate of learning will accrue due to the improved environment.

MORTALITY

What happens to battered children? Many die. In 1962[7] Kempe did the first nationwide survey of child abuse and of 302 cases of abused children, 33 died—an 11 percent mortality. Others have estimated a mortality rate from 5 percent[26] to 27 percent.[27] If an abused child is returned home with no intervention, Helfer[2-] considers that child to be at a 25 percent to 50 percent risk of permanent injury or death.

The number of children who die from parental assault cannot be accurately known. Considering the difficulty in diagnosis, the above figures must be conservative. We know that repeated injury is the rule as opposed to a single episode of abuse. Further, one cannot help but wonder how many children whose deaths have been ascribed to accidental injury or to "crib" deaths may have been the victims of parental assault.[29]

PERSONALITY

What is the personality of a child who has lived in an abusive environment? A critical issue is the potential for rehabilitation of these children's personalities.

No Intervention. Morris et al[30] have contrasted typical behavior with that of the battered child on hospitalization. Most battered children do appear and act differently from their nonabused peers. Common behavior at hospitalization has been noted to include: cry very little in general, but cry hopelessly under treatment and examination; do not look to parents for assurance; show no expectation of being comforted; are wary of physical contact and apprehensive when other children cry; are on the alert for danger and continue to size up the environment; are constantly in search for something from people, as food, favors, services. This is in contrast to the nonabused hospitalized child who clings to parents, turns to parents for assurance, demonstrates a desire to go home and is reassured by parents' visits. Many of these battered children have had previous trauma, and it may be assumed that the personality of children upon hospitalization is secondary to the abusive environment in which he has lived.

What might happen to the battered child as he grows if no intervention has taken place? While the opportunity to study such a population is not possible, retrospective data are available. There is ample evidence that the battered child may grow up to become an adult with violence playing a prominent role in his behavior repertoire. Helfer and Kempe[28] have emphasized that most parents who abuse their children were themselves the object of anger and violence as children. This, incidentally, makes the practice of placing battered children with their grandparents a dubious if not patently ridiculous therapeutic regime. In studies of murderers, a common history of violence in childhood is obtained. Duncan et al[31] interviewed six white, intelligent, first-degree murderers and their families. It was clear that remorseless physical brutality at the hands of the parents had been a constant experience for four of them. Curtis[32] reviews the early literature on this subject and points out the tendency for the child to identify himself with aggressive parents and pattern after their behavior. Easson and Steinhilber[33] saw eight boys, ages eight to sixteen, in psychiatric consultation who had attempted murder, one successfully. In all cases, the parents had been a model for aggression and violence. In an as yet unvalidated report from an eastern city,[34] a consecutive series of 100 juvenile offenders who had assaulted others were interviewed. Eighty percent gave a history of physical abuse by their parents during childhood, 40 percent to the extent of having been rendered unconscious by beatings.

This evidence supports the theory that violence is a self-perpetuating style of life. At this Center, it has not been infrequent to trace child abuse through three or four generations. There most certainly is not a one-to-one relationship between abuse as a child and violence as a way of life in adulthood. Those battered children who have grown to adulthood and not run afoul of the law or child welfare agencies are largely unknown to us. We can only speculate that they may share personality construction of battering parents, although to a lesser degree.

After Intervention. Many of these children are seen after short periods of intervention with active treatment with the parents. After a few weeks from the time of abuse, it may be assumed that only minor changes will have occurred in the child. Allowing that there is variability in the children, the most typical situation is a child who is fearful, distrustful and clings to his caretaker. He tends to be a loner, appearing not to have interest or knowledge of appropriate peer relationships. He shows minimal or no response to praise and little response to limits and controls. He is manipulative and often oppositional—at least refusing to engage with adults or environment despite attempts to motivate him. This child shows a marked apathy to toys and situations which typically interest his age-mates. A few children at this point are quite independent and obstreperous. Occasionally one hears the ward nurse or foster mother comment that she could not blame the parents for battering the child as he provokes anger from surrounding adults. While this more active and aggressive child is seen less often than the apathetic withdrawn child, he perpetuates the notion that many of these children would invite abuse from the most normal of parents.

After several months or years of intervention, the child appears somewhat different. He responds to praise, indeed may seek it out actively. He also responds to controls and limits. He remains fearful and may panic when hearing loud noises or if the examiner raises his voice. His response to his environment is quite striking. Like radar, his "antennae" are constantly searching out the reactions of adults to his behavior. He appears not to be able to use inner ego to monitor his behavior, but must rely on outside clues to gauge his actions. When such a child undergoes testing, he frequently will not continue with a task such as a puzzle or formboard unless, after each step of the way, the examiner reinforces behavior by a smile, a nod or a positive statement.

The typical child tends to be very solicitous and agreeable. Several foster mothers have commented on the agreeableness of the child, indicating he will try to do anything they ask of him. One foster mother in commenting on how nice a particular three-year-old boy was, told how he would sit quietly outside her room in the morning until he heard her stir, and then bring her juice or milk and serve her breakfast in bed. This role reversal of the child includes a willingness to empathize with adult's feelings. While examining a 10-year-old girl, the examiner was drawing geometrical forms for the girl to copy. He made a statement to the effect that it was difficult for him to draw these figures. The little girl quickly reassured the physician that it was all right, that many bright people had difficulty in drawing well.

These children relate quickly to adults, but superficially and indiscriminately. Concern is voiced frequently that the child is apt to go off with any stranger who walks by. Smiles and physical contact are used by many of these children in a manipulative manner with adults they have just met.

As can be imagined, the child at this stage is quite charming, lovable and appealing. Consider for a moment a child who seems to like you immediately, alters his behavior to be consistent with what you want, is interested in pleasing you and in addition is concerned about your feelings. Superficially, this child seems quite nice and healthy. However, on closer scrutiny the child seems shallow. His external being seems quite adaptive, but his inner self is rarely seen and seems tenuous at best. He has difficulty developing deep trusting relationships with special people. His peer relations are casual. He must rely on external rather than self-directed monitors to determine appropriate behavior. While no longer apathetic, his investigative behavior is limited. He gives one the impression of some fragility and brittleness of adaptive abilities.

The rehabilitated battered child often appears quite bright and/or precocious. However, very few of our children have demonstrated superior intelligence scores. One might hypothesize that natural selection or reinforcement in the environment tends to make the survivors of physical assault brighter children. That is, perhaps the brighter child is more capable of adaptation to the abusive environment, making his chances greater of surviving lethal or serious injury. Malone[6] has noted that children living in dangerous environments have certain areas of "hypertrophied" ego functioning, areas of advanced ability. Included is the child's role reversal with parents, such as making decisions for them, taking care of younger siblings. This type of "precocious" behavior is reinforced by their parents. While the child's ability to cope and his areas of hypertrophied ego strength are assets to survival, it is also hypothesized that they are weaknesses, contributing to the child's literalness and inflexibility. Much of this behavior is not transferable to other situations.

Noting the dependency on external stimuli, Malone[6] suggests that it leads to rigid literalness in learning and concreteness of thinking processes. He has studied extensively 21 preschool children living in disorganized families and examined their adaptation to danger in their environment, primarily danger of abuse from their parents. He has found four interrelated characteristics of these children: (1) danger orientation—the distrust, tension and guardedness they display in particularly loaded situations; (2) visual and auditory hyper-alertness—a hyperreactivity to stimuli with much visual and auditory scanning; (3) use of avoidance and denial of un-pleasant and anxiety-provoking situations; (4) hypertrophied ego functions discussed above. He sees these traits as highly adaptive, but in the long run detrimental to successful func-tioning and learning in the classroom.

SPECULATIONS

Erikson's model[35] supplies us a framework to better under-stand the subsequent development of these children. With an extremely serious impediment to development of trust, it is logical that these children have difficulty in mastering auton-omy and initiative. With increasing age and maturity, only with reinforcement of trust will it be possible for these children to develop a mature self-concept and, as adults, to accept and share intimacy.

The delay in language in so many of these children is a case in point. While undoubtedly multifactorial in etiology, it is suggested that the delay in language is related to the child's lack of trust in his environment. These children are reluctant to expose themselves, display initiative or to act without scrutiny of the environment to determine approval or disapproval. Speaking one's thoughts, ideas and feelings can be dangerous for a child. It is difficult for the child to anticipate the effect of his utterances on surrounding adults. To speak is to stake out one's identity and idiosyncrasies. It is also a process of sharing one's inner self with others which must rest on a firm basis of trust and security. It is little wonder then that while motor skills, play and peer relations mature, language continues to lag in development. The part anger and passive resistance play in the deliberate withholding of lan-guage is less clear from seeing these children.

The effects of physical abuse on a child may be catastrophic, including retardation, permanent brain damage and death.

Once a central nervous system insult has occurred, there may be a limited chance for rehabilitation. For this reason, the focus must be on prevention of physical assault. Apart from the actual assault on the child's body, the abusive environment also takes its toll in subsequent neurologic, cognitive and personality development. While early literature suggested that early and prolonged deprivation left children affectionless and detached in their later adoptive homes, follow-up of abused children suggests a greater potential for cognitive and affective adjustment. Taylor's[36] report of 30 children who had been severely deprived for the first 2½ years of life is a pertinent study. In addition to environmental manipulation, the children were each seen for individual therapy and the adopting parents were specially schooled and trained in the peculiar needs of these children. With this active intervention, the potential for affective adjustment seemed quite optimistic. Loomis[37] comments on the need for regular individual therapy for children hospitalized for burns. It may well be that for children who have been assaulted and have spent their earliest months and years in an abusive environment, individual therapy for the child is essential if his fullest cognitive and personality development is to be realized. It is also apparent that the caretakers, be they biologic or foster parents, need help and guidance in understanding these children and knowing how best to respond to their more primitive and aberrant behavioral traits. Treatment of the parents is often centered around their needs and pathology. At the point the child returns to his home, treatment can no longer be exclusively for the parents. The abused child acts, responds and relates in an aberrant fashion. Parents need help in understanding his behavior and feelings and in knowing how to react to him. If one is only concerned with physical abuse, a child may be returned to his home with the rationale that the risk of subsequent physical assault is negligible. If, however, neglect and undernutrition persist, if the abusive environment is basically unchanged, retardation and permanent neurologic dysfunction may be the result.

There is considerable danger in professionals focusing on only one band of the spectrum of maltreatment. Subspecialization in physical abuse, undernutrition, affective deprivation or neglect can and does occur in medical centers. In a report of 50 children with failure to thrive by Bullard et al[38] it was incidentally noted that 10 percent of the children had healed or healing fractures on admission to the hospital. An example of this tunnel vision is the focus on undernutrition as separate from child abuse. Koel[39] recently reported three children hospitalized because of failure to thrive. They did well and were then returned to their homes. Within a few months all were hospitalized again with serious physical abuse that resulted in the death of two of them. A narrow concern with increments in height and weight may result in catastrophic child battering. When one focuses only on the child and ignores his environment, namely his parents, treatment has been incomplete and recurrence or catastrophe may result. Child neglect, abandonment and affective deprivation must also be recognized as points on the spectrum of maltreatment of children.

Placement in a surrogate home may assure the prevention of repeated physical assault. That goal is too narrow. Not only mortality, but morbidity must be considered. Too frequently the child's surrogate home placement is inadequate or inconstant. It is suggested that average normal parenting may not be sufficient for these children. If the child is to spend a period of time in a surrogate home, the foster parents should have counsel about the particular problems and needs of the child. This may take the form of explanation of behavior, the child's fearfulness, apathy, withdrawn distrustful manner. Specific suggestions about child rearing practices may also be needed. It is a common phenomena for foster parents to have considerable ego investment in the abused child's ability to improve in their home. This is usually equated with acquisition of new developmental skills. There is a tendency, therefore, for the foster parents to encourage or demand that the slow child start "growing up" and vindicate their mothering ability by rapidly learning new skills and becoming more independent. This may be the entirely wrong approach to the child. Many of our abused children have essentially missed out on a dependent infant relationship with a giving mother. It is often necessary to allow the child to act more infantile than his chronologic age for a period of time. He may want and need to be fed, cuddled and cared for as a young infant to develop a sense of trust in a mothering figure. There comes a time then when the surrogate mother must then start to encourage more mature behavior from the child. In a sense, he may need to be led through a recapitulation of earlier stages of development. It is not uncommon to see either foster mothers who will not allow the child to act and be treated younger than his age, or, on the other hand, foster mothers who particularly enjoy children who are quite dependent and who find it difficult, then, to help the child mature. The development of more mature behavior is sensed by her as a pulling away of the child from her sustenance. These mothers need help with their expectations and needs just as the biologic mother does. The goal of assistance or therapy for the mother, biologic or foster, should be to provide a growth promoting environment for the child.

SUMMARY

Since Kempe[40] first catalyzed nationwide concern about the battered child, there has been a tremendous amount of interest in these children, and a tremendous amount of energy has been expended to care for them. The focus of most of this work has been towards the following goals: (1) understanding the dynamics of the syndrome; (2) decreasing resistance of professionals to consider the diagnosis; (3) protection of the life and neurologic integrity of the child; (4) legal, medical and social maneuvers to manage the child and family. While these goals have not been fully recognized, impressive progress has been made.

The morbidity of the syndrome is just beginning to be studied. We know that many children die. We now see that even larger numbers of children will be retarded, brain damaged, undernourished and emotionally crippled. This chapter details some of the findings and sequelae in children who have been battered. It must be recognized that subsequent growth and development of these children — physical, neurologic, cognitive, emotional — are dependent in large part upon our ability to develop effective therapy for these children. Rather than an interest in child abuse, we must take an interest in children who have been abused and in their parents. We must look at the family and child to determine the factors operating which are detrimental to the life and development of the child — who happens to have been battered. We must ask: For what are we saving these children? Our therapeutic goals must be broadened. Methods of intervention can and must be developed to maximize the chances for the children to grow and develop into adequate healthy adults without the legacy of retardation, inadequacy, dependency and loneliness.

REFERENCES

1. Gregg, Grace S., and Elmer, Elizabeth: Infant injuries: Accident or abuse? Pediatrics 44:434-439, Sept, 1969.
2. Elmer, Elizabeth, and Gregg, Grace S.: Developmental characteristics of abused children. Pediatrics 40:596-602, Oct, 1967.
3. Elmer, Elizabeth: Identification of abused children. Children 10:180-184, Sept-Oct, 1963.
4. Ebbin, Allan J., et al.: Battered child syndrome at the Los Angeles County General Hospital. Amer J Dis Child 118:660-667, Oct, 1969.
5. Birrell, R. G., and Birrell, J. H. W.: The maltreatment syndrome in children: A hospital survey. Med J Aust 2:1023-1029, Dec 7, 1968.
6. Malone, Charles A.: Safety first: Comments on the influence of external danger in the lives of children of disorganized families. Amer J Orthopsychiat 36:6:12, Jan, 1966.
7. Silver, Larry B.: Child abuse syndrome: A review. Med Times 96:803-820, Aug, 1968.
8. Barbero, Gulio J., Morris, Marian G., and Reford, Margaret T.: Malidentification of Mother-Baby-Father Relationships Ex-

pressed in Infant Failure to Thrive in the Neglected Battered-Child Syndrome: Role Reversal in Parents, Child Welfare League of America G-17, July, 1963.

9. Johnson, Betty, and Morse, Harold: The Battered Child: A Study of Children with Inflicted Injuries, Denver Welfare Department, Denver, Colorado, March 15, 1968.

10. Milowe, Irvin D., and Lourie, Reginald S.: The child's role in the battered child syndrome. J Pediat 65:1079-1081, Dec, 1964.

11. Thomas, Alexander, et al.: Behavioral Individuality in Early Childhood. New York, New York Univ Press, 1963.

12. Spitz, Renee, and Wolf, A. M.: Hospitalism: An inquiry into the psychiatric conditions in early childhood. Psychoanal Stud Child 1:53-74, 1946.

13. Provence, S., and Lipton, H.: Infants in Institutions. New York, Internat Univ Press, 1962.

14. Coleman, R., and Provence, S. A.: Developmental retardation (hospitalism) in infants living in families. Pediatrics 19:285-292, 1957.

15. Prugh, D. C., and Harlow, R. G.: "Masked Deprivation" in Infants and Young Children, in Deprivation of Medical Care: A Reassessment of its Effects, Public Health Papers, No. 14, WHO, 1962.

16. Patton, R. G., and Gardner, L. I.: Growth Failure in Maternal Deprivation. Springfield (Ill.), Thomas, 1963.

17. Chase, Peter H., and Martin, Harold P.: Undernutrition and child development. New Eng J Med 282:933-939, April 23, 1970.

18. Patton, Robert G., and Gardner, Lytt I.: Influence of family environment on growth: The syndrome of "maternal deprivation." Pediatrics 30:957-962, Dec, 1962.

19. Silver, Henry K., and Finkelstein, Marcia: Deprivation dwarfism. J Pediat 70:317-324, March, 1967.

20. Kerr, George R., Chamove, Arnold S., and Harlow, Harry F.: Environmental deprivation: Its effect on the growth of infant monkeys. J Pediat 75:833-837, Nov, 1969.

21. Whitten, Charles F., Pettit, Marvin G., and Fischhoff, Joseph: Evidence that growth failure from maternal deprivation is secondary to undereating, JAMA 209:1675-1682, Sept 15, 1969.

22. Hurley, R.: Poverty and Mental Retardation, A Causal Relationship. New York, Random House, 1969.

23. Perspectives on Human Deprivation: Biological, Psychological, and Sociological. U.S. Dept. HEW, 1968.

24. Wortis, J.: Poverty and retardation: Biosocial factors, *in* Wortis, Joseph, ed.: Mental Retardation, New York, Grune, 1970, pp. 271-279.

25. Birch, Herbert G., and Gusson, Joan D.: Disadvantaged Children: Health, Nutrition, and School Failure. New York, Harcourt, 1970.

26. Helfer, Ray E., and Pollock, Carl B.: The battered child syndrome, *in* Advances in Pediatrics, vol. 15, Chicago, Yr Bk Pub, 1968, pp. 9-27.

27. Radbill, Samuel X.: A history of child abuse and infanticide, *in* Helfer, Ray, and Kempe, C. Henry, eds.: The Battered Child, Chicago, Univ of Chic Press, 1968, pp. 3-17.

28. Helfer, Ray E., and Kempe, C. Henry: The Battered Child, Chicago, Univ of Chic Press, 1968.

29. Adelson, Lester: Slaughter of the innocents, a study of 46 homicides in which the victims were children. New Eng J Med 264:1345-1349, June 29, 1961.

30. Morris, Marian G., Gould, Robert W., and Matthews, Patricia J.: Toward prevention of child abuse. Children 11:55-60, March-April, 1964.

31. Duncan, Glen M., *et al.*: Etiological factors in first-degree murder. JAMA 168:1755-1758, Nov 29, 1958.

32. Curtis, George C.: Violence breeds violence—perhaps? Amer J Psychiat 120:386-387, Oct, 1963.

33. Easson, William M., and Steinhilber, Richard M.: Murderous aggression by children and adolescents. Arch Gen Psychiat (Chicago) 4:27-35, Jan, 1961.

34. Steel, Brandt F.: Violence in our society. Pharos of Alpha Omega Alpha 33:42-48, April, 1970.

35. Erikson, Erik H.: Childhood and Society, New York, Norton, 1963.

36. Taylor, Ann: Deprived infants: Potential for affective development. Amer J Orthopsychiat 38:835-845, Oct, 1968.

37. Loomis, W. G.: Management of children's emotional reaction to severe body damage (burns). Clinical Pediat (Phila) 9:362-367, June, 1970.

38. Bullard, Dexter M., *et al.*: Failure to thrive in the "neglected child." Amer J Orthopsychiat 37:680-690, July, 1967.

39. Koel, Bertram S.: Failure to thrive and fatal injury as a continuum. Amer J Dis Child 118:565-567, Oct, 1969.

40. Kempe, C. Henry, *et al.*: The battered child syndrome. JAMA 181:17-24, July 7, 1962.

8

The Child and His School

KAY DREWS

FOR THE OLDER CHILD who is physically abused, his school may be his only recourse. And yet it is this very source of help that so often lets him flounder and return to his home day after day only to be the victim of continued abuse.

The school-aged child has been somewhat forgotten and pushed into the background in previous studies of child abuse. The strong emphasis has been on the battered *baby*—the child three years of age and under. The school can and should provide a resource for early case finding that would permit the development of a therapeutic family-oriented program. The major question is: If a child of school age is abused or subjected to incest, is the school system prepared and willing to provide help to the child and his family through an adequate and effective system of reporting? Murdock states, "Since its inception, the school (reporting) program has been the greatest single source of uncovering these (abuse) problems in Syracuse."[1]

To help answer this question, a questionnaire was sent to one half of all the school districts in the United States which have a total student enrollment of over 10,000 pupils. The questionnaire was designed to assist in estimating the incidence of child abuse in the school-aged child, to determine whether or not school systems had "standard operating procedures" for handling suspected cases of abuse, and the effectiveness of such a procedure if one did exist. Questionnaires were sent to school superintendents to be distributed to those personnel in their school systems whom they felt would best be able to answer the questions. Of the 363 school programs polled, approximately 34 percent responded. Many school districts returned several questionnaires which had been completed by different individuals within the school system. This resulted in reports being received from administrative personnel as well as teachers, nurses and principals.

In comparing the data provided by the adminstrators with that by the teachers and nurses, one important discrepancy appeared. When asked if the school system had a standard operating procedure to follow when confronted with a case of suspected abuse, 49 percent of the administrators responded that their school system had such a procedure. Only 24 percent of the principals, teachers and nurses indicated that their system had a standard operating procedure. The implications are obvious. It seems pointless for the high-level school administrators, who have very little pupil contact, to have knowledge of a reporting procedure if their teachers and principals, who are actually confronted with the abused child, are unaware of such a procedure. If the teachers and even the principals are unaware of a procedure to be followed, the likelihood of a suspected case of abuse being reported to the proper authorities is poor.

The schools were asked who in the system reports suspected child abuse to the authorities. Several responses listed a number of individuals, and some listed only a single person. Based on the completeness of the questionnaires it became obvious that where one person was responsible for reporting, there was a keener awareness of the problem and how to handle it, and fewer blunders were apparent. When anyone can report, or when numerous people are delegated to report, confusion reigns—with each person interpreting abuse and parental rights through his own eyes. Apparently when only one individual within a given school is responsible for reporting all the cases from that school, the person who assumes this responsibility has full knowledge that a problem exists and recognizes the seriousness of the situation. Although reporting laws vary from state to state, most grant immunity from civil liability to any person reporting a case of suspected abuse in good faith. The school administration should seek legal advice on this point.

Who this individual might be varies in the individual school system. However, the more successful and efficient systems often have a social worker or attendance teacher in the administrative office. The workers receive the calls, visit the parents and initiate the action when a local teacher, nurse or social worker feels a child has been abused. In the Syracuse program "Two (Division of Child Welfare) social workers have been relieved of other duties by the division so that they might devote full attention to the solution of these problems."[1]

INCIDENCE

The respondents were asked to describe in detail a recent case of physical abuse which was, in their view, handled well by the school personnel. The same was asked about a case that was handled very poorly. The purpose of this question was to learn the actual methods that were employed which lead to a successful or unsuccessful result. The responses did not give us this information since most of the answers indicated successful procedures with few unsuccessful incidents described. There was wide variation in the interpretation of "successful" case handling.

The detailed descriptions revealed several important points. Even though the great majority of children who are reported to be physically abused fall into the preschool-age range, our data would indicate a significant incidence of abuse in the older child. This survey has revealed that approximately 40 per 100,000 school-age children are being physically abused by their parents or guardians. This is based on estimates supplied by individual school personnel. They were asked to estimate the number of cases of child abuse seen each year in their school system. The accuracy of these estimates is questionable in that some school systems reported a high ratio relative to their size (120/100,000) whereas other large systems estimated no cases.

A large number of school-age children being abused do not show up in national statistics since many are not taken to a physician or hospital for treatment, and therefore no report is made. The incidence of *severe* physical injury in the abused school-age child appears to be small compared to the abused infant. Consequently many of these children are not reported as intended by the mandatory reporting law. The injuries incurred by the school-age child are often bruises resulting from spankings, whippings and lashing with a belt or cord. The marks are often covered by clothing. If the marks are visible the children are often kept home from school until the evidence fades. One school which serves low income families has compulsory shower baths once a week for grades 3 to 6. This provides an opportunity to observe the physical condition of the children.

INADEQUATE STANDARD OPERATING PROCEDURE

Although it is usually better to have some type of procedure to follow than none at all, we found some procedures where this was not the case. Directions were unclear, details lacking, or merely a reproduction of the state code for reporting child abuse was listed.

A relatively large school system, which answered the questionnaire through a school nurse, stated that they had a standard operating procedure and gave an example of "a well-handled case."

> A kindergarten boy appeared at school after having been beaten severely with a belt. The nurse was called by the principal to examine the child. The principal called the parents asking them to come to the school, at which time she advised them of the school's responsibility if it should occur again. It did happen again. This time a report was sent to the administrative office and no action was taken. The third time that abuse occurred the principal and pupil personnel officer called the youth bureau of the local police. The child was eventually temporarily removed from the home.

The child suffered unnecessary beatings because of the school's poor handling of the situation. If the school authorities had reported the abuse to the authorities as soon as it was brought to their attention, instead of attempting to take matters into their own hands, the child might have been spared the repeated abuse. And yet this case was reported to us as an example of a "well-handled situation."

One county school system in California has recognized this problem by emphasizing that teachers and nurses are *obliged* to report suspected cases *even when their principal tells them not to.* Even though one person in a particular school system is responsible, it must be clear that if any individual strongly suspects abuse the report should be made so that the proper authorities can conduct a thorough investigation.

Children often lie about their injuries for fear of repercussions at home if they admit that their parents beat them. Several examples were cited which illustrated this problem.

One child arrived at school covered with bruises and the teacher sent him to the nurse, who in turn reported the incident to the principal. The principal and the nurse talked to the child and the parents were notified and warned of possible consequences. When the child arrived home he received a severe beating for having exposed the parents to the school authorities.

This problem can be alleviated with proper procedures which would provide a degree of protection for the child. Almost without fail, the schools that cited examples of this type of problem were those schools that took the whole matter into their own hands without notifying a child protective agency. They generally took it upon themselves to reprimand the parents either over the phone or in person. Often the parents were warned that, if the child showed up at school with injuries again, the law or welfare department would be called. Some school personnel felt this to be an adequate approach to deter, through fear, any further abuse. In many cases it only resulted in the child being subjected to more abuse.

SCHOOL-AGENCY COOPERATION

Any program is meaningless if there is poor cooperation between the school and the agency to whom they are to report. Numerous responses indicated bitterness on the part of school personnel who had reported a case of abuse only to have it ignored or improperly handled by welfare departments or the police.

> A girl of junior high school age was repeatedly beaten by her stepfather. The school reported it to the caseworker who said he was too busy to do anything. After pressure from the school the case was assigned to another caseworker. He then said that the school Home Visitor was responsible since it affected her school attendance. The caseworker spoke to the parents, who denied any problems. So he let the case drop.
>
> A young boy who was severely scarred from whippings was reported to the police, then to the judge. The judge refused to act but referred the school personnel to the district attorney. The district attorney told the school there was no law that could prevent parents from beating or whipping their child. The school, therefore, closed the case.

In the midst of this bitterness were reports praising the cooperation of welfare departments. An ideal example of this cooperation came from Wisconsin.

> A county welfare agency, after processing a case of child abuse, notified the school where other children in the family were going. They told the school officials of the known case of abuse in the family and asked them to watch for signs of abuse in the other children. A teacher noted bruises and scars on one of the other children. She reported it immediately to her principal, who contacted the welfare agency. Steps were taken to protect the other children.

Gil[2] states that Baltimore school authorities cooperated actively with their local health and welfare and law enforcement agencies in promotion of the enactment of reporting legislation. As a result, school personnel are included, in the Maryland statute, among those who are required to report.

OPEN-END RESPONSES

The respondents were given an opportunity to make additional comments at the end of the questionnaire regarding child abuse or their feelings about reporting. An overwhelming number felt that emotional abuse and neglect were seen much more frequently than was physical abuse. They were concerned that the former is often much more harmful to the child. In fact, some school systems recalled no cases of physical abuse but reported numerous cases of neglect. There were suggestions that neglect should be included in the mandatory reporting because of its depressing effect on the child's learning and future development.

Another interesting observation by many school officials was that, on occasion, physical abuse was not intentionally inflicted but was strictly the result of parents being unaware of any other method of disciplining their children. The school personnel felt that their going into the home and discussing alternate child rearing methods with the parents often alleviated the problem. A reply from one school stated that staff members consider severe corporal punishment, administered by parents whose cultural patterns call for such discipline, as a form of abuse which is usually handled effectively in a parent-school personnel conference.

Opinions ranged all the way from those expressed by school personnel who wished to counsel the parents and develop a family treatment program, to those expressed by some educators who felt that they should neither become involved with the families nor report abuse to any agency for fear of condemnation for meddling in parental affairs.

An administrator in the largest metropolitan school system surveyed was personally interviewed to gain some insight to how the problem of abuse is handled in a large school system (about a million students). He said he felt that, generally, school children are not abused at home because the parents know that the child is old enough to "snitch" on them and, therefore, would get them in trouble. He felt that parents would fear this risk so they rarely would touch the child. A colleague in this administrator's office stated that abuse did not occur; besides, there was no sense in doing anything about it because they would get nowhere in court, since the judge would feel that parents can do what they want with their own children. These two responses came from the officials who are responsible for educating the teachers within their school system on problems of abuse.

SUGGESTED STANDARD OPERATING PROCEDURE

School personnel must accept their responsibility to the abused children who are enrolled in their system. Their early involvement can be the first step in the establishment of an effective therapeutic program.

From our experience and the results of the questionnaire, a desired standard operating procedure should include the following:

1. Special training programs for *teachers* to enable them to recognize suspected cases of physical abuse.

2. Specific instructions given to the teacher to report *all* suspected cases to a stated individual in her school.

3. The child should be seen by the school physician who would examine the child, interview the parents and report the case to the proper agency.

4. The school must then communicate their information to the agency and develop a cooperative therapeutic plan.

5. A follow-through system should be established by the school to make certain that the case was handled properly and the therapeutic plan is working.

SUMMARY

The cooperation of the school systems responding to the questionnaire provided us with an opportunity to gather most informative and revealing data. The wide discrepancies in the numbers of estimated cases in the different school systems revealed a great need for educating the educators throughout the country. Children will continue to be abused and, in turn, become the abusers themselves unless the schools recognize their role and responsibility in the reporting of their suspicions and developing a close working relationship with the agency that receives their report. It seems unlikely that one school system with 7,600 students would have 26 suspected cases in a one-year period while a school system of 20,000 students had no reports and has done nothing to recognize the problem, hence denying that the problem exists.

The overall attitude of those who responded indicated a desire to learn more about the problems of child abuse, now that their attention had been drawn to it, and to improve certain systems which had already taken effective steps to provide protection to the child. Supplied with valuable suggestions, we were able to develop the recommendations for an "ideal" standard operating procedure.

The school systems which did not respond at all to the questionnaire (66 percent) leave questions in our minds about how these vital people can be reached to realize their responsibility in assisting with the early detection, protection and treatment of the abused children within their school system.

REFERENCES

1. Murdock, C. G.: The abused child and the school system. Amer J Public Health 60:105-109, 1970.
2. Gil, David G.: What Schools Can Do About Child Abuse, American Education, April, 1969.

Part Three

THE SETTING

Where Can Help Best Be Given?

EDITORIAL NOTE

At this point in our understanding of abusive parents and their children it is reasonably clear what type of help battering families need and, with the right kind of effort, that this help can be provided in a practical and realistic manner. The question is where is the best source of help and whose responsibility it is to provide it.

State legislatures have been less than helpful. Mandatory reporting laws have rarely been accompanied by financial aid to implement care once the agency has been notified of abuse. The laws, with all their advantages, have also had the negative effect of letting the physician and hospital "off the hook." They now feel that once the report has been made they no longer have any further responsibility, except to make the child well.

Providing appropriate services to these desperate families is an urgent problem which can no longer be ignored.

9

The Status of Child Protective Services*

A National Dilemma

VINCENT DE FRANCIS, J.D.

IF THE SOCIAL SCIENCES could borrow from the technical sciences to develop a pushbutton method for solving psycho-social problems, it could bring about the creation of instant social work. What a miraculous thought to contemplate.

Should such a fantasy ever become reality social problems would no longer exist, for through the wonders of science we would treat and resolve problems as rapidly as they arose with computerized efficiency.

But there is little immediate prospect for a wedding of these two sciences. To try to resolve human problems with our less than scientific and most imperfect tools is a most difficult task.

The institution of social work is frequently charged with being resistant to change—that it is slow to modify basic programs and functions; that it fails to keep pace with new or changing needs; and that it is slow to adopt or put to use the findings and knowledge coming from the thousands of research and demonstration projects identified with the health and welfare fields. If this picture is true, how ironic it is that the very discipline which seeks to motivate change in the people it serves should itself be resistant to change.

*Reprinted with permission of the American Humane Association, Children's Division.

Social workers talk at great length about gaps in service; about program needs; about rising caseloads; about shortage of qualified staff; and about competition from other fields which drains off talented young people and diminishes the potential for filling social work manpower needs. But all this talk and awareness produce very little actual change.

Resistance to change is a compound of conservative forces which are unable or unwilling to face the consequences of change. Those who are content with things as they are oppose change because their comfort and contentment may be disturbed by change. The insecure guard against change lest their status become less secure and less tenable. And vested interests fear change because of the possible challenge to their prerogatives.

This is true of individuals and institutions.

These forces, united in opposition to change, constitute a negative dynamic which seeks to maintain and perpetuate the status quo.

Practice in many of our social service programs has become institutionalized. Resistance to change has frozen patterns of service and built up attitudes of serene unconcern for the needs of the vast unserved. Many agencies seem content to work with motivated clients only. They serve the "social work hypochondriac" who has real or fancied need for social services. Some voluntary agencies are more comfortable serving a middle-class clientele with problems of interpersonal relationships and with ability to pay a fee for services rendered.

These agencies have moved into a comfortable niche in the hierarchy of social services. They bask complacently in the knowledge that what they do they do superbly well.

It seems to me, however, that the basic question should not be solely "How well we serve?" but "Are we serving the individuals and families who need service most?" Can society justify extending service to those whose needs are moderate but who are articulate, aware and motivated — without concern for people who lack these qualities but whose needs are more acute and more pressing? These are people whose problems have reached crisis proportions. These are people who need help desperately and need it right now. If they don't get help, the weight of unresolved difficulties may, and usually does, bring acute distress to themselves, to their families and to the community as a whole.

Social work administrators rationalize failure to move toward change by projecting blame on external problems — lack of budget, insufficient staff, inadequate space, heavy caseloads, and so on. But are these the only reasons? Is it not possible that we resist change because the status quo is more comfortable — because it takes courage, imagination and dedicated drive to experiment and innovate — to try new methods, to develop new approaches?

Child protective services are not new, but they are different. They impose obligations and require approaches which challenge the status quo. Probably more than any other child welfare program, protective services, in terms of their development, have met the full blast of the negative impact of resistance to change.

It was our conviction of the need to stimulate change in regard to the availability of child protection which prompted us to initiate the study on which this paper is based. If we could document with convincing proof the truth which we have long known, that the development of this basic preventive program has not kept pace with the enormous need, then perhaps it would be possible to stir communities into action on behalf of all neglected and abused children.

That community action on their behalf can be aroused was amply demonstrated by the unprecedented speed with which all 50 states adopted legislation for reporting suspected cases of child abuse.

Thus, the concern to promote more and better child protective services was an overall objective of the two-year study to assess the status and availability of child protective services. The full 328-page report, its 28 major findings, and the state by state analysis support the thesis that this program is grossly underdeveloped.[1]

This paper presents the highlights of those findings.
Specific objectives sought by the study were:

1. To determine which states and communities are currently engaged in providing protective services to neglected and abused children.

2. To identify the auspices and legal bases under which these programs are provided.

3. To assess the size and scope of each such program.

4. To evaluate, in part, the degree to which these programs are able to cover actual need in each community.

WHAT IS CHILD PROTECTIVE SERVICES?

For purposes of clarity let me briefly review the definition of child protective services as used in the study.

The survey was concerned with child protective services as an identifiable and specialized area of child welfare. It is a program which seeks to prevent neglect, abuse and exploitation of children by "reaching out" with social services to stabilize family life. It seeks to preserve the family unit by strengthening parental capacity and ability to provide good child care. Its special attention is focused on families where unresolved problems have produced visible signs of neglect or abuse and the home situation presents actual and potentially greater hazard to the physical or emotional well-being of children.

The specifics of child protective services demand special skills in staff and an approach which seeks out the neglecting family to extend services on behalf of children despite initial rejection or resistance by sometimes hostile or disturbed parents.

The service is usually initiated on a "complaint" or referral from sources outside the family. Sometimes, one parent may report the conditions of neglect resulting from the other parent's behavior; or an older sibling may report the neglect or abuse.

The protective agency has a mandate to provide service when needed and an obligation to explore, study and evaluate the facts of neglect and their effect on children. The agency carries responsibility for maintaining service until the conditions are treated and neglect is reduced. It has the additional obligation to invoke the authority of the juvenile court (or family court) when such action is necessary to secure protection, care and treatment of children whose parents are unable or unwilling to use the help offered by the agency.

WHY THE SURVEY?

In 1956, the Children's Division of the American Humane Association published *Child Protective Services in the United States.* This report summarized the findings of a nationwide survey of the availability of child protective services. That survey was the first national study of this specialized field. It explored services in every state and every county of the nation. It highlighted the fact that child protective services constituted the least developed area of child welfare. The report gave strong support to the inference that foster home or institutional placement of children was being substituted for more constructive planning to preserve the child's own home. Far too many children were placed under court order because court process was invoked when conditions involving neglect or abuse became too gross for the community to tolerate. The absence of child protective services left a wide gap in the community's pattern of social service resources. And the breach was filled by reliance on police or other law enforcement intervention at the point of extreme crisis.

An added objective of the current study explored and identified what changes took place in the one-year period following the 1956 report. However, space does not permit a discussion of the 28 major findings recorded in the 1967 study. This condensed version will relate only to the most significant areas.

First, a review of our findings with respect to the role, in this field, of the voluntary agencies. Protective services under

voluntary auspices were found to exist in only 10 states. This
is a decline of more than 40 percent from the findings of the
1956 survey.

Responsibility for protective services under voluntary auspices is slowly fading away. It was under voluntary auspices
that child protective services began. From 1875, when the
New York Society for the Prevention of Cruelty to Children was
created in New York City,[2] until the thirties, when the Social
Security Act was enacted by Congress, such protective social
services as were available were provided solely by voluntary
agencies. SPCC's, Humane Societies and Children's Aid Societies, although more heavily concentrated east of the Mississippi, were to be found from coast to coast and from border
to border. The greatest challenge to their existence came during
the Depression years when attrition set in because of financial
problems and, more so, because of the growing network of
public child welfare services fostered and promoted by federal
legislation and federal support.

A combination of wholesale agency mergers or the outright
abandonment of service brought these voluntary agencies to
a point of near extinction. Only the more highly motivated,
the more soundly financed and the more adequate, in terms of
quality of services rendered, have survived.

These voluntary agencies provide child protection as their
sole functional program or as a major service in the context of
broader services to children. In most cases the program is
understaffed, but skilled services are given to selected cases
after heavy screening at intake. By self-admission, these
agencies describe their program as insufficient in size to meet
the total need in their communities. This is particularly true
of the SPCC's, whose sole program is concerned with provision
of protective services.

Because of long experience in this field, these voluntary
agencies are keenly sensitive to the needs of all neglected and
abused children. They know that only through the application
of intensive casework may we resolve problems in these

acutely problem-ridden families. However, they find themselves so burdened with heavy caseloads that they cannot
maintain a consistent standard of intensive treatment of the
families they serve. If we add to excessive caseloads, the handicap of inadequate budget and insufficient staff, we compound
the problem and dilute services. The weight of new cases,
with their insistent demands for attention, may force a substitution of superficial service for the intensive casework dynamic inherent to a sound child protective program.

How to resolve the problem without sacrifice of basic principles or quality of service is the dilemma faced by all protective
agencies regardless of auspices.

Some agencies, confronted with these reality factors, have
compromised by becoming selective at intake: "If we cannot
give good service to all neglected children—then we should
serve only as many as can be given intensive service within the
limitations of present funds and staffing." These agencies have
set up screening devices which select cases on the basis of
greatest need. They look not only at the severity of the problem
but also at whether any other agency is currently active with
the family.

This policy is recognized as a stopgap measure, not in keeping with fundamental tenets of "service to all abused and
neglected children." A policy of selective intake negates the
concept of "reaching out" to all who need help and denies the
obligations of the protective function. It is an expediency
dictated by urgent necessity, and adopted with grave
reluctance.

Other protective agencies, responding to their functional obligation to intervene on behalf of all neglected and abused
children called to their attention, view limitation of intake
rather dimly. They see more adequate protection of children
in a policy which offers service more freely but which terminates contact sooner. In other words, the limitation is put at
the other end of the process, after cases have been more fully
explored and some service given. Intensive casework is given

to fewer cases. Many are closed when stress problems are resolved. Others are prepared for referral to other community resources for continuing casework.

Here, again, this approach is viewed as a device made necessary by lack of sufficient funds and staff to do the full job. We look to the day when our frustrations will end; when sufficient money and staffing will give all child protective programs the opportunity to serve neglected and abused children more effectively.

What about child protection under public child welfare auspices?

An overall view of the nationwide status of child protective services reveals marked differences in the patterns of service from state to state. Probably the greatest difference is found in each state's ability to *accept* complaints of child neglect or abuse and in its capacity *to serve* the children and families reported by the complaints. Quite distressing is the fact that many differences, sometimes enormous differences, were found in the pattern of services within states.

But most disturbing is the fact that *no state* and *no community* has developed a child protective service program adequate in size to meet the service needs of all reported cases of child neglect or abuse. In this finding, we are solely assessing the program's ability to respond to complaints on the basis of these criteria:

1. To respond promptly.
2. To explore *all* reports.
3. To assess the damage to children in *all* reported instances.
4. To evaluate the risk to children from continued exposure to neglect.
5. To offer the necessary remedial casework services.
6. To take summary action where warranted through invoking the authority of the juvenile court or family court.

In no sense is this assessment intended to be an evaluation of the quality of services. *We were looking only at the pro-*

gram's capacity for coping with the incidence of neglect and the demand for service posed by the reporting of such cases. The probable increase in all reporting stimulated by more alert case finding under mandatory reporting of child abuse was a factor considered in this evaluation.

However, while the focus of the study was purely in terms of evaluating the quantitative and not the qualitative strengths of these programs, much data reviewed by the staff led to some educated estimates and rather sound deductions about the caliber of service available and offered. Data relating to these informal assessments were concerned with size of staff in relation to the size of the community, educational qualifications of staff, caseload controls, the ratio of supervisory staff to casework staff and specific comments in replies to the questionnaires.

Thus, there is ample documentation and data to support the belief that much of what was reported as a child protective service was in reality nonspecific *child welfare service,* or a nonspecific *family service* in the context of a financial assistance setting. While the spirit and intent to serve neglected, abused and exploited children is present in many of the reported programs—in terms of identifiable and specific *child protective services* — it is often no more than a token program.

Child protective services under public welfare auspices were reported available in 47 states, the District of Columbia, Puerto Rico, the Virgin Islands and Guam. To round out the 50 states—Massachusetts and Nevada have limited protective services with responsibility restricted solely to child abuse cases discovered under newly enacted mandatory reporting legislation. Louisiana was the only state reporting the absence of any protective service programming under public welfare auspices.

While services were found to exist under public welfare auspices in 47 states and the territories, in reality—in terms of statewide coverage—service falls far short of the declared state policy. In varying degree, this was found to be true for all the states reporting a program. The differences between policy and practice seemed to have no correlation with the administrative structure in terms of a state administered or county administered pattern. This finding is documented by qualifying statements made by the state departments of welfare when reporting the existence of a child protective service program.

Phrases such as these were quite common: "Limited service to remote areas." "Forty counties provide limited coverage." "Juvenile courts provide service in some areas." "Some complaints handled by private agencies—some directly by law enforcement officials." "Service actually given varies with the training of the case-work staff and interpretation given the community." "All counties offer child protective services: However, the quality and extent of service varies greatly." "Child protective services theoretically available in all counties—to the degree that referrals come in and to the degree that staff skills permit."

Thus, while some state departments of welfare reported total geographic coverage for their state, the returns on county questionnaires from the same states disclosed the absence of service in some counties and limited service in others. In 30 of the 47 states reporting child protective service, the study either found a statement that services were limited in some geographic areas or found a difference between the report coming from the state office and the returns received from the counties. Almost two thirds of the states reporting a service were found to lack adequate geographic coverage. From the total data examined we have reason to believe that near-full geographic coverage is available in fewer than 10 percent of the states.

STAFFING AND TRAINING

Much has been said and written about the special skills required of staff in child protective services. This is posited on the thesis that problems of child neglect and abuse are frequently referred at a time of crisis. The problems are acute and intricate and often involve deep psychological and emotional disturbances. If these families are to be successfully treated in the best interests of children, then staff must be equipped by training, experience and disposition to deal with the full range of difficult situations common to the protective service caseload.

For the same reasons, caseload controls must be applied fairly rigidly to maintain active loads at manageable levels. Because intensive casework is basic to treatment plans in this field, workers must be free to devote to each family as much time and effort as are diagnosed to be necessary.

Thus, an adequate child protective program must recognize and live up to these two prime requisites:

1. The program must recruit mature, experienced personnel, with the highest social work skills, who are able to establish rapport with parents who throw every sort of roadblock in the way.

2. Caseloads must be tailored down and controlled, to permit the application of those optimum skills in such intensive casework as individual cases may require.

Corollary to the first requisite is the necessity for development of staff skills through planned staff development programs with appropriate content on child protection.

The second requisite — caseload controls — finds successful child protective programs holding caseload levels to between 20 and 25 active cases per worker. Concomitant with this requirement is the need for sufficient staff to allow for the maintenance of tight caseload controls without curtailing intake as a secondary, and less appropriate, means for holding down caseloads.

The data quite consistently described public child welfare staff as not fully trained. A majority of the replies indicated on the average that staffs are composed of some 20 percent to 35 percent of graduate workers, with some 20 percent more only partially trained. Almost all states said they have some staff with bachelor's degrees only; nearly all have some staff without a bachelor's degree.

Control of caseloads through specialized protective service units is not a common practice. Only three states provide protective services exclusively through special units; two more states have specialized units for handling child abuse reports only. Eighteen additional states have one or more specialized protective units serving a single district, county or city.

COMMUNITY COOPERATION

Important to the success of any program is the degree of cooperation received from the community. More than one third of the states cited a need for more community cooperation with their child protective programs. Thirty-eight percent of the states reported it would be helpful to have more cooperation from schools and other social agencies. Forty-two percent described need for more cooperation from the courts.

What are the elements which make for recognition and support from the community?

Recognition implies that the community is fully aware of the importance and value of the child protective program in terms of helping to meet urgent needs of children. It indicates awareness of the preventive role of the service through its focus on stabilizing and strengthening family life. But most of all, it reflects the community's acceptance of the protective service's responsibility to act for the community when it intervenes on behalf of child victims of neglect and abuse.

Cooperation requires that the community-at-large also accepts responsibility in terms of its own role toward neglected children. These relate principally to case finding, i.e., discovery and reporting of children in need of help, and promoting such auxiliary services as are needed to meet special needs.

Resources such as schools, public and voluntary social services, the police and the juvenile court, have more direct roles in a cooperative child protective program. What these roles are and how they may be better used in the interest of children are areas which should be explored by all participating agencies and the welfare planning bodies in the community.

One area which has aroused grave concern is the lack of coordination between services. Frequently more than one agency is serving the family from focal points unique to the functions of each agency. The tragedy is that this segmented approach consumes valuable staff and agency time without truly resolving the basic problem or problems which have produced the surface symptoms being treated.

Protective services are more keenly aware of this ineffective use of manpower because their major service is to the community's multiproblem families — the very group in the community which absorbs the largest share of social services.

These wasteful practices could be greatly reduced with more cooperation in the exchange of information between agencies. Increased understanding about respective roles would improve the potential for more coordination of services. Responsibility for calling the shots should be left with the agency whose relationship with the family is in tune with the family's capacity for positive change. In many, if not in most, instances this would be the child protective service.

LAWS FOR REPORTING CHILD ABUSE

A significant facet of the study deals with an examination of the child abuse reporting laws enacted by all 50 states, the District of Columbia, the Virgin Islands and Guam. The study makes a comparative analysis of these laws, highlighting strengths and weaknesses and pointing to areas where modification is needed.

Only a few of the more significant points can be discussed in this brief report.[3]

NATURE OF REPORT

In 46 states, the District of Columbia, Guam and the Virgin Islands the reporting law was made mandatory. The person or persons cited in the law must report all situations when they know or believe that a child has been physically abused. Four states, however—New Mexico, North Carolina, Texas and

Washington—made their laws permissive. The person or persons cited in the law "may report" rather than "shall report."

What can be said for a permissive law is that it may induce some reporting sources to report because of immunities granted by the law. However, under a permissive law there is danger that the decision may be based on the personal conviction and personal convenience of the potential reporter rather than on the possible consequences to the child if a report is not made.

REPORT TO WHOM

This is the most sensitive area of the whole discussion of reporting legislation. Yet, analysis shows that this is the most confused in terms of legislative action. A critical determination for the lawmakers is the decision about which resource to designate for receiving reports of child abuse. On this important decision rests the effectiveness of the reporting law with respect to achieving the appropriate goals. The right choice will bring into play the appropriate resources. A poor, or bad, choice may produce results not contemplated by the law. It is possible, therefore, for the legislative intent to fail if the tools prescribed to accomplish the goal are inadequate or unsuited on the job.

To be more specific, where the declared legislative intent is to make available the protective social services to prevent further abuse, safeguard and enhance the welfare of such children and to preserve family life wherever possible the logical procedure, consistent with the stated goals, would be to invoke the immediate services of the social agency charged with that special function. This would mean that the reporting should be directed to the department of welfare or the child protective service agency, if separate from the department of welfare. As a second line of "protective social services," an appropriate designation could be the family or juvenile court.

Referral to the department of welfare would involve a psychosocial investigation in each case, with an evaluation of the circumstances surrounding each act reported. The needs of the child victim, the possibility of continuing hazard to the child and the risk to other children in the family would be assessed. Also evaluated would be the potential for a social work treatment of the problem to obtain all the goals defined in the statement of purpose. If a study of the case shows need to assure protection of the child by removal from parental custody, this could be done through petitioning the juvenile court for an order of removal.

On the other hand, given the same declaration of purpose, reaching the stated objectives would be hampered, if not defeated, by selection of some less qualified recourse as the recipient of the report. If, for example, the legislature were to designate a law enforcement agency to receive the report, that choice would not be consonant with the declared intent.

A law enforcement agency would be the police or sheriff or the prosecuting attorney for the community. Their orientation, their functional responsibilities and their *modus operandi* are not in tune with the legislative intent of "invoking the protective social services." Such a choice would be more compatible with a legislative intent to view the occurrence in terms of crimes and punishment. Social services are not a component of the law enforcement function. Law enforcement personnel are trained to investigate and are oriented to determine whether a crime has been committed. While some personnel in large police forces are given special training as juvenile officers, these constitute but a minute portion of the country's police force. Thus, reporting to law enforcement agencies gives little assurance that such reporting will, in fact, invoke protective social services on behalf of the abused child.

What makes for the above mentioned confusion is the fact that the various state legislatures designated a wide variety of resources in the community as the possible recipients of child abuse reports. While the department of public welfare, at state or county level, was most frequently cited as the receiving agency, "appropriate police authorities, the chief of police, or the sheriff or the county prosecutor" were frequently designated. In 14 states the legislature designated one or more agencies as eligible to receive reports of child abuse. It would seem that in these states the choice is left to the person making the report.

Where the reporting source has an option to choose the agency to which he will report, the probability exists that the ultimate community action taken on the report will vary with the agency chosen. Thus, if the reporter chooses an agency within the law enforcement range, the action may be in terms of investigation with prosecution as an objective. However, if the reporter chooses an agency within the protective social service group, the probable action will more likely be related to that specific function.

This seeming flexibility of action made possible by the offer of a choice to the reporter may be the result of a deliberate decision by the legislature to grant such a choice. On the other hand, it may have resulted from indecision on the part of the legislature—a lack of conviction about which is the better course of action—or, more likely, it may represent a compromise of conflicting views. A third possibility is that the legislature wished to provide alternative courses of action in the event that first choices were not available in a given community.

SPECIAL CLAUSES

Discussed under this caption are provisions contained in the reporting law of a number of states and which are not common to the majority. These special clauses fall into four groups. In the first group are provisions relating to the crime of child abuse. The second relates to the creation of a central statewide registry for recording child abuse cases. The third contains a clause which exempts from the reporting mandate all cases of children who are receiving spiritual or religious healing in lieu of medical treatment. The fourth and last group is a miscellaneous category. Most disturbing is the third category related to religious healing.

Religious Healing Excluded from Reporting. The impact of this provision is to exclude from the definition of reportable neglect or abuse the child who is under "spiritual treatment." Quite similar language is found in the statutes of 12 states and the District of Columbia: Alabama, Arizona, Arkansas, California, Colorado, Hawaii, Minnesota, Mississippi, New Hampshire, Ohio, Virginia and Washington.

The intended purpose of the provision is stated clearly in the Minnesota statute: "Provided, however, that no provision of this section shall be construed to mean that a child is neglected or lacks proper parental care solely because said child's parent, guardian or custodian in good faith selects and depends upon spiritual means or prayer for the treatment or cure of disease or remedial care of such child."

We have grave reservations about these exclusionary clauses. In 30 years of practice in the child protective field, we can cite numerous cases where a child's life was endangered by parental refusal to permit needed emergency surgery or a blood transfusion. Where parental objection is based on religious grounds, a neglect petition in the juvenile court seeking a court order to permit necessary medical treatment becomes the only recourse open to the community for safeguarding the child's life. In many of these cases, after court orders were obtained, parents expressed relief at being freed of the onus to resolve the conflict between the prohibitions of their religious tenets and a genuine concern, and despair, for the child's life.

The language employed in these special clauses results in preventing the reporting and identification of a possibly abused child. What is more important, however, is the possibility that the exclusion of these children from being considered "neglected" may also create a bar to the filing of a petition in juvenile court should it become necessary to obtain a court order to save the child's life.

REPORTING LEGISLATION IS NOT ENOUGH

The legislation for reporting child abuse was enacted in all 50 states within a space of time just short of four years. Puerto Rico is the only United States area without a similar law. The speed with which this was accomplished attests to the wide recognition given the problem and to awareness of the grave dangers to its victims. The unprecedented rush by legislators to be counted on the side of abused children came in response to public outcries for urgent action to halt the growing number of battered children.

Passage of these laws has largely appeased public concern. But there is danger that communities may be lulled into a false sense of security based on a belief that these new laws will control, if not erase, the problem of child abuse.

Nothing could be further from the truth. The reporting laws, by themselves, are not enough to control the problem. They do not resolve the problem nor can they prevent the condition, or fact, of child abuse.

Reporting laws are only a beginning. Their chief contribution is that they provide a method for discovering and identifying the child who has been abused. They also serve as a means for alerting a resource in the community to the existence of specific cases as reported. Most of the laws, in addition, impose a responsibility for action on the part of the agency designated to accept reports.

Like the air raid siren these laws, when cases are reported, call attention to a dangerous situation.

To continue the analogy, if there were no civilian defense organization, no air raid shelters, no planned approach for protecting the civilian population—the warning sirens would serve little useful purpose.

So, too, if there are not adequate protective social services available in the community, the reporting law's identification of children in hazard will be meaningless.

The major concern of this study has been to evaluate the nationwide status and availability of child protective services. Our findings are encouraging since we were able to document considerable growth and expansion of these services in the 10-year period between our two evaluations. But there is still a long way to go before child protection becomes a reality in all geographic areas of every state. There is probably an even longer road to travel in terms of establishing in every community a protective service program adequate in size and quality to meet the needs of our country's neglected, abused and exploited children.

REFERENCES

1. De Francis, Vincent: Child Protective Services—A National Survey. The American Humane Association, Denver, Colorado, 1968.
2. The New York Society for the Prevention of Cruelty to Children was created as an aftermath of the Mary Ellen case in 1874. A grossly abused child, Mary Ellen, age nine, was rescued by a church worker, Mrs. Etta Angell Wheeler, who persuaded the American Society for the Prevention of Cruelty to Animals (the ASPCA), organized in New York City in 1866, to intervene on behalf of the child under laws to protect animals. Animal anticruelty laws were invoked because no laws to protect children were then extant. The first child protective legislation, anywhere, was enacted in New York state in 1875, and they provided the legal base for organizing special agencies — The SPCC's — to protect the rights of children. (The Mary Ellen Story, published by The American Humane Association).
3. De Francis, Vincent: Child Abuse Legislation in the 1970's. The American Humane Association, Denver, Colorado, 1970. Provides a fuller and more complete discussion of reporting laws.

10

After Child Abuse Reporting Legislation—What?*

BOYD OVIATT, D.S.W.

THE RECENT REPORT prepared by the Children's Division of The American Humane Association—*Child Protective Services —A National Survey*[1] presents a nationwide assessment of the availability of child protective services. The findings indicate that, though legislation for reporting child abuse exists in all 50 states, no state and no community has developed a child protective service program adequate in size to meet the needs of all reported cases of child neglect, abuse and exploitation. Hence, the primary question posed by the report, and the primary concern of this presentation, "After Reporting Legislation—What?"

It is the thesis of this chapter that public policy must provide for a system of state funding and supervision of protective services, and that the helping professions—social work in particular—must critically examine present methods of providing services for neglected children and their families.

First, a general comment about the study. Richard M. Titmus, Professor, London School of Economics, has stressed the need for research "that enlarges human freedoms, which contributes to a process of community diagnosis . . . brings ethical issues to light . . . and educates society in the need for action."[2] The study completed by The American Humane Association

*Reprinted with permission of the American Humane Association, Children's Division.

identifies a significant social problem and is an excellent illustration of social research which holds the possibility of contributing to the self-realization of man.

A social problem can be considered as a social need which has been culturally recognized and has emerged into community consciousness. When there is a poor formulation of the social problem, our social welfare answers do not always adequately meet the identified human need. Historically, social work has made a significant leadership contribution in the direct day-to-day uncovering and reporting of widespread social problems. This is, of course, one of the essential prerequisites to a community organization effort—that of identification of unmet needs so they become known, labeled and made visible.

The findings of the Humane Association report raise many questions including: What are the roles of the public and the private agency? What is the base for evaluating adequacy of programs? Should a protective service program be a specific program with separate identity, or part of a general welfare and family services program? What is the relationship, if any, between location of administration responsibility and the extent and adequacy of a protective service program? Why have legislators not provided appropriations sufficient to support the development of an adequate service program? Should programs be county or state administered? How can public support be mobilized to push for adequate financial support for protective service programs? Given adequate funds, can social work demonstrate effectiveness in bringing about desired changes in individual and family functioning?

Three general areas will be discussed:

1. The failure of states to identify child neglect as a major social problem.

2. What constitutes an adequate child protective service program.

3. Achievement of a clear mandate and adequate funds for child protective services.

FAILURE OF THE STATES
TO IDENTIFY CHILD NEGLECT AS
A MAJOR SOCIAL PROBLEM

Social policy has often been seen as a "transitory minimum activity of minimum government for a minimum number of . . . people. In this view, social policy is not good business. At the other end are those who have stated that social policies are concerned with the right ordering of the network of relationships between men and women who live together in societies, or with the principles which should govern the activities of individuals and groups so far as they affect the lives and interests of other people." It would appear that the people of the United States have been somewhat slow in accepting as good business a social policy of providing health and welfare services for neglected children and their families.

Although child neglect has been a matter of public concern for nearly a century, there continues to be a lack of firm commitment to a public policy which would insure that protective services would be available to all neglected children and their families. In fact, it was reported that as of 1966, "no state and no community has developed a child protective service program adequate in size to meet the service needs of all reported cases of child neglect, abuse and exploitation."[3]

The goal of developing a satisfactory legal basis for child protective services has been significantly enhanced by the publication of the findings of the ongoing nationwide study of child neglect by The American Humane Association. It is evident that the public has been aroused over the vivid reports and descriptions of child abuse, and legislators have responded with the passage of significant child abuse reporting legislation. However, despite the expanded provision of a legal base for child protective services, such services are not uniformly available.

Has the accomplishment of the passage of reporting laws served to placate the public concern? It is the belief of the public and legislators that abuse reporting laws have resulted in the provision of adequate service programs? How can community concern be aroused to demand the availability of effective services when child neglect has been identified and reported? These are the unanswered questions.

Why has public policy been deficient in establishing and supporting an adequate child protective service program, uniformly available in every state and sufficient to meet the needs of neglected children and their families? Why do the reporting laws of 17 states, the District of Columbia, and the Virgin Islands fail to provide a specific mandate to public welfare departments to provide services on behalf of children? Why do 66 percent of the states report there is a need for more adequate financing to support better child protective programs? Why have 92 percent of the states said more staff was needed? If we look into the fantasied mirror of the Queen in the story of Snow White, expecting to find the answers to these questions, would the reply be: "You have what you have asked *for*?"

Dr. Rino Patti, in a scholarly analysis of public policy regarding child protection in California, suggests that the state had failed to commit itself to the protection of neglected children. He called attention to several factors which may have influenced this lack of commitment, including: "(1) early state policy virtually abdicated to voluntary agencies all responsibility for insuring the availability or quality of services to neglected children; (2) the state had no means of assessing the availability or adequacy of protective services, nor any source of information regarding the prevalence of child neglect. As long as child neglect remained the exclusive concern of the private agency, it appeared to be a problem of small proportions occurring with relative infrequency; (3) when the state entered the picture, it merely authorized county welfare departments to establish protective services at their discretion—as a result, in 1966, only one-half of the county departments in California had instituted services to neglected children in their own homes."[4]

Dr. Patti suggested such a policy deserved what it has produced because: "(1) the limited tax base of counties which restricts the ability of county governments to finance welfare programs; (2) the low visibility of child neglect problems in some counties; (3) probation departments having traditionally been responsible for acting on child neglect complaints and may have resented surrendering these traditional functions to public welfare agencies; and (4) the failure of the state to provide a systematic means whereby these programs could be financed and supervised. Public policy has never authorized a California state agency to exercise regulatory powers over local protective agencies. Consequently, a state agency has been unable to bring about uniformity of administrative operations among counties."[5]

Dr. Patti concluded that in California the major deficiency in public policy has been its failure to provide for a system of state funding and supervision. He believes "without this support and direction, local protective service programs, whether under probation or welfare auspices, have remained underdeveloped."[6]

The American Humane Association report indicated that in the United States, 15 states had county administered programs. The data presented in the study do not permit an assessment of the relationship between the extent of program development and adequacy and whether the program is county or state administered. However, it is generally accepted that the administrative organization of a service program may be instrumental in influencing the emphasis and the course of the service provided. In fact, it has been suggested the "administrative location is program destiny."[7]

One approach to the administrative location of a service agency has been called organization by function. In child protective services this has sometimes led to a blurring of administrative responsibilities between legal and welfare services. Lack of clear administrative responsibility tends to be highly undesirable, in that accountability and specific responsibility for comprehensive program development become blurred. Designation of a single public agency, with specific administrative responsibility, would avoid unnecessary duplication, provide for continuity in services, provide clearness for the public regarding the location of protective services, and facilitate the assessment of the extent of unmet need and the adequacy of existing services.

WHAT CONSTITUTES AN ADEQUATE
CHILD PROTECTIVE SERVICE PROGRAM?

Who is to take the lead in providing services, once the abused child is brought to the attention of a community social welfare resource? In 1966, executives of state departments of welfare consistently reported that child welfare staff were not fully trained.[8] However, if fully trained personnel were available, who is to offer the necessary services to children and families? The Children's Division of The American Humane Association categorically specifies the social worker, stating "successful implementation of the abuse reporting law is contingent upon the availability in every community of a social work oriented child protective service[9] . . . the first requisite points to the need for graduate social workers with experience in family casework or in child welfare, and with sufficient maturity to relate well with uncooperative, immobilized, unmotivated, resistive and sometimes hostile parents."[10]

Are social workers adequately prepared for work in child protective services? The literature does not give consistent direction. On the one hand, a recent article, in discussing social work services for abusive parents, states: "there does not appear to be a need for new techniques—if there are any— but rather a rethinking of old techniques . . . the techniques that we need are not new to the field, but have been old standbys of casework: environmental and supportive help . . . in one case it was recommended that the parents secure a housekeeper to be with the mother who had abused her child during the day while the father was at work; in another case day care was recommended for a young child so that the mother could get some relief during the day. In another, the psychiatrist advised that we should attempt to work with the mother and, failing this, should allow the child to remain in care until he is 6 or 7, since then he will be able to run and defend himself from his mother."[11]

On the other hand, Billingsley, in his study on the *Social Worker in a Child Protective Agency*[12] (winner of the first biennial research award of the National Association of Social Workers) suggests a "certain amount of trained incapacity (in attitudes and skills) seems to exist for professional social workers who engage themselves in child protective services . . . that best social work treatment available may not be sufficient to prevent neglect and abuse of treatment once the process has set in."[13] Billingsley further questions the preparation of social workers stating (1) professional social caseworkers are more prepared . . . for voluntary counseling with middle-class oriented, motivated clients than they are for work with lower-class, unmotivated clients, and (2) the patterns of preferences caseworkers develop for professional activity is somewhat out of line with the reality of work in child protective agencies."[14]

It becomes somewhat disconcerting when one reads "in spite of their widespread use, and in spite of the enthusiasm of their practitioners and their patients or clients, there is not much objective evidence that either psychotherapy or casework is more effective in the relief of distress or disability than simple listening by an untrained empathic nonprofessional."[15]

Is our knowledge based more upon conviction than upon facts? There is little available controlled research concerned with assessment of the effectiveness of social work intervention in protective services. In 1957, a student research group at the Graduate School of Social Work, University of Denver[16] investigated 43 families referred to a child welfare service for child neglect, to determine the outcome of social work treatment. A general improvement was noted in nine of the families who had been seen for an average of 20 months. Little sustained improvement was noted in 11 families. The parents' rights were severed in 12 families. There was evidence of definite continued neglect in six families. In eight families possible neglect was revealed.

A two year before-and-after comparative study of the effectiveness of social work intervention provided by a child welfare department in cases of child neglect is currently being completed at the Graduate School of Social Work, University of Denver.[17] Thirty-six families were examined. It was found that the cases of 17 of the 36 families were closed at the time of the study. Eight of these 17 families were interviewed a year after closing. Significantly, in these eight families there was no evidence of abuse or neglect subsequent to the closing of the case. This finding supported the validity of the agency's assessment. In those families which received services from the agency, where the treatment consisted of a combination of individual and family treatment modalities, the highest positive rating of change in personality and environmental situation was found.

Dr. Leontine Young has reported on the outcome of the initiation of new treatment approaches in protective services.[18] The experimental service program included 125 families referred to a social agency for neglect. Dr. Young stressed the evolving nature of the services in that they continue to change and are modified as new observations and study suggest. The program places primary emphasis on comprehensiveness and continuity of service. Focus is on the integration of casework, education, group work and services adapted to the changing needs of individuals and the family unit. The concept of compensation has been stressed. This refers to the developing of strengths that may compensate for weaknesses. Thus, enabling a father to carry through on a retraining project and the mother to take a part-time job in the evening, with assurance that the father would care for the children while she was at work, led to improvement in the marital, financial, housing and recreational areas, and life was reported as far more gratifying to parents and children. Dr. Young cautions that since this approach places emphasis on structural change, further evaluation is needed to determine if internalization of change has been effected or is necessary. However, it was believed that the compensation improvements were proving to ,be of significant help to both parents and children. By the end of the first year, deterioration had stopped in 90 percent of the families. Furthermore, during the second year, 60 percent of the families showed progress in at least one area of family functioning, with income management and household practices generally improving first. During the third year the families of this study tended toward more family cohesion, showed an increase in their own achievements and took more interest in community activities.

Who, then, is to lead? David R. Hunter suggests social workers; but, perhaps in activity other than direct work with clients, when he states: "First we should realize that social work is not the only system that affects the lives of clients. Often the switches that must be pulled are not in the office of the welfare agency; they are in the chamber of commerce, the board of education, the mayor's office, the urban re-development agency, the employment service, and the trade union. All these groups must participate in analysing the problems and in mounting a common attack on them, and social workers can take the lead."[19]

Billingsley also suggests approaches are needed in addition to casework in extending the role of the social worker in a child protective agency, such as group services, homemaker services, practical nursing services, day care and foster care, and community planning.[20] In addition, Billingsley calls for modification in the curriculum of schools of social work. He proposes that "(1) courses on growth and behavior should give more attention to sociocultural factors; (2) methods courses should include practice materials which deal with the multiproblem and unmotivated client; (3) field placements should include settings providing for work with other than well-motivated clients with ego strengths; and (4) social services should give attention to policy planning related to preventing neglect, dependency and deviance."[21]

The American Public Welfare Association in a 1967 publication, *Public Welfare: Challenge to Validity,* has also called for the social work profession to develop basic new approaches and policies for providing services to the disadvantaged, and specifically questioned "the dubious practice of relying primarily on 'inadequately trained caseworkers' to serve a population many of whose problems are clearly related to a very deprived physical and social environment and a stunted opportunity structure."[22]

Although there is little to point to in the way of evaluation studies, it would seem that the findings of available research suggest that social work intervention can be effective in achieving the objectives of protective services. However, it is also abundantly clear that social work must take a stance which will support ongoing testing, modification and adaptation of traditional methods of assessment and intervention. We have to reach beyond the one-to-one-relationship to deal with affecting change for large groups. Social work must move beyond its long-time primary focus on intrapsychic phenomena, beyond parent-child relationship and beyond the full family. We must develop a knowledge and skill base which will enable us to anticipate, identify and respond to needs and to achieve change wherever it is needed.

ACHIEVEMENT OF A CLEAR MANDATE FOR PROTECTIVE SERVICES

How do we sensitize public opinion in order to mobilize support to provide funds to meet the administrative and service costs of providing an effective protective services program? Since 1962, 50 states have passed statutes to curb child abuse.[23] These laws were enacted within the remarkably short period of five years. What can be learned from the legislative history of these laws? A very informative study of the legislative history of child abuse reporting laws was recently completed and provides some directions.[24] The mass media, the individual, the voluntary association and the executive branch were identified as instrumental in effecting appropriate legislation. The study found that a 1963 "Ben Casey" television program, which focused on the indifference of professionals to the abuse problem, was repeatedly mentioned as a primary source of interest in the child abuse problem.[25] Television, stories in national magazines, and editorials in papers were identified as helping to create a climate favorable to legislation.[26] "As a consequence of this mass communication, a large portion of the public became acutely aware of the problem; in turn many sought to translate their concern into positive action by either individual or concerted effort."[27]

The importance of the individual in the legislative process was also demonstrated. This factor was considered especially noteworthy when considering the current assumption "that individual initiative is no longer significant in promoting social change."[28] Also, in general, these individuals were found to be professionals who deal with children; active laymen were the exception.[29]

Voluntary organizations devoted to child welfare were identified as "in the vanguard to efforts to enact child abuse reporting legislation."[30] These organizations seemed to have a particularly vital role to play in that they are cause oriented rather than political party oriented.

Finally, agencies of the executive department of states were found to have played a significant and often crucial role. Their efforts were effective through initiating study of the problem, formulating proposals and giving recognition and support to individuals and organizations enlisted in the cause of reporting legislation.[31] When sponsoring legislation, it was found that state executive agencies had "generally attempted to include in the effort everybody who conceivably would have an interest in the subject."[32]

It would seem that a community aroused to advocate and support the passage of reporting legislation could also be mobilized to demand the provision and availability of services when child abuse has been identified.

A primary social policy gap in protective services is the insufficient appropriation of funds necessary to provide for the development and expansion of child protective services. If legislators have tended to assume that such services will be funded out of existing state and county welfare department budgets, the true facts have not been brought to their attention. It should be self-evident that the intent of child abuse reporting legislation cannot be effectively achieved without proper financial support from the legislature. The issue was clearly drawn by Robert M. Mullford when he said: "a major function of the child protective movement . . . is to press for increased recognition of this need followed by adequate services under public auspices."[33]

Perhaps one significant factor in the development of sufficient financial base will be the empirical demonstration of the effectiveness of child welfare services in helping children and families. Similarly, tomorrow's program for protective services must be part of the total community system of health and welfare services. Too often we have been in the position of trying to replace the fuse when the whole power line was out. We have been grossly inadequate in translating research findings into practice. For example, the findings of a study of patterns of mothering, by Sylvia Brody,[34] has significant implications for prevention of family breakdown and individual dysfunction. Among several notable findings was the conclusion that adeptness in maternal skill is not spontaneous. Thus, maternal skill is within conscious control and can be learned. Further, it may be asking too much for a mother to cope with the mother role for which she is unprepared.

Pavenstedt[35] has proposed that if sustained interest could be maintained for mothers from their first appearance in a prenatal clinic, through the delivery and into the child's early years, a strong bond would be established that would be invaluable to young mothers who have little or poor contact with women experienced in the mothering role. It is believed that an early relationship with a stable trustworthy person may help to counteract the effect of the mother's immature traits on the child.

Consequently it was proposed that the availability of a maternal and child care worker to establish such contact and to meet the mother's needs would be effective in the prevention of individual and family dysfunctioning.

PROPOSITIONS

In summary, the following propositions are offered as guidelines which, it is believed, would assist in the development of adequate services for neglected children and their families:

1. Every state must commit itself to a public policy which will insure the availability of protective services — a recognition of the necessity for all people to have opportunities to achieve their full potential.

2. The designation of the state public welfare agency with the authority to develop and administer a protective service program, would provide accountability for the provision of at least a minimum level of service and would facilitate the formulation of definitive policies.

3. The policy directing protective services should clearly define the relationship between the law enforcement agency and the protective services agency.

4. If the voluntary agency is to perform its vital role in developing and demonstrating effective protective services, increased private and public financial support is required.

5. The professionals engaged in providing protective services must assume a strong leadership role in mobilizing the public backing necessary for achieving adequate financial support.

6. Personnel engaged in protective services must test, modify and adapt current practices in terms of their impact on clients' lives.

7. Controlled research is necessary in order to facilitate the development of effective protective service methods.

In conclusion, one might question the supposition of some people, that nothing new is required of social workers practicing in protective service settings. Rather, it would seem that social work practice must be modified as a result of varied and changing problems of our society. We must accept the necessity and challenge to examine, test and modify current methods. Arnold Toynbee said, "The greatness of man or a nation is measured by response to challenging new ideas." So it must be with a profession.

REFERENCES

1. Child Protective Services – A National Survey. The American Humane Association, Children's Division, Denver, Colorado, 1967.
2. Stein, Herman D.: Planning for the Needs of Children in the National Plans of Developing Countries, "Social Progress Through Social Planning – The Role of Social Work." Proceedings of the XIIth International Conference of Social Work, International Conference of Social Work, New York, 1956, p. 189.
3. *Op. cit.*, ref. 1, p. vii.
4. Patti, Rino John: Child Protection in California 1850-1966: An Analysis of Public Policy. Unpublished Doctoral Dissertation, University of Southern California, 1967, pp. 348-355.
5. *Ibid.*, pp. 348-354.
6. *Ibid.*, p. 355.
7. The writer is indebted for this phrase to Norris E. Class, Professor, School of Social Work, University of Southern California, Los Angeles.
8. *Op. cit.*, ref. 1, p. vii.
9. *Ibid.*, p. ix.
10. *Ibid.*, p. 25.
11. Brown, John A., and Daniels, Robert: Some observations on abusive parents. Child Welfare 47:89-94, Feb., 1968.
12. Billingsley, Andres: The Social Worker in a Child Protective Agency, mimeographed, National Association of Social Workers, New York, 1964.
13. Ibid., pp. 142-146.
14. Ibid., p. 146.
15. Aldrich, C. Knight, M.D.: Impact of community psychiatry on casework and psychotherapy, Smith College Studies in Social Work 38:(#2)109, Feb., 1968.
16. Unpublished Master's Thesis: Outcome of Protective Services to Children in Denver, Graduate School of Social Work, University of Denver, 1958.

17. ————: Before and After the Fact: Protective Services to Children, *ibid.*, 1968.
18. Young, Leontine R.: An interim report on an experimental program of protective services. Child Welfare 45:376, July, 1966.
19. Hunter, David R.: Social Problems and Social Work, Social Casework, November, 1963, pp. 44-597.
20. *Op. cit.*, ref. 12, p. 145.
21. *Ibid.*, p. 148.
22. Public Welfare: Challenge to Validity, prepared by the Technical Assistance Project, American Public Welfare Association, Chicago, July, 1967, p. 11.
23. Paulsen, Monrad, Parker, Graham and Adelman, Lynn: Child abuse reporting laws—some legislative history. George Washington Law Rev 34:482, March, 1966.
24. *Ibid.*, pp. 482-506.
25. *Ibid.*, p. 488.
26. *Ibid.*
27. *Ibid.*, p. 490.
28. *Ibid.*, p. 488.
29. *Ibid.*, p. 491.
30. *Ibid.*, p. 493.
31. *Ibid.*, p. 497.
32. *Ibid.*
33. Mullford, Robert M.: Development of Child Protective Services in the United States. In the Interest of Children — A Century of Progress. The Children's Division of the American Humane Association, Denver, Colorado, 1966, p. 26.
34. Brody, Sylvia: Patterns of Mothering. New York, Internat Univ Press, 1956.
35. Pavenstedt, Eleanor: A study of immature mothers and their children, *in* Caplan, Gerald, ed.: Prevention of Mental Disorders in Children. New York, Basic, 1961.

11

The Medical Center
Child Abuse Consultation Team

HARRIET DELNERO, M.S.W., JOAN HOPKINS, R.N.,
and KAY DREWS

MOST CHILD ABUSE case reports generate from health facilities. The hospital staff is placed in the unique, and sometimes un-enviable, position of being the first service oriented profession-als to be involved in 60 percent to 80 percent of abuse cases. This, coupled with our recommendations that the immediate responsibility of any social worker, nurse, teacher and police-man is to see that any child suspected of being abused be taken to a hospital emergency room or clinic, places consider-able responsibility upon the hospital staff.

The complexities of handling the multiple medical, legal, social and psychiatric problems that are present in every case of suspected child abuse require the direction and guidance of a highly skilled hospital consultation team. Only with this form of guidance can we expect the diagnosis, treatment and therapeutic program to follow a smooth and reasonably organ-ized pattern. Nothing is more chaotic and frustrating for a physician and/or social worker than to stumble through their first case of child abuse without some form of assistance from someone who has had experience with the problem.

Every active pediatric service will find it most beneficial to delegate *one* pediatrician, *one* social worker and a coordi-nator (to be discussed subsequently) to consult on every sus-pected case of child abuse that is admitted to the children's unit. Thus, early consultation will turn confusion, and seemingly endless problems, into a positive therapeutic program for both the child and his family as well as a meaningful educational experience for the resident or private physician.

The individuals delegated to this team must have the time and motivation to develop the skills and to acquire the factual knowledge necessary to carry out their role as the child abuse consultants for the hospital.* Many cases require a significant degree of personal commitment which may seem most unrewarding at first. It is only after the long-term follow-up has been completed that this effort will be seen to have been worthwhile.

Although many practicing physicians have the capabilities to become excellent child abuse consultants, most will not be able to devote the time necessary to deal with the many details. In most instances it is advisable for these consultants to be part of the salaried staff within the pediatric and social service department of a particular hospital. A full-time pediatrician and social worker might spend up to 30 percent of their time as child abuse consultants within a hospital where 30 to 50 abused children are admitted each year.

When hospitals within a community are unable to staff such a team, or if there aren't enough cases to warrant each of them having one, then it is advantageous for a group of hospitals to establish a *joint* consultation program. One physician within such a community can be delegated to receive the necessary training which would enable him to serve as a consultant at several hospitals. In this situation the consultant might well be a practicing pediatrician. Since this physician will be invaluable to the child welfare agency within the community it would be to the agency's distinct advantage to pay the physician for these services. This will permit him to take the necessary time away from his practice to perform this consultation adequately. This type of joint endeavor hardly seems feasible, however, unless one of the hospitals has at least one social worker who

* Training programs are now available in Denver and London to assist physicians and social workers in obtaining these skills.

can spend part of her time working with these families. An alternative would be to have the local child welfare agency delegate a social worker to a hospital to handle these cases and work on the consultation team.

There are few subspecialties of medicine which provide the individual physician with such a multiplicity of situations and challenging encounters. The child abuse specialist (both pediatrician and social worker) must be readily available as a consultant to the emergency room and/or admitting physicians. The problems which arise during the diagnostic process and care of the battered child are too multifaceted to be handled by an inexperienced physician or social worker.

These specialists must develop the ability to gather appropriate historical data, interpret physical findings and laboratory results, maintain a meaningful communication with many social and community agency workers, understand their own feelings about parents who physically injure small children, meet their responsibilities to the courts, and maintain a long-term follow-up program as part of the therapeutic plan for the child and his parents. Using both a pediatrician and a social worker who have extensive experience in this difficult area of child care greatly facilitates the diagnostic and therapeutic process.*

The child abuse consultants also have a very definite commitment to those individuals in their institution and community who are seeking further education in their particular fields. Pediatric residents are, for the most part, reluctant to become involved in cases of child abuse because they fear the unknown. When given the necessary support by a pediatric consultant, a specially trained social worker, and a child abuse coordinator, this reluctance often disappears. Some even become active participants in helping specific families.

There are few problems in medicine that will provide a pediatric or psychiatric resident with so much insight into medical, social, family, legal and community needs as will a case of child abuse. Long-term follow-up of an abused child and his

* The physician is referred to *The Battered Child* ("The Role of the Physician") for a more detailed discussion of his role.

family, with appropriate guidance, will provide most students with a significant learning experience in comprehensive care. Many residents are even anxious to go to court when the child abuse consultants prepare them and accompany them to the hearing in order to provide necessary expert testimony.

A significant amount of the ongoing educational commitments to the community (social agencies, judges, nurses, law enforcement officials, lay groups and graduate students) must be met by members of the child abuse team. Most of this training is performed at the request of those involved. On occasion, however, certain groups must be educated without their recognizing this need. Under these circumstances the educational program should be initiated, with great tact, by the child abuse team.

THE SOCIAL WORKER

The hospital social worker may often be the central person responsible for maintaining good communication with other members of the consultation team, house staff and the family. Even though the social worker's major role is to contribute an assessment of the social situation as it relates to the overall medical/social problem, it may well be that she is asked, on occasion, to go far beyond this role of early evaluation to one of supporting the needs of the family.

A clarification of some of the functions of the medical social worker on the team is essential. First, she must develop an understanding of the abusive parents and obtain and assess the pertinent social information. Second, she must collaborate with, and provide consultation to, members of the medical staff who are making an attempt to understand and work with the child and his family.

UNDERSTANDING THE SOCIAL SITUATION

Although the social worker must have a complete understanding of the psychodynamics of parents who injure their small children, of equal importance in this helping process is her need to understand her own feelings before and during her work with these parents. She faces one of her most challenging clients when she meets a suspected abusive parent. The more she understands her feelings and those of her client, the more energy and effort she has to devote to the helping process. The primary role of the hospital-based social worker is to gather information but, in so doing, she begins a very important therapeutic relationship, which unfortunately must be transferred to someone else rather soon in the treatment program.

The gratifications received from working with parents who abuse their small children are of a different nature than those received from other clients. The limitations of these parents, both in communication and in establishing a relationship with others, bring the social worker face to face with extreme degrees of testing, demands, anger and hostility which are often expressed in a most devastating fashion. Many social workers feel uncomfortable in this setting, knowing that most of the data they gather will be used to document a case of abuse. They must be convinced of the importance of obtaining this data, and that the information will eventually be helpful in establishing a treatment plan for the family.

Every move of the worker will be closely observed by the client. Misinterpretation is common, requiring the social worker to be constantly alert to her own actions and reactions as well as those of her client. These parents are imbued with the idea that they are going to be rejected. They are deeply suspicious of the motive of others and are preoccupied with the feelings that advantage will be taken of them.

> Mr. and Mrs. T were being seen by the medical social worker for the first time. Shortly before the interview, the doctor discussed with them medical findings following an accident in which their son had allegedly fallen from his bed onto a carpeted floor. They had been told that their son had suffered severe head injuries.
>
> At the time of the interview, the parents were angry and suspicious. They spent the initial part of the interview ventilating their anger, projecting this primarily upon the social worker. They looked on her as someone who was there to

take their child, and they felt she thought of them as "gypsies" because of their living patterns. The social worker told them quite honestly that she was confused by this impression they had of her, and asked what she had said or done that may have given it to them. The mother quite angrily stated, "You used the word inflicted . . . ." By acknowledging and clarifying the issue with them, the social worker was able to move her relationship with them into a more meaningful and helpful phase.

The social worker must gather certain data about the family of the abused child if she is to add relevant social information to, and assist in, the assessment of the medical diagnosis and treatment plan. She should not feel that any particular area of information is "off limits" or that she must obtain every piece of information. The "complete" story will unfold at the dispositional conference, when all the information which has been gathered will be shared. Care must be taken, however, that the efforts to obtain this information do not hinder the attempts to "reach out" to these "hard-to-reach" and "resistant" parents. They are individuals who, in varying degrees, have a fear of failing and of being accused of being "bad," and who harbor feelings of being "unloved." They must be reached, and trust must be established, if they are to be helped. The social worker must extend herself by going *to them,* by being available at the hospital (occasionally even on nights and weekends), for in very few instances will they come to her. They desperately need help in seeking and in establishing a therapeutic relationship.

Mr. and Mrs. J. had been seen by the medical social worker on the day of their one-month-old daughter's hospital admission for head injuries. Due to the nature of their baby's injuries, more information had been requested regarding the parent-child relationships. Following this initial contact, in which they had revealed information indicating severe problems in the area of child care, Mr. and Mrs. J. failed to keep all appointments with the social worker. Instead, they would appear on the ward late in the evening, expressing a great deal of anger and hostility toward the medical staff.

A home visit was made by the social worker. During the visit, Mrs. J. began to talk a great deal about her attitudes toward the child, about her marriage and about her early life, including how she used to be beaten severely by her mother. This information followed the social worker's comment about how good Mrs. J's coffee was. As the worker was leaving, Mrs. J. stated in a shy, diffident manner, "Will you return . . . no one has ever told me I did anything good before."

The crisis which leads to hospitalization provides a valuable opportunity for intervention with a family that is generally not motivated and is frightened of receiving help. We do an injustice to the child and family if we do not take advantage of this opportunity to become involved.

There are several techniques utilized by the medical social worker, once contact has been made, to obtain the parents' trust. Four deserve attention:

1. You, the social worker, must clarify your role and why you are involved. To do this you must relay your genuine feeling that you are there to help the parents. This expression of interest in helping may be met with great resistance, for the parents may not be able to admit the need for help, or know how to accept it. Both tact and honesty must be utilized in stating, to the best of your ability and knowledge of the parents at that moment, their need for help. Be honest. Your client will be the first to know when you are not. In being honest, you may encounter anger from the parents, but you should handle that anger calmly and with understanding.

2. Listen and observe what your client is doing and saying. Allow the parents to define the starting point of their need. They come to the hospital with a multitude of problems. Seek out the area *they* consider the most problem-filled and devastating. If you do not understand what is said and done, clarify this with them. Hold them and yourself to the reality of what is being said. Be reasonably certain that an understanding has been reached not only by them, but by you. Often the pertinent in-

formation regarding their attitudes, relationships with the family, etc. will be revealed as you listen and guide them in what they are saying and thinking.

You may not learn all the "facts" you need to know in order to complete your evaluation and assessment in the first or second visit, but you will have opened an important door for these people. You have assisted them to seek help, possibly for the first time in their lives, through the very fact that you listened and made every attempt to understand what they were saying. Listening establishes contact, as well as trust, because we hear what the client is saying and show our understanding by clarifying what we both do and say.

3. Direct your attention and interest toward the parents. A client can be lost quickly if the social worker overemphasizes the child and underemphasizes the parents. Allowing the parents the opportunity to talk about themselves, their needs, their ideas, their fears, helps to build the essential trust necessary to extend further help to the family.

4. Do not become obsessed with the need to identify who abused the child.

COLLABORATING WITH THE MEDICAL STAFF

The house physician or resident is one of the first persons to see the abused child and his family in the hospital setting. Unless the patient has been referred by an agency and/or outside physician, he must be the first to recognize the evidence of possible abuse. How he deals with the parents during this initial contact can frequently mean the success (or failure) of providing subsequent help for the parents. One aspect of his success during this contact is his understanding of the parents. The medical social worker can contribute to this understanding and be most helpful to the physician.

The resident faces, like each of us, many challenges when he sees his first abused child. Perhaps one of the most difficult is his personal reaction to the situation. Several reasons exist for these difficulties: Inadequate medical education and orientation; inability to accept parents' anger; inability to accept the fact that parents could abuse a child; inner conflict over which takes precedence, rights of a child or rights of parents, and so forth.

Collaborating with, and providing consultation to, the medical staff is not without difficulties. When the hospital-based social worker is recognized and accepted professionally by the house physician, the difficulties are significantly less. When this is not so, or there is a breakdown in communication between the physician and team members, efforts to reach the parents will be more difficult. The physician who has the first contact with the parents must support the entrance of the social worker. If he fails to see her as providing a service that can assist him and the family, communication will usually be hindered, if not virtually impossible to accomplish.

The hospital-based social worker must feel comfortable in turning over a large amount of the logistical problems, which are so common in these cases, to a competent coordinator. This delegation of duties will save countless hours and make the lives of both the social worker and the parents much more bearable and meaningful.

THE CHILD ABUSE COORDINATOR

There is nothing more frustrating for members of a family, already confused and under stress, than to find themselves engulfed in the maze of poorly coordinated medical and social services.

When an abused, neglected or deprived child comes to the attention of the medical center staff, he requires the services of many specialty departments and community agencies. It is not unusual to find pediatrics, neurosurgery, orthopedics, psychiatry, social service, welfare, public health, police and the courts possibly all involved with the care of the battered child and his family. Each person or service may be called upon to help in providing protection for the child and/or to assist his parents. The coordination and organization of these services are mandatory if a positive therapeutic relationship is to be developed.

A Team Coordinator is usually the only person in the group who devotes all of her time to the program. She must, therefore, bring into common action and direction those persons who are working on a case involving child abuse so that they may work together in a smooth, concerted manner. She is employed for the specific purpose of easing the problems confronting both the parents and staff. Since she does not have to parcel out her time with numerous other responsibilities, she may well be the only steady, prodding figure in the overall effort to help prevent further injury and to make certain that the plans for disposition are implemented. Her presence and influence are felt in the beginning, when the child enters the hospital, and are maintained throughout the treatment program.

The basic qualifications of this individual are best described by her inherent qualities rather than educational background and degree. She must be able to work comfortably, strongly and diplomatically with professionals as well as with families of any income or educational level. She must not buckle under when strong forces are pulling in two different directions, but rather be willing to make herself heard and recognized as she directs two or more forces into one common plan.

Although there are many agencies which might find it advantageous to employ such an individual, the hospital seems to be the most suitable place for her to work. Since early involvement of a most knowledgeable person is the keystone to the development of a positive therapeutic program, and since 70 percent to 80 percent of the suspected child abuse cases are reported from hospitals, the placement of the coordinator in this setting is most beneficial.

The ready availability of medical, social, psychiatric and diagnostic services is most advantageous. Coordinating these with the professional services within the community can result in the early development of a positive therapeutic program for both the child and his family.

The Team Coordinator functions best with a clearly defined list of responsibilities which serves to clarify her role. The responsibilities which allow her to turn potential confusion into an orderly therapeutic system fall into the following broad categories: early case involvement; maintaining communications; case finding; locating "lost" families; maintaining records; public relations; and helping the parents.

EARLY CASE INVOLVEMENT

The most important factor favoring the medical center setting as the desirable location for the full-time coordinator is the need for early case involvement. This can mean the difference between total confusion and a combined effective effort toward a common therapeutic goal.

When a child who is suspected of having been physically abused is brought into the hospital, a rapid and thorough diagnostic evaluation is of paramount importance. Although the house physician or resident in charge of the case is perfectly capable of dealing with the evaluation of the injury, he usually requires a significant degree of guidance in handling all the other ramifications of these ofttimes involved situations.

This early involvement can begin even before hospitalization, since the Team Coordinator is the key person in the hospital to accept referrals for diagnostic evaluation from community agencies, private physicians, school personnel and public health nurses.

MAINTAINING COMMUNICATIONS

The Team Coordinator attempts to alleviate the confusion between hospital staff and community agencies by making certain that one group is aware of the others' presence and goals by maintaining, encouraging, or arranging for long-term communication and a close working relationship between agencies. She also must communicate with parents and discuss with them what to expect next, thereby avoiding surprises which often result in a disastrous lack of trust. The presence or lack of communication among all concerned can make or break a case.

Welfare agencies seem to be particularly prone to working independently rather than as part of a team. They are responsible for the protection of the child and "supervision" of the parents—a vital responsibility, indeed. An agency often does not want to risk making a mistake by sharing this responsibility with another agency.

The concern about "overlapping services" frequently arises in dealing with families who abuse their children. To some people, having the public health nurse, the child welfare worker and the lay therapist all working with the family could be termed "overlap"; to a battering parent this can be the sign that "someone really cares." These workers must all be oriented toward the same goal. Frequent conferences arranged by the coordinator help keep everyone aware of that goal and informed of the current follow-up by each person.

Extensive overlap can be prevented if information obtained at the hospital for use in determining if a child has been abused or neglected is shared with all concerned, especially the lawyers and courts. The coordinator sees to it that this information, including the hospital staff's recommendations for disposition, *is* shared.

CASE FINDING (OLD AND NEW)

Another vital role is the identification of abused children which may have inadvertently been missed in an emergency room or pediatric clinic. A weekly review of all x-rays taken of injured young children often serves to identify abuse which may have been otherwise overlooked.

A coordinator often finds herself playing private detective. Discovering a questionable case of abuse is one thing, but locating the family may be another problem. The abusive family is often the family on the move. One mother of a battered baby moved 18 times in a year and a half. One often must use a great deal of ingenuity to track down the families. Common methods used include cornering the local mailman, contacting school personnel to try to find out where school records may have been sent, talking with neighbors, and so on.

An accurate record must not only be maintained but be made available to hospital personnel. All involved personnel must be kept up-to-date on the patient's status. This record must include the names of all persons, both in and out of the hospital, who are working with the family. A file of past, present and *potential* cases is also kept for reference, as well as an up-to-date record of available information on all active cases.

PUBLIC RELATIONS

Many groups and organizations are clamoring for more information on child abuse. Recent publicity about the problem has made more individuals aware that they themselves might have been, or perhaps will be, confronted with a difficult decision regarding an abused child. Most people are unaware of the legal protection provided for those reporting in good faith, or know how to recognize a case, or know anything about what type of person injures a small child. Calls are received from individuals and organizations to arrange instructional programs. The coordinator is in a position to make certain that an authority on the subject will be available and that he or she knows of a particular group's range of interest. Education of the public is a goal shared by all those who have worked in the field of child abuse, and these programs may be one of the better methods of achieving this goal.

GUIDING THE PARENTS

Parents are often in need of someone to be a friend and guide them through these hard times and red tape. The overwhelming complexities of such things as finding the x-ray department, making follow-up appointments, understanding hospital admission procedures, seeing to it that their other children are taken care of, meeting the social worker, preparing for the visit from the child welfare worker, can add to the anxiety that the parents already feel. If someone can assist them with these problems and even cater to them a bit, such as offering them a cup of coffee, providing them with an opportunity to express their feelings, or interpreting certain procedures to them, the parents often become less hostile. This sets the stage for a long-term therapeutic relationship.

Understandably, abusive parents often do not appear to appreciate the help being offered to them. Someone must be available to listen to them when they become angry with the doctor, psychiatrist, social worker, nurse or the court. Assisting the therapeutic team to develop the "mothering role" can, in some situations, be a most important role.

A coordinator, particularly when new on the job, must face the fact that she herself has feelings about parents who abuse children that often hinder her in her work. She may have very angry feelings toward these parents and yet realize that they must be overcome. As she tries to understand and help the parents, she too must be understood and helped. This problem cannot be resolved easily, but it is lessened when she can talk to someone who has handled a large number of cases and has also dealt with the same inner feelings.

It is vital that she have consultants available for backup. In her contacts with agencies, she speaks for the medical and psychiatric team. When she speaks, she must know that she will be supported by her colleagues. This, of course, means that she must discuss cases regularly with the hospital staff so that she is presenting information accurately.

THE DISPOSITIONAL CONFERENCE

We have found it extremely helpful to organize an inter-agency-hospital dispositional conference during this period of early diagnostic evaluation. These conferences clarify who needs to be involved, in what capacity, etc. They often mean immediate help for the parents and child, and can cut through significant red tape. They should be held as soon as feasible after the child is admitted to the hospital (within the first 72 hours if at all possible). Communication among those who wish to help the family is a problem from the moment the first person reaches out to the abusive parent. Each must know what the other can or does offer the family in order to provide both the continuity of care and long-term help that are so essential (see Chapter 12).

The major purpose of the conference is to share the information that has been gathered and to develop a long-term treatment plan for the family. An added benefit derived from these conferences is that they serve to increase trust as well as communication between all those involved with the problem. In difficult cases, follow-up conferences will be necessary. In areas where several cases are seen each week or month, a regularly scheduled conference is often easier to establish and continue.

The question of the child abuse report is no longer one of debate. Each state now requires a physician (and many others) to submit a written report of his findings on all suspected cases of non-accidental injury to children.* The question that arises in most people's minds is what actually constitutes the requirements for a report to be made. In general a *suspicion* of abuse is all that is necessary. Concrete evidence is not required; in fact, the search for "who did it" is so futile that it should not be pursued with any degree of vigor. We would like to propose that the written summary of the dispositional conference be considered as *the* report. This, then, will contain all the available data and recommendations.

The report must not be thought of as a threat to either the parents or the physician. In many respects it is a request for help—help in the data gathering, the arranging for a disposition, the protection of the child, and providing treatment for the parents. When the physician and/or parents need help in any of these areas a report should—in fact, *must*—be made.

Actually, there are *two* reports to be made—a verbal and a written one—and their timing is most critical. They should be made *only* after the parents have been told that such reports *must* be made, what they will contain, who will receive them, and what will happen after they are received. The verbal report must be made soon after the child is admitted

*The American Humane Association (Denver, Colorado) has recently published an updated listing of all the reporting laws.

to the hospital. This notifies the protective agency of the problem and mobilizes its services. There is nothing more upsetting to both parents and social workers alike, or more detrimental to the development of a treatment program, than to have a home visitor arrive unannounced. The written report should come *after* the hospital staff and the protective service workers have gathered *and shared* all the available data. This is the only way in which the report can be meaningful.

SUMMARY

The pediatrician, social worker and coordinator, who comprise the child abuse consultation team within a given hospital, can work together with the hospital staff to implement the beginning of a smooth flowing therapeutic program for the family and a meaningful educational experience for those in training within the hospital. Many of their efforts will go unnoticed unless there is close cooperation with the community child protective service. A mutual trust *must* be developed between these two vital service programs. This is discussed in detail in Chapter 12.

(The editors have recently become aware of the term SCAN, a program initiated by the staff at Mott Children's Hospital, University of Michigan. SCAN refers to Suspected Child Abuse and Neglect. This term is both appropriate and descriptive and its adoption by other centers is encouraged.)

12

The Consortium

A Community-Hospital Treatment Plan

Ray E. Helfer, M.D. and C. Henry Kempe, M.D.

THE DEVELOPMENT of any meaningful therapeutic program must begin with the realization that child abuse is a serious manifestation of abnormal rearing within a family structure. Any treatment program must be directed toward helping the family by making the home safe, thereby enabling the child to be reared in a more "normal" manner. By their very nature, the problems of child abuse encompass the responsibilities of many disciplines within a given community. Herein lies the basic difficulty confronting every community which tries to provide services for these children and their families.

Our social system is not geared to a rapid exchange of knowledge and information between its various disciplines. In fact, many of the subdivisions of this system often compete with or duplicate the work of each other; all too often, even a degree of distrust develops between them. The implementation of the suggested child abuse treatment program presented here, mandates that these problems be resolved within a community if the program is to be successful. One encouraging note should be mentioned: The implementation of this type of program often has a very positive effect on improving communication and trust between the many disciplines involved.

The program that we have found to be most helpful can be implemented both in a small community or a large metropolitan area. The major obstacle is related to the ability of the many disciplines within a community to develop a *combined* treatment plan.

Often a number of traditional rules and regulations must be bypassed if the ultimate goal of helping these children and their families is to be realized. The major difference between implementing a plan in a large metropolitan area and a small community is that the larger program must be thought of in smaller segments and the actual metropolitan area divided into several geographical, easily defined areas. If one attempts to develop a *single* child abuse treatment program for the City of New York or Chicago, for instance, he will immediately be confronted with undue frustrations and stumbling blocks. A large city must be looked at as a conglomeration of many smaller segments, each of which must often be approached separately. It is advisable to begin with a single demonstration project, using one small predefined area within the metropolitan region, before attempting a larger and more definitive treatment program. The basic concepts of the treatment plan do not change, however, and can be adapted to either the small community or the large metropolis.

This treatment program is based upon the concept that the initial phase of any child abuse case must be considered, in the large majority of instances, as a diagnostic medical/social problem. It is clear that the professionals within either setting cannot gather all the data that are required to develop both the diagnosis and a realistic disposition without the close cooperation of the other.

This suggested treatment program is schematically depicted in Table 1, which places the community-based professionals on the left-hand side and those within the hospital setting on the right. On the far right of the table is a time scale consisting of four unequal separate segments—the first 24 hours, the next 72 hours, 2 weeks and, finally, the period of time encompassing approximately 6 to 9 months.

Probably the single most important factor for the success of any therapeutic venture is the realization that a coalition between the community and the hospital must be developed, a coalition which must be built upon mutual trust and dependency. Without this basic factor the program will not be successful and the problems inherent in the family structure will be enhanced.

A nonaccidental injury to a child, which normally occurs within the home, is usually followed by one of three things (see Table 1). Either the child is taken directly to the hospital emergency room by his parents or the case is reported by someone to the police or a child welfare agency. When one of these last alternatives occurs, the child should be taken directly to the emergency room by the police or agency. All emergency room physicians must recognize that the *suspected* diagnosis of nonaccidental injury to children mandates admission to the hospital, which will greatly facilitate the necessary diagnostic evaluation. (This concept has been discussed further in Chapter 5.)

Once the child has been admitted, and someone on the child abuse consultation team (see previous chapter) has consulted with the parents about the necessity of making a report to some community authority, a phone call is then placed to the protective service agency. In some communities this phone call is directed to the police department. If this be the case, a close working relationship between the police and protective service *must* be developed, since the police-type criminal evaluation is not necessary or even warranted in most cases of child abuse (see Chapter 16).

Once the phone call has been made, a concurrent evaluation program is initiated both by the protective service and the child abuse consultation team within the hospital. The social worker on the consultation team should have the benefit of Parent Aides or other lay helpers to assist her in implementing the initial or primary treatment program. (This aspect of therapy has been discussed in Chapter 3.)

The first 48 to 72 hours after the child is admitted to the hospital is used for the gathering of data that will be necessary to present at the dispositional conference, which is held no

TABLE 1. *Ten Steps to Treatment*

NB: PARENTS MUST BE GUIDED THROUGH THESE STEPS WITH DELICATE PRECISION.

BY THE COMMUNITY	BY BOTH	BY THE HOSPITAL	TIME
1. Parents, child welfare worker or police, take child to hospital emergency room.			
		2. Make preliminary diagnosis and admit ALL suspected cases of nonaccidental injury.	24 Hrs.
		3. Phone report of SUSPECTED case to child protective services.	
4. Begin evaluation of home by protective services.		4. Begin evaluation of case by child abuse consultation team.	
	5. Dispositional conference at hospital or protective services, attended by ALL parties involved. *		72 Hrs.
6. Involve courts, if applicable. **			
	7. Implement dispositional plan OUT-OF-HOME WITH TREATMENT — HOME WITH TREATMENT		2 Wks.
8. Maintain case as long as problem warrants.		8. Follow all children in the family in special follow-up clinic.	

TABLE I. *Ten Steps to Treatment* (continued)

BY THE COMMUNITY	BY BOTH	BY THE HOSPITAL	TIME
	9. LONG-TERM TREATMENT PROGRAM		6 to 9 Mos.
	a. Protective Services Social Worker		
	b. Hospital Social Worker		
	c. "Private" Agency Social Worker		
	d. Supervised "Parent Aides"		
	e. Special Day Care Centers		
	f. Crisis Centers		
	g. 1/1 Psychiatric Care		
	h. Group Psychiatric Care		
	i. Mothers Anonymous		
	j. Neighborhood Centers		
	10. RETURN CHILD HOME (If Removed) WHEN HOME HAS BEEN MADE SAFE.		

* The written report of this conference should be attached to the formal Child Abuse Report which is required by law and submitted.

** The decision regarding court intervention must be decided upon with each individual case—depending on type of case and cooperation of the courts (see Chapters 13 and 14).

[181]

later than 72 hours after admission. If the collection of data
is handled in an understanding and parent oriented manner,
this same period of time can be used for the initiation of the
primary therapeutic relationship with the parents.

Although the child abuse coordinator should be the person
to initiate and organize the dispositional conference, which
should probably be held within the hospital setting, it is
basically the community-hospital personnel who share all the
data that have been collected and develop a reasonable and
feasible treatment plan for the family. This dispositional conference should be followed up by a summary report to the
welfare agency. This summary is considered the "report" required by law. One should take note of the link between the
protective services and the hospital at the dispositional conference. It is at this conference that the trust and respect for
each other's discipline will develop, a necessary entity if the
child and his family are to be helped. (The concept of the
dispositional conference and the role of the coordinator within
the hospital were discussed in the previous chapter.)

One of the most important decisions that must be made at
the dispositional conference is whether or not the courts should
be involved in the case. There is a great deal of "prejudging"
which takes place at this point in time. Many agencies refer
less than 10 per cent to 20 per cent of the reported cases to
the courts. Agencies often feel that a case will be lost to them
if the court is involved, or that they will be treated poorly in
this setting, and therapy in some way will be compromised.
The courts, consequently, receive a very skewed population
of abuse cases. They no doubt could be more helpful if involved more frequently.

One hopes that the relationships with the juvenile court system, within a given community, are such that the judge's role,
which is of extreme importance, will not be usurped by any
agency. Many communities have been able to develop close
working relationships with the courts, which permit them
to be very helpful and therapeutic in the large majority of
cases. This, unfortunately, is not true in other communities,

in which case a great deal of effort must be made to improve these critical relationships. (The role of the court and law-related professionals is discussed fully in Part Four.)

Another important decision that must be made at the dispositional conference is the type of long-term treatment program that will be implemented for a given family. Several alternatives exist (see Table 1), many of which are discussed fully within the text. The type of treatment program that is initiated will, of course, depend upon available community facilities, such as specialized day care or crisis centers, and upon such factors as the willingness to use lay aides. Whatever treatment program is recommended, and often more than one may be indicated, a special follow-up clinic within the hospital setting must always be a part of this long-term therapy. The diagnostic consultation team, together with interested house and staff physicians, should be available on a regularly scheduled basis for ongoing long-term follow-up for each child and his parents. This staff must work in conjunction with others who are involved in the therapeutic program. The Team Coordinator accepts as her major responsibility the implementation of this follow-up clinic and makes certain that very few, if any, children are lost to follow-up (see previous chapter).

A third major decision that must be made at the dispositional conference is to try to determine how long it will be before the home can be made safe for the child's return. It is conceivable that this could be achieved within the period of time of hospitalization, in which case the child may indeed be discharged directly to his home. On the other hand, it may well be determined that more time is required to implement the treatment program. When this is necessary the child may be discharged from the hospital to an out-of-home placement for a few months. It is our feeling that when this latter course is taken it is mandatory that the court be involved in the decision. We realize, however, that many communities have not established a positive relationship with the court which will curtail this type of program to be developed. One hopes that these communities will constantly strive to improve their relationships with the juvenile court system so that the courts can assume and carry out their responsibility in these difficult situations.

Although the reporting laws have served many useful purposes, they have resulted in one serious problem. The physician and hospital often assume they no longer have any role in the case once the problem has been reported. This concept could not be further from the truth. On the contrary, their responsibilities are just beginning. It is hoped that the ongoing relationship between the hospital and community will serve to erase the major differences that exist which limit the degree of cooperation between these two vitally important groups of professionals. We can no longer afford the "luxury" of autonomous programs, which fail to respect the needs and roles of each other. This is especially true when it is realized that the information that is necessary for a disposition to be made must be gathered by several different individuals, working together for the common goal of making the home safe for the child's return.

In our experience neither the community protective service program nor the hospital consultation team can operate in a vacuum. The skills required for a comprehensive therapeutic program for these families are not found in either of these service programs. Only through the development of a consortium where there is mutual trust and dependency upon each other can we hope to develop a meaningful plan which will prove helpful. It is our feeling that this consortium will and can be realized if the plan depicted in Table 1 is implemented for each and every case.

Part Four

THE COURT AND THE LAW

A Positive Role

EDITORIAL NOTE

The role played by the courts, lawyers and police is often thought of as punitive and/or authoritarian in handling cases of child abuse. This is a traditional concept which is against the new thinking in judicial process as well as inconsistent with our empirical experience in trying to help these children and their families.

A positive role must be established by those who provide services in this segment of our social system. This will permit these professionals to become an adjunct to the therapeutic endeavors and will move them away from the adversary concept of dealing with abusive parents and their children.

IN MEMORIAM

Jack Isaacs devoted his life to helping abused and neglected children by his selfless efforts and unparalleled understanding of family law and the legislative process. The lives of thousands of children serve as living memorials to his unyielding efforts.

13

The Battered Child and the Law

Judge James J. Delaney

THE LAW IS CONCERNED with the battered or abused child in two contexts. Universally, child abuse is proscribed by law and defined and punished as a crime. The law also treats such conduct as a civil matter, justifying court intervention on behalf of the child under the *parens patriae* doctrine.

CHILD ABUSE AS A CRIME

Criminal laws on child abuse are generally of local concern, although there are some federal statutes which, at least incidentally, also relate to children. These include the statute which makes kidnapping for ransom a capital offense (the Lindbergh Law) and one prohibiting transportation of females across the state line for prostitution (Mann Act).

State laws are quite uniform in defining as a crime child beating and other forms of child abuse. Many criminal codes (a body of laws on a given subject is often referred to as a "code") contain a "Wrong Against Children" statute. Even in the absence of a specific child abuse law, all criminal codes include such offenses as "assault," "assault with a deadly weapon," or "felonious assault." Assault, also called "simple assault," is injury inflicted without use of a weapon or instrument, and is generally considered a minor crime or misdemeanor. When assault is with an instrument which might cause death, the offense is usually classed as a major crime or felony. A stick or strap or fist, not considered a "deadly weapon," may well be lethal when used in an assault on a child.

Other criminal statutes which protect children are those covering statutory rape, indecent liberties, incest or similar sexual misconduct.

Violations of state statutes are prosecuted by a state or district attorney in a state court in the name of "The People of the State of ———." The penalty for minor offenses is usually a fine or confinement in a local jail for a term not to exceed a year. Felonies are punishable by prison terms, generally of from one to 10 years, although some states use indeterminate sentences, not to exceed a maximum provided in the statute.

In addition to the types of state statutes discussed above, many incorporated areas have adopted city ordinances which parallel some of the state laws. Most cities have ordinances relating to sexual offenses, assault and forms of child abuse. City ordinances differ from state statutes in that they apply only to offenses committed within the city, and the penalties are limited to a fine or short term in a local jail. When an offense is a violation of both a state law and a city ordinance, the usual procedure requires reporting both to the state and city prosecutors. The former takes precedence, but if the state elects not to prosecute, then the city or local prosecutor may charge a violation of the ordinance. An offender is seldom charged for the same offense in both courts.

The criminal codes of most states have been in effect for a long time and are generally quite standard in their definition. Criminal statutes have been reviewed by appellate courts, both federal and state, to the extent there is remarkable uniformity in their interpretation. This does not imply there is equal uniformity in application. State prosecutors have considerable latitude in determining whether to prosecute an alleged offender and whether to charge a felony or misdemeanor. Hence, based on the custom and culture of a community, variations may occur in deciding where an exercise of reasonable parental authority stops and child abuse begins. Community attitudes toward different racial and ethnic groups may also cause variable standards in the law's application.

THE CRIMINAL PROCESS

The criminal prosecution of an abusive parent merits critical examination. First, we need to look at the methods by which the law exacts its toll, and the effect on those most directly concerned, the parent and the child. Second, we must assess the results obtained in terms of lasting benefits and detriments to these same parents and children.

A criminal proceeding, once set in motion, is formidable, impersonal and unrelenting. It is supposedly the public conscience censoring a fellow member; its aim is primarily punitive rather than therapeutic.

The accusatory process usually begins with a written statement called an "information," filed by the public prosecutor with a court. The action is entitled, "The People of the State (or Commonwealth) of —— against ——, Defendant." It then goes on to say that the defendant (the accused parent), "on or about —— in the County and State aforesaid —— feloniously, willfully and maliciously did assault and wound the person of ——, contrary to the provisions of the statute and against the peace and dignity of the People ——." There is no word of concern for the child, nor reference to preservation of the family. This is the People against an individual, set to avenge a wrong against society.

In response to the "information" the court authorizes an arrest warrant to issue, directing a law enforcement officer to take the accused person into custody. To insure that he will be available for future court proceedings, the court usually fixes bail, which may range from $300 to $5,000, a sum forfeited if he fails to appear as ordered.

The first court proceeding brings the alleged offending parent before a judge or magistrate to receive formal notice of the charge and of his rights as an accused person. This advisement also covers the privilege against self-incrimination and the right to counsel, including right to a court-appointed attorney if the defendant is indigent. At the time of being formally charged, called the "arraignment," the accused parent is required to admit or deny the charge. If he is still in jail, unable to post the prescribed bond, the judge may reduce the bond or even release the defendant on a "PR" or personal recognizance bond, i.e., his personal, unsecured promise to appear when requested to do so.

Between the original court appearance and the time of trial, the defendant's attorney learns all he can about the offense charged and tries to discover and evaluate what evidence the prosecutor has to prove the case. This evidence may include statements of witnesses, photographs of the injured child, the defendant's own admissions. In this interim, too, "plea bargaining" may occur. Depending on the strength or weakness of the state's evidence, the severity of injury and the public climate, the prosecutor may agree, in exchange for a "guilty" plea by the defendant, to reduce the charge to a lesser offense, as from "Felonious Assault," a felony, to "Simple Assault," a misdemeanor.

If the accused parent denies the charge and elects to go to trial, the state must be well buttressed with evidence if it is to obtain a conviction. The injured child is often an infant who cannot relate what happened. Even when old enough to testify, if the child has remained with the parents, their subtle suggestions and review of the incident may affect his recollection and statements to the extent that his version at the trial is sometimes far different from the original given the investigators. This latter account may even be exculpatory. Neither the accused parent nor spouse can be required to testify. Hence, the state is often left with evidence of child injury without being able to prove "beyond reasonable doubt" (proof which excludes any hypothesis of innocence) that the injury was caused by a battering parent as alleged.

PREDICTABLE RESULTS

A parent accused of the crime of child abuse, if acquitted, generally feels he has been vindicated, that his conduct was justified and the jury has, in effect, found his "corrective" parental measures acceptable. Thus the parents' battering tendencies may be reinforced, although his ordeal will prompt him to become more cunning and subtle.

Upon a plea of "guilty," or in event of a conviction, the parent, unless a previous persistent offender, may, as a matter of right, apply for probation. A presentence or probation investigation is conducted, usually consisting of form-type inquiries to present and former employers, advising them the parent has been convicted of child abuse, inviting comments as to his character and reputation. Occasionally, such investigation may include a psychological or psychiatric evaluation. The presentence report contains a good deal of factual data about the accused, his background, education, employment history, economic status, personal habits. Seldom does it probe or reveal the true reason for the offender's conduct. The report usually concludes with a recommendation that probation be granted or denied. Infrequently does it chart a positive course of supervision or treatment.

If probation is granted, all too often probation services consist of a printed list of prohibitions proscribing association with criminals, possession of firearms, keeping of late hours and use of alcohol or narcotics. Periodic reporting, in person or by mail, including any change of address, is required, and the probationer may not leave the court's jurisdiction without permission. High on the list of requirements may be repayment of court costs assessed against the defendant. Since child abuse is repugnant to most persons, and because few probation officers have training in, or understanding of, the pathology of child abuse, it is rare, indeed, when probation services actually have any therapeutic result. More often such surveillance, punitive and repressive, merely makes the offender more cautious. It does nothing to abate his hostility or increase his understanding of how to deal with the underlying emotional problems which are, and will continue to be, the source of child abuse.

Case History. This illustrates the results of the criminal process:

> P. was an Air Force tech. sergeant on foreign duty. His wife, 23, and their daughter, age 2, continued to live in a trailer at their last stateside duty station. Mrs. P.'s own family lived in another part of the county, and she had few friends or confidants where she lived.
>
> A complaint of child abuse, made by neighbors, resulted in investigation and a criminal prosecution. Mrs. P. was represented by court-appointed counsel. At the trial, when the state concluded its evidence, the case was dismissed for lack of proof "beyond reasonable doubt." Because of this outcome, the civil abuse case was also dismissed and Mrs. P.'s child was then returned to her, with no follow-up surveillance or service. Within three months she had killed the child.
>
> On a prosecution for homicide, Mrs. P. was convicted of manslaughter and was given a short prison term.

Comment. Mrs. P.'s present whereabouts are unknown. It may be assumed she may bear other children. If she cannot manage her frustrations and irritation, she may kill or injure one or more of them. It is unfortunate that this woman, when desperately in need of help, did not receive the kind of timely treatment which would have prevented her child's death and perhaps have enabled her to fulfill her role of wife and mother.

CONCLUSION

It can be seen that the criminal process as a solution to child abuse is usually totally ineffective. Probably it has some deterrent effect on the parent capable of controlling his conduct, but its chief value lies in satisfying the conscience of the community that the wrong to a child has been avenged. That the true causes of the battering parent's conduct have not been sought out and treated is of little concern.

THE CIVIL LAW AND THE BATTERED CHILD

There are, of course, those who believe courts should not be concerned with treatment and prevention of social ills. Fortunately, this appears to be a minority view.

These comments are meant to explore and discuss the ways in which the juvenile and family courts can be an effective resource in treating, even preventing, child abuse. The true aim of the law should be to give us a better way of life. If we use courts only to arbitrate commercial disputes and punish public offenses, we restrict one of our most effective resources. The true goal of a good legal system should be to make the law work for the people it serves.

We are all too familiar with physical abuse, the beating and cruel repressive treatment which maims and sometimes kills. This form is obvious. Less apparent, but equally harmful, are the more subtle forms: Withholding love and affection, indifference, inconsistent discipline, poor nutrition—the many ways in which a child is denied the chance to grow and to develop his mind and body. These, too, leave their permanent disfiguring marks.

Those close to the problem, who see parental abuse and neglect at firsthand, know it is these abused children who become delinquent, who grow into the adult offenders, who become the social misfits who fill our institutions and form the hardcore relief cases; who themselves become poor parents. We will never reduce juvenile and adult crime until this fact is realized and we do something about it. The law must be invoked, not only out of humane concern for the child, but out of enlightened self-interest for all. That's the case for the juvenile court's broad involvement in abuse and neglect.

TRADITIONAL METHODS AREN'T GOOD ENOUGH

If courts are to deal effectively with this widespread social evil, both judges and lawyers must be willing to modify traditional legal process. The cherished adversary system assumes the only way to judicial truth is through competing lawyers, each advancing his own cause, with the judge as a referee. This must yield to, or at least share with, another system in which other disciplines also join in the fact-finding and decision making, one in which justice is seen, not as blind, but as alert and understanding and compassionate and concerned.

The law can never serve the true ends of justice until lawyers and judges alike view the battered child as more than a legal problem. Each must commit himself to the ultimate welfare of the child and parent rather than to win or lose or obtain the end the client seeks, or to reach a purely legal verdict, regardless of its effect. This is not to say that the traditional judicial process must be scrapped; quite the contrary. But while the strict adversary system and the rigid rules of evidence which often exclude essential information, may be good enough for the court of the marketplace, it falls far short of what a truly competent court can do in dealing with the complex emotional and psychological problems of the troubled family. These people not only desperately need the ministrations of the physician and behavioral expert, but the firm insistence of a court which can insure those services are accepted.

Other portions of this book have discussed fully the emotional, physical and environmental factors which spawn child abuse. These signs are as obvious as symptoms of typhoid or tuberculosis; ignoring them is just as dangerous.

Courts are charged with administering the law so as to alleviate these factors, just as a public health agency is responsible for preventing communicable disease. If we view the court only as an impartial arbiter, meting out punishment for a legal transgression, we limit the court's power and influence to "after the fact" matters and ignore its great potential for prevention and social change. If the courts are truly to reflect the conscience of the community, they must also be understanding, compassionate, forward looking and involved, reaching out to troubled parents before serious abuse occurs. Impersonal observation from the sideline is not enough.

AN ADEQUATE CHILDREN'S CODE –
A PREREQUISITE TO CHILD PROTECTION

The foundation of a judicial system which is to deal effectively with child abuse is law which recognizes that such conduct is of social and medical origin, not solely a legal issue. Reasonable harmony in commercial law has been reached by the adoption of uniform codes. Presently there is no uniform children's code in general use, although such are available. The Children's Bureau, National Council on Crime and Delinquency and the National Council of Juvenile Court Judges have each developed model juvenile codes. All are similar, and each recommends the law be administered by a special children's and family court, either as a separate entity or as part of a court of general jurisdiction.

An adequate child abuse law, in addition to usual statement of purpose, definitions and procedural provisions, should include:

1. Specific reporting provisions, including a mandatory requirement that physicians, and medical and hospital personnel, schools and public agencies report suspected cases of abuse, abrogating the physician-patient confidentiality privilege. The law should likewise encourage reports from individuals and should grant immunity from civil damage actions to all who make reports in good faith, even for reports which prove unfounded.

2. Well-defined responsibility of the police or public welfare agency, requiring prompt and thorough investigation of all such reports, with clear-cut channels of referral for protection of the child.

3. Broad jurisdiction of the court to protect any child within its boundaries, regardless of the residence of the parents.

4. Right of hospital or protective facility to provide emergency care and shelter for a limited time.

5. Authority of a court to make unilateral orders for temporary removal of a child from a parent, pending the filing of and a hearing on a petition or complaint in neglect and abuse, where reasonable grounds are shown to justify such action.

6. A limit on the degree of proof so that child abuse may be established by a preponderance of evidence rather than beyond reasonable doubt.

7. Where an infant or child too young to testify on his own behalf sustains unexplained injuries, a rebuttable legal presumption that the child has received such injury at the hands of the parents or guardian.

With the experience gained by nearly 70 years' operation of juvenile courts, and the model codes already drafted, there is little excuse today for any state to be without an effective court system or adequate laws to protect the battered and abused child. All 50 states have adopted some form of this law, yet many fail to meet the needs of children because of ineffective administration and because courts haven't been provided with the needed services and facilities.*

NEED FOR COMMUNITY'S CONCERN
AND INVOLVEMENT

The true extent to which a juvenile court may assist with the socio-legal problems of the community is seldom fully understood by the various agencies or by the individual citizens; sometimes even by judges and lawyers.

Social welfare workers, public and private, are prone to try to cope with behavioral problems far beyond their capacity to modify with gentle persuasion or "casework services." Fear that the caseworker-client relationship may suffer, distrust of a misunderstood judicial process, and sometimes justifiable disillusion with the court's dispositions, often prompt the social agency to struggle with problems far beyond its capability.

The public schools, also a front line observer of child abuse and neglect and its symptoms, remain aloof, ignoring such evidence because it's not considered an "educational" problem and "they don't want to get involved." Another deterrent is lack of clearcut channels through which such problems may be referred.

* The reader is referred to Paulsen (see Bibliography under *Law/Police/Registry*) for a more complete review on reporting laws.

The police are inclined to investigate child abuse and neglect in terms of criminal conduct and determine referral solely on the basis of criminal evidence.

Even the private citizen who sees child abuse at firsthand seldom takes the initiative in reporting it for fear of "getting involved." If he does make a timid, anonymous inquiry about what to do, he is told that unless he is willing to be identified and will appear in court to testify against his neighbor, nothing can be done.

Hence, in a judicial approach to the treatment of child abuse, a massive program of community education is needed. The court must be seen, not solely as a punitive, avenging agency whose services are sought only as a last resort, but as another resource, along with the social and behavioral scientist, the physician, legal services, the police and other community agencies concerned with prevention, detection and treatment of child abuse and neglect.

THE JUDGE

It seems axiomatic that a judge who deals with problems of child abuse must be more than merely "learned in the law." To approach the problem intelligently, he must know the pathology of child abuse and the family dynamics which produce it. He must be able to see it as more than the willful act of a cruel or depraved parent which can be corrected by punishment. He should know that a criminal prosecution, even if the charge is sustained, may have little real effect in the parents' emotional growth; that if the charge is dismissed or the parent acquitted, such action may reinforce the parent's conviction of the rightness of his conduct and increase his hostility toward those who might have helped him. The judge should remember that, even though the parent is punished, the child, (and perhaps others yet unborn) will again be in the parent's custody. Surely if the factors which produce child abuse have been ignored, further abuse will most probably occur, the only change being greater care on the parent's part to conceal his conduct.

Hence, perhaps the foremost ingredient in adequate judicial handling of the abusive parent is a competent, sophisticated judge who understands the factors which produce the battered child and the battering parent.

This is not a natural ingredient of a judge's background. Most were practicing attorneys, trained in the adversary system. Thus, they tend to project such system to all judicial problems. The judicial process is basically fact-finding, by a judge or jury, of "what happened" and "who did it" without much emphasis on "why." Therefore, under the adversary system, especially in a criminal proceeding, the area of inquiry is limited by rules of evidence and constitutional safeguards to a degree that the true anatomy of the problem, the "what," "who" and "why" in their proper relation, is seldom revealed. As with the iceberg, only the superficially exposed portion is seen; the parents' deep-seated emotional conflicts and their source are ignored. Since the problem is oversimplified by emphasizing the result rather than the cause, the treatment is usually ineffective. To be adequate, the judge must avoid such limitations; he must acquire the know-how and develop a social conscience which enables him to go beyond these traditional limits.

Does the judge then have to be a psychiatrist and a social worker? No! No more than a corporate president need be an accountant, lawyer or production manager. It is enough that he look at more than the legal side; that he receive the help of the medical and social specialists.

THE LEGAL PROCESS

Because of the very nature of the offense and the almost certain danger to the child, any known cause of apparent child battering should be brought into the legal process of investigation, referral to court and a court proceeding.*

The quality of this process determines the kind of results obtained. To deal effectively with child abuse, all parts of the

* For comments on the Gault Decision and its effect upon abuse and neglect petitions, see Chapter 15.

system must have the same goals. These include the immediate protection of the child, ascertaining the reasons for parental abuse, treatment of such causes and, ultimately, a permanent return of the child to a well-adjusted home, preferably his own. If any part of the process malfunctions, if the investigator overlooks pertinent facts or increases parental hostility, if the attorneys or the court are concerned only with the legal aspects of the case, or if evaluation and appropriate treatment are not accorded the parent, supported by judicial supervision, the legal process may well fail the child, the parents *and the community.*

The following steps suggest the way in which each part of the legal process may be most effiective.

PRE-JUDICIAL EVALUATION

The prelude to actual court appearance is important.

State law provides for reporting child abuse to the police or public welfare agency or both. Facts to support court action are developed by a police officer, a social worker, or other noncourt personnel. In some cases the child may already be in protective custody and sometimes the parent may be in jail.

The way the parents are handled in this initial stage often sets the tone for all that follows. In child abuse cases, the investigator's natural reaction is indignation and anger. A skilled juvenile officer or child protective worker will repress such emotion and reserve judgment. He can perform his duties, even while taking the parent into police custody, or removing the child from the home, humanely and objectively. This is not meant to infer that a battering parent deserves special consideration or preferred treatment. Rather, the investigatory stage and pre-court process should concern themselves principally with the child's injury and protection. The issue of the parent's guilt is important to the extent needed to invoke the court's jurisdiction. Statements or treatment which increase the parent's hostility or heighten anxiety serve no useful purpose and make the ensuing judicial process more threatening than therapeutic. Because of improper pre-court handling, the court process may be impeded because needlessly created anger or apprehension prevents the rapport with the accused parents which promotes intelligent communication. For these reasons, the skill and sophistication of the community's police and child protective services may influence the court's ultimate success in dealing with the abusive parent.

A word of caution here! In the initial investigation of alleged child abuse, a police officer or social worker may reach a personal conclusion that, although abuse probably occurred, the evidence is too scant to warrant referral to court. Hence, the abusive parent may go unchallenged and parent and child denied needed treatment.

In *all* cases of suspected child abuse and neglect, a referral should be made to a competent welfare or court intake worker for further assessment. Experience shows that, even where strict proof of abuse or neglect is lacking, the parent, when confronted with the facts available, may ask for help and submit voluntarily to the court's jurisdiction.

Further, although present facts may leave the investigator in doubt, information that had been learned about other abusive parents may support the findings by revealing a pattern of parental mistreatment.

THE PETITION

Due process of law requires that the parents be informed in writing and in plain language of the reason for the court's concern and intervention, and of the relief sought. This written statement is usually called a "petition." Its phrasing should be factual rather than accusatory. Thus, instead of "You are accused of abusing and neglecting your child," the petition may read, "The child is alleged to be abused or neglected in that he fails to receive adequate care and supervision." A technicality? Perhaps; but an essential distinction. The former increases the parents' defensiveness and hostility; the latter may invite cooperation and a call for help.

The petition usually also forewarns that, if the child is found to be abused or neglected, the court may determine his future custody. It may even terminate parental rights. These points are stated, not as threats to the parents, but to apprise them of the seriousness of the proceeding.

EVIDENCE

Limited uses of written reports and other types of evidence which might be excluded under strict evidentiary rules may be provided for by statute. Most juvenile codes distinguish the degree or "quantum" of proof required in neglect cases from that needed to support a petition in delinquency. The former is preponderance; the latter beyond reasonable doubt.

The state is sometimes at a serious disadvantage, where injuries to infants and small children occur, because the child can't testify and the parents cannot be compelled to do so. Hence, even if the injury is clearly established and no satisfactory explanation given, there may be no real evidentiary connection between the injury and the parents.

To meet this need, some state laws provide that, where serious, unexplained injury to the child occurs while in the custody and under the control of a parent, and such is established by competent evidence, there is a presumption that the injury resulted from the neglect, indifference or abuse of the parent. The parent may rebut this presumption by a showing to the contrary, but the fact of abuse or neglect is considered established if he fails to do so.

Many juvenile codes provide for the use of written reports without the writer being present. There is generally a provision, however, that upon proper advance request, either party may have the writer appear for further questioning in regard to the report.

Such liberalization of evidentiary restrictions speeds up the handling of juvenile cases without sacrificing any real protection for the persons affected.

THE PRETRIAL CONFERENCE

A frank pretrial discussion between counsel and court, in which a full disclosure of known facts and opinions is revealed, narrows the controverted issues. It also establishes which reports can be used and whether the writer of a report should be required to appear to give personal testimony. Obviously, there are many situations where strict adherence to rules of evidence would either repress the evidence totally or destroy an otherwise desirable relationship between parents or between a parent and relative or neighbor.

Such disclosure, which could never occur in an open adversary proceeding, allows the court and attorneys to evaluate all evidence. The abusive parent may be seen as one desperately in need of help. If this is so, and the court assures that its disposition will be therapeutic rather than punitive, the conference may result in a stipulated or consent decree.

Where this occurs the court, state's attorney, respondents and their attorney, and those who will supply the helping services, all have a voice in developing a plan for the family. It permits all to share the responsibility for protecting the child, leaving him in, or returning him to, parental custody only when safe to do so. Making the plan an order of court insures that it will be followed.

THE TRIAL

Where a child abuse case cannot be settled in a pretrial conference (there will always be some lawyers and judges who will insist on strict adherence to the adversary system, and some cases which simply don't lend themselves to such disposition) a trial is necessary.

The child abuse trial, especially if the occurrence was flagrant and if pretrial publicity was overzealous, may attract a crowd of morbidly curious spectators. Whether such trial should be public or private is largely discretionary with the judge and the wishes of the involved parents. If the parents want a public trial they are entitled to one as a matter of right. However, as a means of improving parental care, it is ineffectual. The naïve assumption that a mentally ill or emotionally disturbed parent can be "shamed" into being a better parent through public exposure, is an obvious fallacy.

A private hearing, conducted in the judge's chambers, and with only those directly interested present, is more conducive to reaching the truth with a minimum of hostility than a public, adversary trial. This is a critical time in the life of both the child and the parents. The hearing should be unhurried. The judge not only should allow all time necessary to solicit the legal details which give the court jurisdiction and form the basis for subsequent court action, but he should also invite the parents to express their feelings and discuss their problems as they see them. Where it is established that a child has been battered or abused by a parent, it is the judge who must make the dispositional judgment. Regardless of the seriousness of the offense, the object should be to reunite the parent and child if possible. Based on sound professional advice, the judge should use the court's authority to insist the parents follow the prescribed course of treatment as a condition to considering a return of custody. To insure that the court's directives are followed, periodic reviews by the *same* judge should be scheduled to assess progress.

Admittedly, the conference method of conducting a child abuse trial is time-consuming. Yet a judge will seldom face a more important decision. If he returns the child to the parents prematurely, or because not enough evidence was presented to retain the court's protective jurisdiction, he may well invite further abuse, even the child's permanent injury or death. Probably every metropolitan court has recorded several such gross and needless failures. On the other hand, if the child is detained in protective custody longer than necessary because no plan is evolved for treatment of the family and a guarded phasing back of the child into the home, he may become so isolated from his family that he loses the chance to return. This alternative spawns the permanent institutional or foster home inmate.

At this point, some may say a judge just doesn't have time to go into all this detail. This is nonsense. If the legal system can justify spending five months on a criminal trial, or six months on a libel action, it doesn't make sense to deny a troubled family an hour or two of a court's time. What may be needed is a reassessment of the use of judicial time. A system which allots 95 percent of the court's time to criminal matters and commercial law and about 5 percent to juvenile and family problems should be examined critically.

DISPOSITION

Assuming child abuse is judicially established, what then? Obviously, punishment of the abusive parent is not an objective; this is or was the role of the criminal court. Yet separation of the child and parent is often necessary. Unless the reason is carefully explained, the parent may equate separation with punishment.

The judge must make it clear that the parent's conduct is unacceptable; than a return of custody cannot be considered unless and until this conduct is modified. Change, to be real and lasting, generally requires the help of a behavioral specialist, a psychiatrist, a psychologist or social worker. It is the judge who must set the stage for such counseling and allow these specialists the time needed to treat the parent effectively. It is not enough for the court to prescribe such treatment; the parent must be made to *want* help. To provide the needed incentive, the court's order may state that the child will be returned to the parents only on the combined recommendation of the treatment specialists. If the parents have the capacity to understand what the judge is saying, this exercise of choice is a reliable test of the parents' true feeling for the child. Generally, one who rejects help, after a full explanation of the need and expected benefits, is in effect also rejecting the child, regardless of his protests to the contrary. If he accepts such an offer, it is the first step on the road to change. The kind and duration of counseling or treatment, of course, vary with the person, his motivation, intelligence and the nature of the problem.

To discourage parents from "unloading" children on the court, support payments in keeping with the parents' financial ability should be assessed.

To gauge the parents' progress, and to make it clear that the court will remain concerned and involved, periodic reviews should be scheduled. If after a reasonable time, generally not more than a year, it appears the parent cannot or will not change, and the child cannot, in the foreseeable future, be returned, an alternate plan is needed. The court should seriously consider termination of parental rights, thus freeing the child for adoptive placement or other permanent planning. Sometimes, faced with such action, a parent will voluntarily relinquish the child or may agree to permanent placement with a relative acceptable to the court.

Appropriate help for the abusive parent is available in most metropolitan areas although, for the uninitiated, securing it may be difficult. The court must aid in directing the parent through the social service maze and often must use its authority to insure that treatment is afforded.

Courts in less affluent and sparsely settled communities have fewer treatment alternatives; sometimes they appear almost nonexistent. Yet even the smallest hamlets have some social services from a public welfare agency. There are clergymen with skills in counseling. Military and veterans' facilities, with behavioral specialists, may be available to parents who are now, or have been, in military service. Many mental health centers have traveling specialists who see patients regularly in their own communities on an outpatient basis. Volunteer services, built around business and professional people who use their skills in part-time individual and group counseling, are another resource.

There is also increasing experience with Parent Aides and other supervised lay therapists, who are willing to provide the intense personal commitment of a loving friend which both parents often need. The resources of adults willing to take on these difficult families exist in all communities. (This was discussed in Chapter 3.)

SUMMARY

Unless the present trend can be changed, child abuse is here to stay. A massive educational program and united community effort are needed if this social evil is to be recognized, identified and eradicated.

Traditionally, courts have the respect of the community and a reputation for concerned objectivity. Thus, a judge seeing child abuse at firsthand, is in a strategic position to serve the community by focusing attention on the extent of the problem, its causes and suggested solutions. This does not mean he has, or should have, all the answers. Rather, he can be the catalyst, helping to bring together the professional community, the lawyer, physician, social worker, police, the clergy and the educator. These disciplines, acting in concert, with a planned information program, can do more in a few weeks to explain the nature and extent of child abuse than can be accomplished by individual disciplines in a lifetime. Once the problem is recognized, its causes identified and the needed facilities and services defined, hopefully the community will provide the support and the funds.

The facilities needed to combat child abuse are generally already available in most communities.

First, and most important, is the understanding of the problem and the needs. Most news media will unite to aid in this spread of information. A volunteer speakers bureau can be organized. Many knowledgeable specialists will devote a great deal of time to an information and education program.

Second, most communities have social workers, police, and medical and behavioral specialists. What is needed is to make them "partners" in dealing with the problem of child abuse.

Third, most areas have a children's home, or the equivalent of this type of facility. Foster homes are also in use nearly everywhere and if additional or better ones are needed, there are plenty of concerned citizens who would gladly provide family care for an abused and neglected child if asked to do so, and if fairly compensated.

Fourth, every area is served by a court. Its effectiveness should be a matter of public concern. If it is not meeting the needs of the community, it can and should be changed, by enlargement, education, training, addition of staff; by whatever is necessary to permit the court to function adequately.

Finally, in terms of actual cash outlay, it is difficult to say whether additional funds must be provided, or whether it is a matter of a changing emphasis in spending and a more efficient use of funds that have already been appropriated. Even if additional money is required, it can be justified on the ground that the safety and well-being of children cannot be measured solely in terms of dollars. A further argument for spending today to reduce child abuse and neglect, is the far greater future cost we continue to pay for our failure to reach and abate the problem at its source.

Child abuse is predictable and preventable! Causes of child abuse can be detected and treated. Abused children can be protected. The abusive parent can be changed; the abusing and neglecting family strengthened; the child and his family reunited. We have only to care enough to act.

14

The Family Court in an
Urban Setting

JUDGE JUSTINE WISE POLIER and KAY McDONALD, LL.B.

EXTRA DIMENSIONS OF CHILD ABUSE
IN A BIG CITY

IN A LARGE CITY, the problems of parents who abuse their children become accentuated in the same way that loneliness is emphasized and suicides increase during holidays when some people feel excluded from what others are, or seem to be, enjoying. A picture has been drawn of "abusive" parents who live in a house on a residential street with Venetian blinds closed as symptomatic of their failure to participate in church or community activities and of the walls of isolation built between themselves and normal relationships outside the home.

Isolation, whether imposed by the outside world or by the self, becomes more difficult to cope with or overcome when parents live in a city tenement in a poverty area. The shifting tenants, the overcrowding and the anonymous quality of life prevent or discourage others from even noting how their neighbors live. Similarly in the high rent areas, isolation may be a way of life called "privacy." Even the pervasive city noises and acceptance of the "city way of life" often preclude helping one's neighbors — let alone strangers — or reporting what could call for citizen action in a smaller community. Troubled, lonely and self-isolating families are among the first to be sealed off from such help or concern.

The rape of a girl in the city, her unanswered screams, and her pitiful death by stabbing on a city street was widely reported. Interviews with people noted that the screams only induced some to shut their windows, thereby removing themselves from hearing, feeling or trying to help the victim.

Lack of timely intervention on behalf of an abused child must therefore be seen as only one of the many tragedies resulting from pervasive dehumanization and depersonalization in the big city. Like a degenerative virus, such dehumanization has invaded the lives of individuals, impaired their perception, their sensitivity and their capacity to respond to the needs of others.

In evaluating city people who may seem less than human or humane in their sense of responsibility for the welfare of others, one must be aware of many factors that have affected their attitudes toward those they do not know. There is an increased fear of personal danger in the cities; there is a sense of impotence in regard to the ability to change the surrounding world. The sheer size of problems that impinge upon life in the city dwarfs the sense of independent strength.

The virus of dehumanization has, likewise, invaded the institutions that have been developed in big cities to deal with social problems. Both public and private agencies, created to render services, are all too often seen as remote, disinterested bureaucracies administered by remote control. Consequently, they are viewed with suspicion and avoided by the ordinary citizen who does not wish to become involved in the problems of neighbors, but might seek help from an agency if he knew where to go and felt assured that he would be well received.

Some justification for such feelings is found in the fact that, in 1969, 50 percent to 80 percent of the children reported abused in the boroughs that compose New York City were members of families receiving public assistance; yet, only 5 percent of the reports came from public assistance workers.

Depersonalization is also reflected in the preliminary court proceedings in child abuse cases. The prosecuting attorney assigned to present the case, the lawyers assigned to represent the parents, the representatives of the protective services and their counsel, and finally the judge are usually all strangers to the parents and unfamiliar with their family background, their lives, their neighborhoods and their problems.

At an initial or preliminary court hearing, when the dynamics of the parental conduct are still unknown, the specific alleged act must loom largest. The general expectation that the court must divine the future and protect the child in such a situation inevitably leads to anxiety. The prosecutor, the protective services and even defense counsel must be burdened by fear that failure to remove a child from his home may endanger the child.

One young and dedicated lawyer, who represents many poverty stricken people, said, "Child abuse cases are the only ones I have begged off taking. When I did take one, I got a dismissal. I never knew whether that was right. I don't know what happened to the child."

In a metropolis, there is an additional source of fear due to the ease with which families may move or disappear. This too affects the decisions of the protective services and the court. The high turnover of staff in the public services, the rotation of judges and the unpredictable periods of disinterest and intense interest in the battered child on the part of the press, all contribute to pressures for child removal when a child abuse case is brought to court. The absence of immediate diagnostic services to guide the court adds a further element of uncertainty which invites decisions to take the "safe" course of removal.

When stories of child abuse are published, the reflex response of the general public is to demand punishment for the parent and removal of the child. Descriptions of injuries inflicted on a child evoke a sense of horror, fury and the feeling that no punishment can be too great for such a crime. The thousands of children brought before the court as neglected are viewed in a quite different light or are largely ignored by the public. There is no public clamor to punish the parent or to secure appropriate services for the child. Indeed, there is little interest in, or support for, helping the parent become a better parent.

THE ROLE OF THE JUDGE[*]

The education of physicians for service to abused children and their families is still all too limited. Consequently, the judge is rarely the beneficiary of special skill or knowledge on individual cases brought before the court. Just as further education of physicians is needed in this field, so too there is great need for further education of lawyers and judges. Child abuse has been aptly described as a disease of the battering parent. But it must be also added that both child abuse and child neglect reflect a social disease, a disease where the parental illness and societal neglect combine to destroy children.

> Recently a child of 12 was found dead in the home of a neighbor as the result of an overdose of heroin. Extensive newspaper publicity searched out every detail of the family's history. The Department of Social Services, which had known the family situation for many years, responded by filing a petition to have four younger half-siblings found neglected and subject to removal. The press followed this case with grim determination.
>
> It was only after the tragedy that an outstanding clinic reached out to help the mother and found her in need of medication as well as psychotherapy. On the urging of the court the Department of Social Services found an apartment in place of the furnished room in a miserable tenement that had been the home of this family for many months.
>
> This court did not remove the children. At the last hearing it was found that despite, or perhaps because of, the tragedy, the mother for the first time was receiving and responding positively to the help she had long needed.

This case illustrated that if judges are to meet their responsibility, they will need far more help from physicians and psychiatrists. They will also need far better service from

[*]The editors realize that there is a certain degree of overlap (both in similarities and differences) in the views expressed by Judge Polier and those by Judge Delaney (Chapter 13). This was felt to be necessary in order to give the reader a more complete view of the problem. Judge Delaney's observations are made in Brighton, Colorado, while Judge Polier's experiences are derived from New York City.

social agencies than they have received in the past if public pressure for punishment of the parent is not to compel unwarranted removal of children. At times the judge must be the initiator by going out of his way to develop the communications necessary for this cooperation to be developed.

When a child abuse petition is brought before a judge, the formal allegations of injury to a small child frequently raise an image of a "parent-monster" bent on evil, a veritable devil. In startling contrast when the parents are brought before the court, they generally appear to be sad, insecure, burdened and frightened human beings. In this setting, they evidence no stigmata to distinguish them from the rest of the human race.

At the initial hearing the judge must protect the constitutional rights of the parent to counsel and a fair hearing. The judge must also decide whether the child is at significant risk in the home and whether removal is needed for protection. Immediate removal may allay the judge's worry over what may happen to the child; it may also protect the judge from public criticism. To yield to this consideration for his own sake rather than for the child's protection is to abdicate his responsibility as a judge and violate the rights of both parent and child. It sometimes seems that judges and prosecuting counsel at the initial hearing may not fully appreciate the long run emotional costs to both child and parents where immediate removal is ordered when it is not in the best interest of the child.

If at the end of the fact-finding hearings, the court enters a finding of abuse, this completes only one stage in the judicial process. Investigation of the home by probation officers and social agencies, expert testimony on the mental and emotional condition of the parents, and the potential for working with the parents to make the home safe and healthy for the child — all still lie ahead. When the judge has received all the evidence, he must then make an order of disposition that will determine whether the child must be removed from the home for a period of time or whether the child can remain at home under court supervision.

It is at this point that the juvenile court judge is challenged by the concept of individualized justice. In recent years it has become fashionable to proclaim that the concept of individualized justice, developed at the turn of the century, is no longer of value and should be given a decent burial. What its original proponents urged was that courts should not regard the criminal or delinquent act as controlling in the disposition of cases. Courts should rather aim to see the defendant as a whole person with all his weaknesses and strengths, and make the disposition most appropriate to achieve his rehabilitation. There are few areas of judicial disposition where this approach could be more constructive than in the disposition of child abuse or neglect cases.

Tragic as it is, courts must today recognize that the goal of replacing punishment with treatment, the goal of replacing incarceration with rehabilitation, and the goal of individualized justice for children have all receded in the absence of the social nurturing needed to provide the skills and services required for these objectives. As a result of the failure to implement these goals, recent emphasis has been placed largely on procedural reforms such as the right to counsel, the right to confront witnesses and the right against self-incrimination. These reforms, while valuable, have the additional advantage of seeming cheaper than providing substantive services for those who are mentally ill, engaged in deviant behavior, or are poor. Paradoxically, while adversary proceedings are becoming the fashion of the day and are resulting in dismissals of more cases, there is also a growing demand for harsher sentences. There also has not been any substantive improvement in the services to children and their parents essential to the rebuilding of the home, except in a few pilot projects.

The judge, unlike the prosecutor, defense counsel or John Q. Citizen, who has reacted with anger against the abusive parent, must still seek to determine what disposition is truly in "the best interest of the child." This phrase, while sometimes misused to justify whatever is done, places a heavy responsibility upon the judge to search all possibilities at the dispositional stage. He must face the consequences to a child of removal to an overcrowded shelter, of life in an institution, of living in a succession of foster homes, and of the danger of progressively attenuated relationships with the natural family. He must also face the risks involved in leaving the child in a home where intensive service to, and continued treatment of, the parents is essential but may, despite promises and good intentions, not be provided.

> After a charge of manslaughter and a period of hospitalization to determine her sanity, a mother, responsible for the death of her four-year-old child, was permitted to plead guilty to assault. She was placed on probation for five years conditioned on her continuing in therapy. Her subsequent termination of treatment was discovered only on a further outside complaint. A second hospitalization was followed by restoration to probation. Following difficulties with the probation officer and removal by the family to another county, probation requirements were reduced to the sending of postcards by the mother stating she was still in treatment.
>
> Removal to a third county was followed by the mother lodging a complaint of assault against her husband. Psychiatric studies in the court clinic again revealed the need for intensive treatment for the mother, and that she had been attending a clinic on less than a monthly basis.
>
> Review of the voluminous record showed she had appeared before 10 different judges, had been hospitalized three times, had attended two clinics, and that three separate probation services had been involved in a period of four years. No steady or continuing service had been rendered either to strengthen the family or to provide preventive services adequate for the protection of the children remaining in the home.

A CLOSER LOOK AT THE COURT'S ROLE—
CASES BROUGHT TO COURT

It is not possible for the writers to evaluate services in other large metropolitan areas at this time. We shall, instead, report on what has developed in New York City and seek to identify the various parts of the "system" that endeavors to protect children, and the degree to which they mesh or fail to mesh with one another. In an attempt to present the current picture objectively we have examined statistics, studied reports and cases that came before the courts, analyzed a sample number of cases in depth, and conferred with representatives of both public and private protective agencies. We have also drawn on many years of experience in the Family Court.

Under New York legislation all persons and agencies are required to report suspicion of child abuse to the Protective Services Division of the Department of Social Services. The number of such reports has skyrocketed during the past two years. The records show that the number doubled from 1967 to 1968. They more than doubled from 1968 to 1969, which included an eight-month period following a great deal of newspaper publicity and the 1969 legislation on child abuse. The total number of child abuse cases reported to the Protective Services Division in New York City were as follows:

1966	210
1967	369
1968	730
1969	1,829
1970	2,800

A breakdown of the cases reported in 1969 reveals that the vast majority reflect what might be better classified as situations of neglect requiring assistance or counseling to the family, and placement of children where indicated, rather than true cases of "child abuse." This was inevitable since the definition of a "neglected child" in the Family Court Act[2] was far broader than the definition of an "abused child" in the 1969 law.[3]

An analysis by the Bureau of Child Welfare of child abuse reports shows that 90 percent of the cases reported to its Protective Services warranted investigation and follow-up. Between 60 percent to 65 percent of the families were found to require long-term supportive services, and 10 percent to 15 percent of the children were placed through voluntary agreements between the parents and the Bureau. Only 10

percent were referred to the Family Court for action and of
this comparatively small hardcore group, the court removed
the children in approximately one quarter (27 percent) of the
cases.[4] Such removal thus constituted only 2.5 percent of the
reported child abuse cases.

INCIDENCE AND DISPOSITION

In response to the legislative mandate requiring the establishment of a separate child abuse part in the Family Court,[5]
a Central Trial Term was developed in Manhattan to hear
child abuse petitions from all five boroughs for the first five
months following the effective date of the legislation.[6]

The recording of petitions in the docket book from all
counties during this period was examined in order to determine
the volume of child abuse cases requiring court intervention
as seen by the public and private protective services, the
police, the criminal courts and the Family Court judges. It
must be realized that these months spanned a period that reflected heightened interest in child abuse following an incident
publicized earlier that year.

A word of caution is needed, however. The referrals to court
for authoritative action also vary in accordance with the prac-

TABLE 1. *Court Referred Child Abuse Cases in N.Y.C. June Through
October, 1969*

COUNTY	NO. CASES	POPULATION	NO. PER 100,000 (5 MONTHS)	FIGURES PROJECTED FOR 1 YEAR	
				NO. OF CASES	NO. PER 100,000
Bronx	58	1,475,000	4.0	139	9.4
Kings (Brooklyn)	101	2,620,000	3.8	242	9.2
N.Y. (Manhattan)	82	1,745,000	4.7	197	11.3
Queens	18	1,990,000	.9	43	2.2
Richmond	3	280,000	1.0	7	2.5
New York City	262*	8,110,000	3.2	628	7.7

* 7 entries in docket book do not list county of origin.

tices and services of protective services in the various counties, the practices of referring hospitals, and the decisions of judges as to which neglect cases should be referred for treatment as child abuse cases. Since the figures were drawn from the first five months after the enactment of the new law they may also reflect the response to the heightened anxiety of that period concerning child abuse.

One other source of referral to the court is the medical examiner. Surprisingly few cases come to the court's attention from this office. Examinations of these reports to Protective Services show 25 child deaths, between 1964 and 1969, which were reported as raising suspicion of homicide.

Reviewing these reports reveals that 14 of the deaths were described as due to physical injuries including skull fractures and contusions; five as due to asphyxia; three to starvation or severe malnutrition and in three no cause was given.

The Assistant Director of the Office of Psychiatry of the Department of Social Services has expressed concern that there are a number of codes used by the medical examiner to classify causes of death which are suggestive of parental neglect, and he urges the need for closer liaison between the Department of Social Services and the Office of the Medical Examiner. The medical examiner has supported legislation to require more complete reporting.

A paper presented by Dr. Milton Helpern, Chief Medical Examiner of the City of New York, and two colleagues, on deaths of children in their own homes, emphasizes the need for systematic study of all infant deaths including "crib cases."[7] The authors note that, in the absence of extended injury, crib deaths have too often been certified without autopsy as due to various kinds of pneumonia. In a subsequent statement, Dr. Helpern urged careful investigation of the circumstances, and a complete autopsy in every infant death. He expressed concern about physicians who are satisfied with inadequate explanations by parents or guardians, and stated that excuses offered by a physician for not reporting suspicion of abuse "are a rationalization of (his) unwillingness to become involved." He emphasizes the importance of long-term follow-up after the reporting in view of the evidence of "repeated assaults."[8]

When the docket book was closed on December 4, 1969, six months after the Central Abuse Term was inaugurated, the record showed that there had been findings of child abuse in 85 cases of the 269 cases in which petitions alleging child abuse had been drawn. A separate or additional finding of neglect was entered in 33 cases. There had been dismissals in 80 cases and three petitions had been withdrawn. No adjudications had been made in 66 of the cases which were still awaiting fact-finding hearings.

The 85 findings of child abuse included some findings based on the drug addiction of a parent. Although the 1969 statute referred to a parent or other person "who has been adjudicated a narcotic addict," some judges interpreted this as giving them power to make a finding of child abuse if a parent admitted drug addiction before the court, or if a child demonstrated withdrawal symptoms shortly after birth.[9]

ECONOMIC STATUS

The Director of the Children's Division of the American Humane Association, Vincent de Francis, J.D., in a letter dated January 19, 1970, writes:

> From what I have seen of statewide statutes on child abuse, a majority of cases are reported in the larger urban areas. Sources of referral are predominantly hospital personnel in hospitals serving minority families in deprived pockets of the community. A consequence of the reporting is a bias in terms of identifying child abuse as a phenomenon associated with minority families in underprivileged areas.
>
> We found this same bias in our study of sexual victimization of children.
>
> The paucity of reports from private physicians or from other than public hospitals cannot be viewed to mean that abuse does not occur in families which do not use public facilities. Our 1962 study of more than 600 cases reported in the press in every state documented the existence of the problem at all levels of our society.

This position is supported as one examines the sources of referral to the Protective Services of the Department of Social Services, and by the negligible number reported by private physicians.* It is also supported by the different ways in which the reporting of mental illness for those using public facilities and those able to secure private treatment are handled. In juvenile court cases, probation officers secure a Social Service Exchange listing of a family for information. If a parent or child has been in a city or state hospital that fact will appear. However, attendance at a private sanitorium or treatment with a private psychiatrist is not reported.

It appears that the right of privacy is regarded as more sacred for those accustomed to privacy than for those who cannot afford it.

NEW YORK COUNTY—19 CASES REVIEWED

Eighty petitions alleging child abuse came from New York County (Manhattan) and were filed at Central Term during the first five months following the enactment of the child abuse legislation in June, 1969. By taking every fourth case as a sampling, 19 cases were secured.

In 10 of the 19 cases the finding of child abuse had been made.† One half (5) of such findings were based on narcotic addiction of a parent. Four of the cases had been dismissed‡ and action was still pending in January, 1970, on the remaining five. Neglect petitions had preceded the child abuse petitions in 10 of the 19 cases.

---

* The Director of Psychiatry for the Department of Social Services of the City of New York is now engaged in a study of abuse. He reports that of the 1,117 suspicion of abuse reports received from July, 1969, to December, 1969, only eight came from private physicians.

† In three cases an additional finding of neglect was entered. In two cases neglect petitions on which findings had been made were discharged to the child abuse petition, so that only the abuse petition remained active.

‡ The charges had been made by one parent against the other in three of the four cases dismissed.

No clear-cut picture emerges of what one may reasonably expect to happen after a finding of abuse. Review of the cases raises many questions as to who will assume responsibility for services to the abused or neglected child, his siblings, or the family.

In some cases siblings were included in the original petitions or in accompanying neglect petitions. In other cases they were not included. In some cases children were paroled under supervision by probation to persons who had shown interest in the child. In others, children were discharged to the Department of Social Services or placed with voluntary agencies, away from the natural parents, for 18 months. *There was little evidence of acceptance of full responsibility by any single agency for intensive work with the natural parents toward return of a child once the child had been removed.* While some efforts will undoubtedly be made by individual probation officers· or staff members of the Bureau of Child Welfare toward strengthening the family, such efforts will in all probability be far down on the list of priorities for overburdened staff once a finding of child abuse has been made and the child has been removed.

In some cases children in one family are divided between those included on a *neglect* petition and the child or children in regard to whom a separate *abuse* petition has been drawn. In such instances disposition is even more likely to result in separate placement of siblings. Where this occurs there is danger that no single agency will assume the major responsibility for working with the family toward its stabilization and the return of all the children. At times it was possible to identify as many as eight to 10 medical, legal, judicial or social "intake" workers with no one person accepting the responsibility for the care of the child or his family.

Even where the Protective Services Division had initially made meaningful efforts to strengthen a family, these efforts were terminated when the case was referred back to a public assistance agency or to the court on child abuse petitions.

It is quite clear from this review that when the child is placed by the court in a child care agency, despite comprehensive responsibility for work with the family, the care of the child and not the problems of the parents becomes the center of interest.

As cases are read one discovers that clues to the need for help — and even requests for help — had been ignored well before the child abuse occurred.

> A father had sought medical help because of drug dependency and had been referred by a voluntary hospital to a city hospital for psychiatric observation. He was not accepted and told to return. Several months later, after quitting a good job, he again sought help from the voluntary hospital. This time he was given a letter urging his admission by the city hospital which once more failed to find room for him. He left his wife and child for a few weeks. Then upon his return, the alleged abuse of the infant occurred.

One Family Court judge has written about a four-year-old child who was taken, with a critical head injury, to the emergency room of the same hospital that had rejected his mother's earlier appeal for help when she felt unable to control her whippings of this child.

LONG-TERM GOALS AND INTERIM STEPS

This limited survey of the handling of child abuse in a large urban area points up the need for the clarification of goals, the need for the development of ways to achieve them, and also the need for interim steps that should be taken without delay.

There can be little question that the goals must be the creation of services that will prevent child abuse wherever possible, and services to treat the whole family when child abuse has occurred.

Such goals will require establishing a program of outreach services on the part of physicians, well-baby centers, day care centers, schools, social agencies and hospitals to help identify vulnerable families and provide them with timely help. Members of the outreach groups will need help in developing the skills to identify parents who should be given special attention.

They will also need skilled guidance so that they will be able to lessen, rather than increase, the isolation, *self*-isolation and fear that has been found to be common among parents who harm their children. The treatment goal will require that needed services shall be available, so that identification of problems will not be followed by further denial of what is necessary to help these families. This, in turn, will mean community insistence on adequate government aid to service such programs.

Short of achieving such goals there are interim steps that can and should be taken without delay:

1. A registry of child abuse reports, for use in suspicious cases, needs to be centralized and available 24 hours a day, 365 days a year. Physicians in hospital emergency rooms, where children who have been injured are most frequently brought, should be able to clear names at any time. This is especially important in cities, where families move frequently and can go from hospital to hospital (see Paulsen in Bibliography, under *Law/Police/Registry*).

2. A registry must be more than a switchboard. It must be a service manned by skilled people on call to meet emergencies without delay whenever they occur.

3. Requirements for reporting of suspicion of abuse should include not only immunity for reporting, but sanctions against those who fail to report. This is important in view of the dearth of reports by private physicians.

4. While Protective Services should be centrally administered, its operative services should be decentralized. Staffs of local centers must be familiar with and responsive to both local problems and local resources. Hopefully, the local service centers will be linked with hospitals in the same areas which will develop specialized teams to render service to the abused child and his family.

5. Local service centers should be developed first in the areas where the highest incidence of cases arises (see Appendix B).

6. Protective Services must be given adequate and qualified staff so that it can fully investigate and provide the follow-up service needed to protect the child and secure voluntary cooperation from the parents whenever that is possible.

7. Protective Services must develop cooperative relationships with public and voluntary agencies so that when a child is at risk and parents agree to voluntary placement, appropriate foster home or other specialized residential care will be immediately available.

8. Hospitals should develop teams including pediatricians, social workers and psychiatrists to provide diagnostic skills and follow-up service for the abused child and his family. Such services are essential if children are not to be removed unnecessarily and if children are to be returned to their families as soon as the home is made safe (see Chapter 5).

9. Hospitals should be given the power to hold any child regarded at risk until the court can provide a hearing and determine whether such abuse or neglect has occurred.

10. The authority of the Juvenile (or Family) Court should be invoked when there is evidence of abuse and when voluntary cooperation of the parent is inadequate to safeguard the welfare of the child.

11. The Juvenile (or Family) Court has a two-fold responsibility at the initial fact-finding hearing. It must see that the constitutional rights of the parent are protected and it must safeguard the welfare of the child. When a fact-finding hearing warrants a finding, the court must be able to call upon probation officers for a full and independent investigation and to call upon its psychiatric staff for an evaluation of the parents, when that is indicated, before a disposition is made. Above all, the court must be committed to determining in accordance with all information available what is truly in the best interest of the child. The exercise of judicial authority must be seen as a procedure invoked to determine what can be done either to rehabilitate the family, or, if that is not possible despite conscientious efforts over a reasonable period of time, to terminate

parental rights. Just removing a child indefinitely from his home cannot be seen as an adequate final disposition.

REFERENCES

1. Letter from Director of the Bureau of Child Welfare, Department of Social Services, New York City, to writer, dated Feb. 4, 1970. Manhattan, Brooklyn, and Staten Island, 80 percent of the reports were families on public assistance; Queens, 50 percent on public assistance; Bronx, 60 percent on public assistance.
2. Sec. 312.
3. Family Court Act, Sec. 1012, Added L. 1969, C 264.
4. *Supra*, note 1.
5. Family Court Act, Sec. 1013, Added L. 1969 c. 264, Sec. 2 eff. June 1, 1969.
6. On Dec. 4, 1969, the last of the cases remaining in the Central Trial Term were returned to the county of origin.
7. Helpern, Devlin and Ehrenreich: Sudden Deaths at Home of Infants Under One in Apparent Good Health, presented Congress of the French Speaking International Association of Legal Medicine, Montpellier, France, October, 1968.
8. Letter to Judge Polier, Feb. 10, 1970.
9. See, Matter of Three "John" Children, 61 Misc. 2d. 347 (1969). Dr. Michael M. Baden, Associate Medical Examiner for the City of New York, has expressed his grave concern about the deaths of small children of heroin addicts due to mis-or non-feasance rather than malfeasance—where death appears to be the result of the inability to properly care for a child rather than the result of any purposeful will to harm.
   The 1970 amendments specifically include such situations within the jurisdiction of the court as neglect cases. *Supra*, note 6 Sec. 1012 (B).

15

The Role of the Lawyer in Child Abuse Cases

JACOB L. ISAACS, LL.B.

IN RECENT DECADES a significant development in the handling of court cases involving families and children has been the assimilation into the judicial process of bodies of knowledge and techniques developed by disciplines other than the law. The issue of the "best interests of the child," raised in custody disputes, neglect and dependency proceedings and other cases involving family disruption, is now often evaluated and determined in medical and psychiatric terms. Social work objectives and techniques have been accepted almost uniformly as legally permissible tools for the investigation, evaluation and formulation of judicial dispositions in a wide range of family cases. This development, coupled with the spread of avowedly socially oriented family and juvenile courts, has engendered considerable uncertainty as to the role legal counsel has in family litigation.

Nowhere is this confusion more evident than in the handling of child abuse and neglect cases.[1] Public concern over the scope and significance of the problem of the battered child is a comparatively new phenomenon. Participation by counsel in any significant numbers in child abuse cases in juvenile or family courts is of even more recent origin. It is small wonder that the lawyer approaches participation in these cases with trepidation. X-ray and other medical techniques, as well as psychiatric evaluation—subjects normally alien to the lawyer—have become the principal tools not only for identifying instances of parental battering but also for legally establishing parental culpability and guiding judicial action. The lawyer's dilemma is compounded by the fact that strict adherence to traditional ethical concepts of advocacy might ultimately result in exposing a child to further and more serious injury.

The proper role of the lawyer in child abuse and neglect cases will have to be forged in the crucible of actual experience. However, some of the misconceptions can be avoided, and uncertainties dissipated, by examining the need for and role of the lawyer in child abuse proceedings from a new perspective and against the background of recent developments.

At the outset, the limits of this discussion should be defined. Almost all states have cruelty-to-children statutes of one form or another which subject parents or other legal custodians to the possibility of prosecution in the criminal courts. The role of counsel in these criminal cases is deliberately omitted from this chapter for several reasons. First, most knowledgeable legal authorities, as well as medical, psychiatric and social work experts, agree that criminal courts are inappropriate forums for dealing with the personal and familial problems underlying child abuse.[2] Second, the role of counsel in the prosecution and defense of a criminal proceeding is so well defined by ethical tradition and practice as not to require further elaboration. However, paralleling the criminal statutes in almost all jurisdictions, are statutes vesting in family or juvenile courts civil jurisdiction over cases involving neglected and dependent children, these terms being normally so defined or interpreted as to encompass the abused child.[3] The avowed purpose for the exercise of such jurisdiction is not to adjudge and punish but rather to protect the child, provide treatment for the parent and, ultimately, rehabilitate the family if possible. It is the role of counsel before the juvenile and family courts which presents novel problems and to which this discussion is directed.

Juvenile courts are, at least to some extent, the product of the accumulation of knowledge about human behavior that began to be developed in the fields of psychiatry, psychology and social work about the turn of the century. Increased attention to the behavioral sciences brought with it dissatisfaction with the application to children and family problems of procedures designed for adult criminals. The philosophic rationale for the new juvenile courts was a vision of the court as fulfilling the role of *parens patriae*—the wise and benevolent substitute parent.[4]

In the context of this view of the court, the notion was widely accepted that a lawyer could serve little purpose in this new and enlightened judicial approach other than obstruction and pettifogging.[5] Accordingly, for almost half a century the presence of counsel in the juvenile court was a rare phenomenon. A survey conducted as recently as 1963 indicated that, in almost 50 percent of the courts studied, lawyers appeared in neglect and dependency proceedings in only from zero to 5 percent of such cases.[6]

Experience demonstrated, however, that excessive rejection of traditional legal safeguards and procedures carried with it the potential for serious abuse of individual rights.[7] The jurisdiction of the new juvenile courts could frequently be invoked on the basis of vague allegations of presumably antisocial behavior. Judges wielded great power, shielded from the glare of public scrutiny and freed from the limitations on the arbitrary exercise of judicial discretion normally provided by the presence of counsel.[8] Evidence of recurrent instances of infringement of basic constitutional rights in the juvenile court process brought with it a rising wave of criticism.[9]

An important by-product of this critical reevaluation of the juvenile court concept was a reversal of the earlier thinking which had discouraged participation of lawyers in these courts, and a demand for increased legal representation of children arose.[10] The State of New York pioneered in this field with the creation by statute, in 1962, of a system of "law guardians" to provide legal representation for minors in neglect as well as in juvenile delinquency cases.[11] The tremendous impact of this innovation can be appreciated if it is realized that in

1959 less than 9 percent of all children involved in delinquency and neglect proceedings in the City of New York were represented by counsel whereas in the period from July 1, 1968, to June 30, 1969, law guardians appeared in about 92 percent of the juvenile cases and private counsel in an additional 5 percent.[12]

The growth of legal representation in juvenile and family courts was given tremendous impetus by the decision of the United States Supreme Court in *Matter of Gault*[13] in which legal representation of minors in juvenile delinquency cases was elevated to a constitutional right. The *Gault* case does not extend such constitutional mandate to neglect or child abuse cases. However, the expanded legal services created throughout the nation to meet the *Gault* requirements have frequently included provision for the representation of children in neglect and child abuse proceedings.[14]

The influx of lawyers into neglect and child abuse proceedings has not been accomplished without considerable difficulty. While the lawyer's role in the trial phase of juvenile delinquency cases was delineated with minimal difficulty, lawyers themselves still approach their participation in neglect and child abuse cases with great wariness. The report of a judicial investigation recently conducted in New York City into the handling of a case in which an allegedly neglected child, returned to her home by the Family Court and ultimately killed by her stepfather, was critical of the performance of the law guardian who appeared for the child and expressly noted the uncertain conception of the lawyer's role in these cases.[15] It is hoped that succeeding portions of this chapter may serve to dissipate at least some of this confusion.

THE NEED FOR AND ROLE OF
COUNSEL FOR THE CHILD

Although some skeptics continue to express doubt as to the utility of legal representation for children in neglect and child abuse proceedings, this residual opposition is unwarranted.[16] The preoccupation of the county or city attorney—

or any other person acting in a quasi-prosecutorial role—with the necessity of establishing culpability is too great to insure single-minded attention to safeguarding the long-range interests of the child. Counsel for the parent obviously cannot furnish the child with truly independent representation since the potential for conflict of interest between the parent and child in this type of case is manifest. Even the judge cannot adequately serve as protector of the legal and social interests of the child without seriously sacrificing the appearance of impartiality. It is interesting to note that in the State of New York, although many judges were initially dubious about intervention of law guardians in neglect proceedings, during the past judicial year counsel have been assigned to represent the child in 99 percent of all neglect cases in New York City and in 56 percent of all such cases in other areas of the state.[17]

The term law guardian used to describe counsel for the child under the New York Family Court system seems a particularly apt description of the proper function of the counsel in neglect cases. It connotes in the first instance the traditional obligations of the effective advocate. However, the use of the modifying word "guardian" would also seem to indicate the intention to expand counsel's role beyond advocacy alone. The concept of "guardianship" requires that not only the legal rights but also the general welfare of the minor be thrown on the scale in the weighing by counsel of his course of action.[18]

Despite disclaimers to the contrary, neglect or child abuse proceedings normally partake of most of the essential elements of an adversary proceeding. However, counsel for the child in a neglect or child abuse proceeding occupies a position substantially different from that in which a lawyer normally finds himself in other litigations, since he is not required to take an adversary position. He is not called on either to prosecute or defend, but rather to insure that there is presented to the court all relevant facts necessary to adjudication and disposition, and to exert his efforts to secure an ultimate resolution of the case which, in his judgment, will best serve the interests of his client.

One should not be deceived, however, by the apparent simplicity of this description of counsel's function. The ultimate decision as to the course of action to be taken by counsel in any given case is basically nonlegal in character and imposes upon the attorney an awesome responsibility, the implementation of which may affect the entire future or life of his client for good or ill.

Counsel for the child can play a meaningful role at each stage of the neglect or child abuse case. In many jurisdictions court probation staffs, public welfare officials and other public and private agencies are invested with considerable discretion to attempt to deal with, and adjust, cases of child abuse or neglect on a voluntary basis and without formal judicial intervention. It is rare that counsel is brought into the case at this pre-judicial stage, but in those instances where he is involved before formal proceedings have been instituted he can play a crucial role in the decision as to whether formal judicial proceedings will be initiated.

Once a child abuse proceeding has been started, and even before the issue of the culpability of the parent is heard and determined, counsel for the child may be faced with the necessity of taking a position on the issue of whether the child should be removed from its home during the pendency of the legal proceedings. Thus, at a very preliminary stage, the lawyer will be faced with the difficult task of weighing the risk of further and perhaps more serious injury to the child against the potentially traumatic impact of separation of a child from its family and familiar surroundings for even a limited period. Obviously, an intelligent decision will have to be premised on careful evaluation of whatever data is then available concerning the family's social or legal history, the nature of the injury sustained by the child, and such expert medical, psychiatric or social work evaluation of the parents as may be available. While doubt must almost always be resolved in favor of protecting the child, counsel would be remiss if he invariably recommended removal of the child as the safe way out and without considering the possibility of alternative temporary protective measures.

Once preliminary questions have been disposed of, the judicial process in child abuse cases falls into two principal stages: First the determination of the culpability of a parent, if that is put in issue, and then the ultimate disposition of the matter based on such determination. The first stage is primarily legal in nature and encompasses many of the procedural aspects common to trials of other issues in other courts. The second phase is primarily diagnostic and social in nature.

In the first stage, it is the proper function of counsel for the child to insure that there is presented to the court all relevant facts bearing in the nature and extent of the injury sustained by the child. These facts include the circumstances under which such injuries were inflicted, and any other proper evidence bearing on the responsibility of the parents, whether by acts of commission or omission, for the infliction of such injuries. Of course, the main burden of presenting evidence on these issues rests on the public or private agency seeking to sustain the complaint or petition, and on counsel defending the parent. However, since each of these contending forces is concentrating on presenting that evidence which supports their respective positions, much of the ultimate responsibility for a full and objective presentation of the facts rests on counsel for the child.

Once the liability of the parents for the acts of abuse has been established, a wide range of dispositional alternatives may be available to the judge. Temporary or permanent removal of a child from its home may be directed. Under some circumstances such removal may be obviated by the removal or institutionalization of the offending parent. Where less drastic remedies are required, the child may be returned to its home under probation supervision or under some other regimen of public or private treatment, counseling or assistance.

In good juvenile and family courts the dispositional process involves extensive investigation and evaluation utilizing the diagnostic techniques and recommendations of experts in the social work, medical and psychiatric fields. It has been accordingly suggested that because of his essentially nonlegal orientation, counsel for the child can play no meaningful role at this stage. However, experience has demonstrated the contrary.[19] Counsel's single-minded devotion to the interests of the child and the child alone enables him not only to protect the child but the whole process from arbitrary action and prejudice. He can serve as a counterbalance to unreasoned pressures exerted on the judge by newspapers and the public. He can serve as a procedural watchdog, making sure that disposition is based upon complete and accurate facts and valid expert opinion. He can even participate meaningfully in the formulation of the ultimate plan for disposition if properly supported by available consultative services.

The services of counsel for the child frequently will not terminate with the initial disposition of the matter. As will be later indicated, the very nature of these proceedings often requires the court to review the status of the matter at periodic intervals, and modifications of the original disposition are common. Of equal importance, the presence of counsel for the child gives the child legal standing to obtain appellate review of a determination deemed to be erroneous or injurious to the child's welfare and to seek a stay of such determination pending the appeal. Vigorous prosecution of appeals in appropriate cases is not only a permissible function for counsel for a child but a necessary aspect of proper representation.

Much of the discomfiture expressed by lawyers as to their proper role in representing children in neglect or child abuse proceedings seems to stem from the fact that many of the judgments required of a lawyer are social in nature rather than legal. Lawyers might feel somewhat more comfortable if they would stop concealing the necessity for making such judgments.[20] Recognition of this function, however, carries with it the responsibility to conduct an independent investigation, and to acquire sufficient knowledge of the techniques utilized in the diagnostic process to make informed decisions.

Concededly, the role of counsel for the child imposes an awesome burden of specialized competence and capacity far beyond that normally required of the practicing attorney. To the lawyer who is titillated by the intricacies of a corporate merger or antitrust litigation, it will hold little appeal. To the lawyer who views law as a meaningful mechanism for the adjustment of social conflict it will present an irresistible challenge.

THE ROLE OF COUNSEL FOR THE PARENT

The rapid expansion of legal services designed to provide representation for the child in juvenile court cases has not been parallelled by a significant expansion in services available to the indigent or near-indigent parent who finds himself accused of abusing or neglecting his child.[21] While legal services programs initiated by the Office of Economic Opportunity have ameliorated the situation somewhat, the alleged offending parent is often hard put to obtain effective representation despite the fact that, in criminal court proceedings, the right to such representation would normally be constitutionally guaranteed.

It is difficult to conceive of a party in a court proceeding more in need of independent legal representation than a person charged with brutalizing his child. Even before the charge is proved, newspaper and other media may well have almost condemned the accused as a social outcast. The misdeeds he's charged with may automatically align the entire court staff against the alleged offender. Who but counsel can stand between the accused and public hysteria?

While the role of counsel for the parent is better understood by most lawyers than that of counsel for the child, the complexities of that role are often overlooked or unduly simplified. At the time he first meets his client, the lawyer must overcome the same problem confronted by the physician, the social worker, the psychiatrist and any other person who comes in contact with a parent accused of inhuman treatment of his child—namely, to avoid revulsion. Such feelings, at the beginning, may irreparably alienate him from the client. It is only by acquiring some insight into the motivations which turn a parent into a child beater that the attorney can achieve the level of understanding and compassion that permits him to serve as an effective advocate and counselor.

Physicians, psychiatrists, social workers and teachers who are able to establish some form of relationship of trust with a parent apparently involved in child abuse, might well advise such a parent to obtain legal counsel before a formal judicial proceeding has even been instituted. As previously indicated, the possibility of pre-judicial voluntary adjustment sometimes exists. By working with the investigatory and treatment agencies in the fomulation of a voluntary plan of treatment and family rehabilitation, counsel may not only avoid the formal accusatory process, and the attendant loss of employment and permanent damage to the family relationship, but may also insure that the objective of protecting the child and restoring him to his family with safety can be achieved as quickly as possible. In this connection it should be noted that an eminent family court judge, who presided over a substantial number of child abuse cases, recently noted that the more economically privileged child abusers do not usually wind up in court because of the belief that such parents have resources to deal with parent-child problems without formal public intervention.[22] Counsel may assure equal opportunity for the less affluent parent.

Many lawyers have expressed concern about the "ethics" of a lawyer zealously defending a person believed by the lawyer to be a child beater. Such fears mistake the ethical responsibilities of the lawyer. The organized bar in recent years has strongly emphasized that the defense of unpopular clients and unpalatable causes is one of its essential responsibilities in a democratic society. The child beater, no less than the rapist or the murderer, is entitled to full and effective legal representation in the courts. Moreover, if the client insists upon his innocence, it is the function of the court and not the lawyer to determine the issue of guilt or innocence. If the client persists in denying guilt, it is not only the proper function but the duty of a lawyer to insist that the allegations of the charge be proved by whatever quantum of proof the law requires.

The role of trial advocate should not, however, be permitted to obscure the equally important role of the lawyer as counselor. Advice to a client to admit culpability and even to waive some legal rights is not always a violation of a lawyer's professional trust. In various fields of the law, consideration of the totality of a client's long-range interest often compels counsel to advise a client to forego immediate legal advantage, or technical legal rights, in favor of some more important ultimate objective. Similarly, in child abuse cases, the lawyer, in his role as counselor to the parent, may properly look beyond the immediate outcome of the case to the ultimate rehabilitation of the family. For example, could it be seriously argued that a lawyer is derelict in professional responsibility if he advises his client to admit responsibility (even where such culpability might not be established at a trial) when the lawyer knows that, without some therapeutic intervention, his client will be continuously exposed to the temptation of inflicting even more serious injuries on his child and will subject himself to more serious punishment in the future?

Where the responsibility of the parent for the injuries sustained by the child is a contested issue, the lawyer has a duty to defend his client with the utmost vigor and resourcefulness. The lawyer in a juvenile or family court, no less than in any other court, must stand as the ardent protector of his client's constitutional and legal rights. He must bring to the task the usual tools of the advocate—familiarity with the applicable law, the ability to logically present the pertinent facts, and the facility for forceful and persuasive exposition of his client's cause.

There are rarely any eyewitnesses to episodes of parental battering of a child. Accordingly, parental responsibility is often difficult to prove. Despite this, however, the lawyer defending the parent has a more complex and difficult task in many child abuse cases in a juvenile court than would counsel defending such a case in a criminal court. Although the burden of proof rests with the accuser in child abuse cases, the courts, utilizing a doctrine of *res ipsa loquitur* ("the thing speaks for itself"), developed in negligence cases, have held that the mere showing of the existence of injuries which would normally not occur but for parental acts or omissions is sufficient to require the parent to come forward with proof to otherwise explain the injuries.[23] While this presumption is probably justified as a matter of social policy and expediency, it nevertheless imposes a greater burden on the part of the parent to prove his innocence than would be required if he were being prosecuted in a criminal court. Moreover, whereas in criminal proceedings the burden of proof must be sustained beyond a reasonable doubt, in many jurisdictions a finding of child abuse or neglect may rest on a mere preponderance of the evidence.

The difficulty of counsel's task is compounded by the fact that the issue of guilt or innocence may well hinge on technical, medical or psychiatric testimony. Thus counsel must have sufficient familiarity with x-ray and other diagnostic techniques to conduct a meaningful cross-examination of expert witnesses and to adduce rebuttal evidence. He must also be sufficiently conversant with the jargon of psychiatrists to understand and evaluate their testimony.

Normally in a criminal case, once the judge or jury has determined the issue of guilt or innocence, the function of defense counsel ends except for the usual rhetoric employed in the appeal for clemency on sentencing or the following-through of an appeal. In child abuse cases, however, the finding of culpability may only be the beginning of the opportunity for effective legal representation.

Observation of the actual activities of counsel in the ultimate disposition of neglect and child abuse cases has indicated at least eight separate functions which the lawyer can productively perform at this stage of the case.[24] As in the case of the lawyer for the child, he can insure impartiality by acting as a counterbalance to the hostility and pressures exerted on the court by the very nature of the issues. He can assure that the basic elements of due process are preserved, such as the right to be heard and the right to test the facts upon which the disposition is to be made. He can make certain the disposition is based upon complete and accurate facts and that all the circumstances which shed light upon the otherwise unspeakable conduct of his client are adduced. He can test expert opinion to make certain that it is not based on mistakes either arising from the factual premises on which it rests or the limited expertise or lack of it on which the conclusions derived from these facts are based. He can give the frequently inarticulate parent a voice in the proceeding by acting as his spokesman. His relationship with the parents may even enable him to give the probation department or other auxiliary staff of the court new and meaningful insights into the family situation. Finally, and equally important, he can interpret the court and its processes to the parent and thus assist the parent in genuinely accepting a proper disposition by the court.

Neither the task of counsel for the child nor that of counsel for the parent normally ends with the initial disposition of the case except where psychiatric or other factors demand immediate and permanent severance of the child from the family. Even if the final disposition directs removal of the child from his home, it should also normally contemplate some form of continuing therapeutic regimen for the family, with the ultimate objective of family rehabilitation and restoration of the child. Accordingly, there may well be various postdispositional proceedings requiring the participation of both counsel for the parent and that of the child. These proceedings may involve modification of the previous disposition of the court for the purpose of modifying or terminating the custodial status of the child, or enlarging, reducing or otherwise changing the therapeutic measures being directed toward the parent.[25]

TRAINING OF COUNSEL

The previous discussion would certainly seem to indicate the need for a high degree of specialized training and experience for lawyers handling child abuse and other types of family matters. Unfortunately, until recently, little cognizance of this need was reflected in law school curricula. A survey conducted in 1964 among all American Bar Association approved law schools indicated that almost one third of the schools provided no substantial coverage in any course dealing with juvenile and family court matters.[26] Only a limited number of schools reported advanced courses in this area.

It is apparent that counsel in child abuse cases must be thoroughly familiar with both the substantive and procedural law which governs the proceeding in which he is participating. In addition he must know how to read and evaluate, at least to a limited degree, medical diagnostic reports and the reports of psychiatrists, psychologists and probation officers. He must have at least a passing familiarity with the medical and psychiatric literature in the field of child abuse and be acquainted with treatment techniques and their potentials and limitations. He must know the range of alternative dispositions which are available to the court and have at least general knowledge as to the community resources and facilities which may be called upon as therapeutic agents.

This description of a lawyer's armament will undoubtedly invoke dismay from traditionalists who view the lawyer's incursions into other disciplines as incompatible with his traditional function. The fact is, however, that lawyers have frequently assimilated the expertise of other disciplines where necessary for effective representation. Thus counsel who specialize in personal injury cases often acquire a considerable body of knowledge in the field of medical jurisprudence. Counsel who handle mental incompetency proceedings must, of course, be familiar with various medical and psychiatric concepts. The patent attorney is frequently called upon to demonstrate substantial expertise in areas of engineering, chemistry and physics. As much as many lawyers would yearn for the earlier and simpler days, the increasing complexity of society often makes it necessary for the lawyer of today to develop competency in fields not strictly encompassed by the study of law. There is reason for hope that the law schools' increased recognition of this fact, and the rising demands of law students for greater relevance in their studies, will produce greater emphasis on fulfilling the training needs of the "family" lawyer.

REFERENCES

1. The term "child abuse" would seem to ordinarily encompass any nonaccidental acts or omissions of a parent or legal custodian resulting in physical or emotional injury to a child. For legal purposes, however, the term "child abuse" has usually been reserved for cases involving the "battered child"—i. e., the child who has sustained serious physical injuries as a result of nonaccidental means and for which the parents are responsible or legally accountable. The term "neglect" is legally used to describe children deprived of minimally accepted standards of food, shelter, medical attention and other care or proper guardianship, or who have been abandoned. See distinction between definitions of neglect and abuse contained in New York Family Court Acts, Secs. 1012 (e)-1012 (f).

2. See, e. g., Paulsen: The legal framework for child protection, 66 Columbia Law Rev. 679, 1966; Dembitz: Child abuse and the law, The Record, Association of the Bar of the City of New York 24: (#9) 613, Dec., 1969; Terr and Watson: The battered child rebrutalized: ten cases of medical-legal confusion, Amer J Psychiat 124:1432-1439, April 10, 1968; Kempe: The battered child and the hospital, Hospital Practice, October, 1969, p. 44.

3. See Paulsen, *supra*, n. 2; Gil: The legal nature of neglect, 6 N.P.P.A.J. 1, 1960; Paulsen: The delinquency, neglect and dependency jurisdiction of the juvenile court, chap. 3, *in* Rosenheim, M., ed.: Justice for the Child, New York, Free Press, 1962.

4. For a good discussion of the historical and philosophic background of the juvenile court in this country see the opinion of Mr. Justice Fortas in *In re Gault*, 387 U.S. 1, 1967.

5. See, e.g., Alexander: Constitutional rights in juvenile court, 46 A.B.A.J. 1206, 1209, 1960.

6. Skoler and Tenney, Jr.: Attorney representation in juvenile court, J Fam L 4:77, 1964.

7. See *In re Gault, supra,* n. 4, pp. 540-548.

8. See, e. g., *In re Diaz,* 212 La. 700, Sup. Ct, Louisiana, 1947, where a child was removed from its mother and placed in an orphanage because the mother, while in a physician's waiting room and upset by the complaints of the doctor that the baby's crying was annoying other patients, slapped the child until its buttocks were red.

9. See, e. g., Paulsen: Fairness to the juvenile offender, Minn L Rev *41*:547, 1957; Antieau: Constitutional rights in juvenile courts, Cornell L.Q. *46*:387, 1961.

10. See Schinitsky: The Record, Association of the Bar of the City of New York *17*:10, Jan., 1962; McMullen: The lawyer's role in the juvenile court, Prac Law 8:49, 1962.

11. N.Y. Fam. Ct. Act §§ 241-249; see Isaacs: The role of the lawyer in representing minors in the new family court, Buffalo Law Rev *12*:501, 1963.

12. See "Family Court—Unfulfilled Mission," Fifteenth Annual Report, Jud. Conf. of State of New York, 1969, p. 321.

13. See ref. 4, *supra.*

14. In 1969 the provision for law guardians in neglect cases in the New York Family Court Act was implemented by legislation expressly requiring law guardians to represent children in child abuse cases, N.Y. Fam. Ct. Act, §§ 241,243, 249.

15. Report of Judiciary Relations Committee on the handling of the Roxanne Felumero, Supreme Court of the State of New York, First Judicial Department.

16. The "law guardian system" in New York rests on an express legislative finding that "counsel is often indispensable to a practical realization of due process of law and may be helpful in making reasoned determinations of fact and proper orders of disposition." N.Y. Fam. Ct. Act § 241.

17. Fifteenth Annual Report, N.Y. Jud. Conf., supra, footnote 4, p. 322. Judge Justine Wise Polier, of the New York Family Court, described the performance of law guardians in neglect cases as follows: "The provision for a law guardian to represent the child in the Juvenile Court has proven to be of great value in assuring full presentation of the evidence, interpreting the court's role to the child and his family, and securing a fair hearing at the initial stage of the proceeding." Polier: A view from the bench, NCCD, 1964, p. 67.

18. See Isaacs, *supra,* ref. 11.

19. See Treadwell: The lawyer in juvenile court dispositional proceedings: advocate, social worker, or otherwise, Juv Ct Judges J *16*:105, 1965; Isaacs: Proceedings of Section of Family Law, American Bar Association, Chicago, 1964, p. 49.

20. "In my opinion the attorney must act as neither advocate nor social worker alone, but as a combination of both. In juvenile court dispositional proceedings, I believe it wise for the lawyer to amalgamate the functions of a lawyer and the functions of a social disciplinarian. The new and revolutionary setting of the juvenile court, even judging from its very first inception, allows no less. In fact, it demands this type of representation." Treadwell, *supra*, ref. 19.

21. Paulsen: Juvenile courts, family courts and the poor man, Calif L Rev 54:694, 706,1966.

22. See Dembitz: Child abuse and the law, *supra*, ref. 2.

23. See, e. g., *In re Young*, 50 Misc. 2d 271, 270 N.Y.S. 2d 250, Fam. Ct., N.Y., 1966. In 1970 this presumption was enacted into law in the State of New York, N.Y. Family Court Act Sec. 1046 (a) (ii).

24. See ref. 19, *supra*.

25. See, e. g., *In re Bonez*, 48 Misc. 2d 900, 266 N.Y.S. 2d 756, Fam. Ct. N.Y., 1966.

26. Skoler: Law school curriculum coverage of juvenile and family court subjects, J Fam L 5:74, 1965.

16

The Police

MAJOR RUDOLPH A. PITCHER, JR.

THE PROPER MISSION of law enforcement agencies relative to the child abuse phenomenon continues to remain unresolved. The general disagreement over the most suitable role for the police, which existed among the social work, medical, law enforcement and legal professions in the early sixties,[1] has not been substantially modified with the passage of time. There is still no interdisciplinary consensus in this area despite the marked expansion of available knowledge and child protection services which have occurred as a result of widespread public concern and intense multi-professional interest generated over the last decade.[2]

Law enforcement agencies generally have highly formalized procedures or, as a minimum, time tested precedents to guide them in their activities involving unlawful behavior. There is a notable lack of specific guidelines for police encountering domestic offenses totally confined to the family unit, however. Perhaps the most glaring example of all exists in cases where parents criminally assault their children. Although model roles for the other professions concerned with the child abuse phenomenon have been defined with increasing clarity, little progress has been achieved in delineating police functions in a coordinated, combined community approach to the problem.

Law enforcement agencies must be recognized as having a legitimate interest in the social problem created by families in which children are victims of physical aggression. They have traditionally possessed a general mandate to enforce law and

order and protect life, limb and property within their jurisdiction. Though states vary in the substance of their child
cruelty laws, all denounce criminal assault. These statutes are
applicable whether a child or adult is the victim.[3] The police
have a legal duty to enforce all laws and a social responsibility
to protect all persons, regardless of age or relationships, from
the harmful aggressive behavior of others.

Crime and delinquency prevention is also an important
aspect of police services. A few studies have ominously suggested a relationship between a childhood marred by the brutality of a caretaker and subsequent delinquent and criminal
behavior.[4] Establishing this possible link may well result in law
enforcement agencies becoming even more interested and involved with cases of child abuse in the future, thereby enabling
them to perform their traditional functions more effectively.

The definition of an acceptable police role in dealing with
cases of child abuse has been particularly hampered by the
tendency of some members of the social work and medical professions to stereotype all law enforcement officers as "authority
figures" whose mere contact with abusive families is undesirable due to a possible detrimental effect on subsequent family
therapy. They have tended to deny outright or severely limit
the role of the police in any model child abuse prevention and
protection program for communities. Differences in agency resources and the unique organization and functions of law enforcement agencies make this viewpoint unrealistic.[5] For the
child welfare agencies to have the same capabilities in the field
of child protection as the police currently possess, they would
have to greatly expand their personnel and equipment resources, organize along the lines of law enforcement agencies
and confer peace officer status on their personnel. This does not
seem too likely to occur in the forseeable future.

The attitudes of the law enforcement profession on the handling of child abuse cases are continually changing toward favoring a less punitive approach. This transformation has been very
gradual, and a strong tendency to rely on "tried and true"
police procedures, primarily oriented toward criminal prosecu-

tion, continues to exist in many law enforcement agencies across the nation. Such an approach cannot be justified for cases of child abuse on the grounds of community protection, since abusive parents are seldom a threat to anyone outside the family. Neither can it be justified for deterrence value, due to the highly charged emotional climate normally associated with an incident of abuse. Incarceration of a convicted abusive parent achieves only a temporary period of safety for a child victim, at best, and prisons cannot be expected to improve parental caretaking abilities. At worst, this respite for the child is gained at the cost of the family's means of support or the potential for adequate future child care in the same family.

The gap between the conflicting professional viewpoints in the role of the police seems to be closing at the theoretical level at least. A spirit of interagency cooperation, particularly between the child protective and law enforcement agencies, is required for an effective community program for child protection. The question would no longer seem to evolve around how to minimize police involvement in child abuse cases but, rather, the specific functions the police should perform as a team member in an efficient program.

The efforts of all professions and agencies concerned with the battered child syndrome within a community should be focused on resolving cases in the child's best interests. All other considerations should be secondary and the desirability of maintaining family integrity, excessive emphasis on traditional parental "rights," and community demands for retribution should not be allowed to cloud this central issue. When the twin goals of child welfare and abusive family rehabilitation are incompatible, priority must be given to the former. Acceptance of this basic philosophy, and a willingness to be flexible and cooperative in meeting the needs of individual cases, are keystones in any coordinated, multi-institutional child abuse prevention and treatment program.

Law enforcement agencies across the nation have many unique capabilities and characteristics which can be of value in the area of child protection. Police services are universal in that their police power mandate covers every geographical area of the country. Police organizations normally possess manpower, communications and vehicle resources sufficient to provide around-the-clock services. This, combined with standard deployment practices, enables them to respond to a situation in a manner that no other public service agency can begin to approach. Equally important is the degree to which they pervade society. Of all public service agencies, the police are the most visible and familiar in local communities.

Unlike most other public service agencies, law enforcement agencies of the various states have marked similarities in organization, operational and administrative procedures. Interstate, as well as intrastate, police communications are also relatively highly developed. The police thus have a capability for the expeditious exchange of information, coordination of activity and timely reaction across state lines that is unparalleled.

Although a model role for law enforcement agencies in cases of child abuse can be generally defined, the need for individual consideration of each case necessitates complete and continuous coordination, particularly with the child protective agency. There should be few overlaps of services to engender interagency hostility nor gaps to invite tragedy. Assignment of basic responsibilities followed by thorough coordination is the only means of avoiding both. In some communities the delegation of a specially trained juvenile officer to the child welfare department has served to achieve the desired goals.

The broad area of community child protection must be recognized as an appropriate function of the child protective agency.[6] Police may be able to perform parallel functions in the intervention, investigation and adjudication processes, but they do not have the training or resources for family therapy. Since a need exists for a single coordinator of all agency activities in each child abuse case,[7] this responsibility should rightfully be assumed by the child protective agency caseworker, with the few exceptions to be discussed later.

Police efforts should be directed at complementing child protective agency services as needed in areas where they are inadequate and in supplementing them where possible for maximum program efficiency in areas where they are adequate. There must be limitations based on practical considerations, however. Except in situations where child protective agency personnel are not available,[8] extensive police involvement in cases of child abuse should be restricted to those that are serious enough to warrant more than superficial medical attention. Most such cases normally involve the legal elements associated with the offense of aggravated assault.

THE POLICE IN DETECTION AND REPORTING

The law enforcement agency may make its greatest contribution to a combined community child protection program in the area of case finding. The extent and nature of police services within the community provide them a singular opportunity to detect abusive families, particularly where preschool children are the victims. Police on routine patrol assignments, or responding to certain complaints such as domestic disturbances, often enter residences while performing their duties. They are in an excellent position to observe all family members. The common police practice of semi-permanently assigning the same officer to a relatively limited patrol area is also favorable for case finding. Patrol officers frequently accumulate a great deal of information about "problem families" in their area, from both direct encounters and informal sources developed through prolonged association.

It would seem expedient to capitalize on this existing capability of the police. This could be achieved most effectively by instructing all police officers in the child abuse syndrome during recruit training and by providing periodic refresher courses to maintain their alertness. Training programs conducted by an experienced social worker of the child protective agency would be desirable not only to insure quality but also to enhance interagency understanding.*

*Some of the techniques are suggested in the chapter on interviewing (see Chapter 4).

Although the uniformed patrol officers should be alert for indications of abusive families while performing routine duties, they should be cautioned against pressing for explanations from the parents—or other caretakers the child might have—of suspected injuries. They should also be cautioned against taking direct action in suspected child abuse cases except in emergencies, such as when there is immediate danger or obvious injury to the child. In these situations the police should have an arrangement with a local hospital to accept and evaluate these children on a 24-hour basis. In all other cases they should complete their initial assignment and, upon departure from the residence, report their suspicions as expeditiously as possible for immediate referral to the child protective agency.

The available professional literature pertaining to physical abuse of children reflects considerable controversy over whether the recipient of reports generated by the mandatory reporting laws should be the social welfare or law enforcement agency. On a theoretical plane there are arguments favoring both, but as a practical matter the capabilities of the two agencies at the *local* level should be the determining factor. Where the social welfare agency has an around-the-clock capability to receive and respond quickly to incoming reports, that agency probably should be the one to receive them in the interest of maintaining continuity of all child protective services and in recognition of their prime responsibility in this area. Where these capablities are not available, the feasibility of a bi-agency central referral unit should be explored. If this is not possible, arrangements should be made with the telephone company to have all nonduty hour reports of child abuse to the child protective agency rerouted to the juvenile unit of the law enforcement agency.

Open channels of communication are absolutely essential to the early identification of abusive families. There can be no reluctance on the part of medical personnel, agencies responsible for child protection, other welfare services, law enforcement departments and probation offices to exchange information if an established system is to function successfully. In order to avoid duplication of efforts, city and county governments should maintain a central information file for all public services dealing with families. If this is not practical, each agency should use initiative in screening their day-to-day workload for information of probable interest to other agencies. For example, copies of all police reports of suspected child abuse, drug abuse by a parent or unusually aggressive parental behavior, in terms of frequency or violence, should automatically be forwarded to the child protective agency. The child protective agency should share an up-to-date list of abusive families, who are receiving treatment, with the law enforcement agency so that reports of any and all subsequent police encounters with these families are duly forwarded for consideration.

THE POLICE IN INVESTIGATION AND EVALUATION*

Current police training and experience in standard criminal investigation practices must be recognized as inadequate preparation for child abuse cases when child welfare and family rehabilitation are accepted goals. On the other hand, certain other attributes cultivated by this training and experience, such as techniques of observation, familiarity with rules of evidence, and testimonial competence, are particularly valuable in the investigation process, especially if juvenile family court proceedings or criminal trials result. Police also have the legal authority to enter a home, remove a child or make an arrest when there is a need and reasonable grounds. There is every reason to believe that police practices and the implementation of the social worker's expertise in family problems are compatible and mutually beneficial.

Joint investigations of serious cases of child abuse are a practical means of capitalizing on the strengths of both professions. The viewpoint of the police investigator, grounded in realism,

*The editors appreciate that some of the suggestions made by Major Pitcher go far beyond the "tried and true" of police work. Their inclusion emphasizes our strong feeling that their adaption, even though difficult, would benefit all concerned, especially the battered child and his family.

would probably also create a desirable balance with that of
the social worker, who sometimes tends to be overly optimistic
in assessing the degree of child danger and potential for change
within the abusive families. In addition to preventing antagonistic parallel investigations due to overlapping areas of responsibility and activity, joint investigations have the added
advantage of encouraging interagency cooperation in sharing
information from files and sources available to each, which are
often quite different.

Some would argue against providing the police with the
identification and other information pertaining to abusive families that is developed by the child protective agency. Such
argument is usually based on the view that community prejudice against child abusers is detrimental to any attempts at
family therapy and that confidentiality of casework within the
sphere of the social work profession is therefore justified. Certainly the confidential nature of such information must be re-
spected to enhance the possibilities of successful casework,
but unnecessary restrictions should not be imposed at the cost
of a comprehensive, cooperative child protection program. The
police have an equal interest in achieving the goals of the program, and their potential value in this area is great. This cannot be fully exploited, nor can wholehearted interagency cooperation be long maintained, if communications are completely
one-sided. Law enforcement agencies are equally well experienced in working with confidential information.

The social work and medical professions have also tendered
arguments against active police participation in cases of physical abuse of children, other than homicides or incidents, that
are unusually severe or heinous. Concern with parental defensiveness and attenuation of receptiveness to therapy engendered by uniformed "authority figures" with badges[9] is easily
negated by the use of plainclothes police investigators. Since
battering parents are generally suspicious by nature and are
seldom positively motivated toward seeking outside help,[10] it
is doubtful if a civilian-attired police investigator, who identifies himself as an officer, would substantially increase a parent's

negative reaction over that which he would feel with a social caseworker. Indeed, there is some indication that a suggestion of authority may even be beneficial.[11]

The argument against standard police investigative practices, except where criminal prosecution is the desired goal, is valid however.[12] Consequently, police officers assigned to the investigation of child abuse cases should be carefully selected and specially trained. A sufficient number of investigators should be qualified within a law enforcement agency to allow for their availability around the clock, seven days a week, through a shift or on-call arrangement.

Individuals selected for this duty, whether full-time or as an additional duty, should be chosen not only for experience and competence but also for attitude. They should be cooperative and understanding, have a sincere interest in helping children and troubled families, and possess good judgement. Tradition bound and "hard-nosed cops" would not be desirable candidates.

Training of these police investigators in all aspects of child abuse, including the treatment strategy, should be intensive and continuous. The formal instruction should be conducted by highly qualified and experienced social welfare personnel and physicians, to insure the quality and timeliness of material presented as well as to foster interagency respect and an appreciation of other agencies' views and problems. Periodic meetings of agency executives, caseworkers and police investigators to discuss problems and establish working policy are beneficial in achieving program ends.

In large law enforcement agencies with specialized functions, assignment of these special investigators would most logically be with the juvenile unit. Their duties would center around coordinating law enforcement activities in the area of child welfare with the child protective agency, and the joint investigation of serious child injuries suspected of being caused by a parent or other caretaker. When child protective agency services are not available, due to resource limitations, these special investigators should respond to all reports of suspected child abuse. Other duties include liaison with police patrols in the field, securing evidence from child abuse cases, case findings, and maintaining special files of proven and suspected cases to allow for timely response to inquiries from law enforcement agencies of other jurisdictions. These investigators would also serve warrants and make arrests in such cases, as required; and also, upon request, they would escort child protective workers performing casework with particularly hostile families or in especially high crime areas. In some communities it may even be desirable for the police office to initiate and file the dependency petition in family court.

To avoid conflict between child protective agency caseworkers and police investigators on joint investigations, a working balance must be struck. Police investigators should have prime responsibility and investigative dominance in cases of homicide; wanton child torture, such as multiple cigarette burns; in cases where the parent or guardian has an extensive police record for other offenses; and when the suspected abuser is someone other than a member of the child's family. Examples of the latter would be paramours or babysitters. In all other cases the child protective agency caseworker would have the responsibility of directing the family investigation, including timing and technique of questioning.

Police investigative efforts in serious cases of abuse should center around determining whether an incident of physical abuse of a child did in fact occur, and the circumstances surrounding the incident. Concern with identifying the perpetrator and establishing proof sufficient for prosecution should be secondary. Active participation should be limited to necessary nonthreatening questions for clarification, careful observation, and minimal collection of physical evidence done as unobtrusively as possible.* The latter activity should be necessary primarily where an instrument has been used. Photographs and written statements should be taken at the time of initial intervention only if absolutely necessary, but notes should be jotted down and expanded into final form as soon as possible after departure from the residence.

*See Chapters 4 and 5 for a complete discussion on data gathering.

An important determination at initial intervention is the need for emergency removal of the child from the home. This assessment is based on the hazard to the child if left with his family. Where a child bears visible signs of injury it should be routine procedure to have him admitted to a hospital for medical evaluation and treatment. Where there are no observable physical signs of abuse, the decision on emergency removal must rest with the child welfare caseworker.

Immediately upon completion of the initial investigation, the child protective agency caseworker and police investigator should compare and evaluate available information and coordinate the further investigative activity required. The caseworker should screen available welfare files while the police investigator, working through routine police channels, including questioning of local police patrol officers, should look for indications of parental deviant behavior in the past. Responsibility for questioning neighbors and for extended family interviews, in order to try to substantiate suspicions, should also be determined at this time.

The police, often being involved in the most urgent of situations, continually have to set priorities. It is imperative that the child be protected. Many of the points made elsewhere in this book will be helpful to a police officer to obtain the knowledge and skills required to establish these priorities. Protecting abused children is imperative; doing it in such a manner that a positive therapeutic program is thereby developed is another matter.

THE POLICE IN DISPOSITION AND FOLLOW-UP

It is imperative that police child abuse investigators establish and maintain close and continuous liaison with the public prosecutor. Where the public prosecutor's office is large, with a number of appointed assistant prosecutors, only one should be designated to receive reports of child abuse offenses to insure continuity of disposition.

When a criminal statute has been violated, as is nearly always the case in incidents of child abuse, the investigating police officer is responsible for filing a report of all the facts surrounding the offense with the public prosecutor. The prosecutor makes the final determination whether the perpetrator will be prosecuted. This is based on the substantiability of available evidence, the balance of interests of the child, offending parent and community at large, available alternative means of disposition and limitations on prosecution resources. His decision to prosecute may be made at any time after a criminal statute has been violated within the period defined by the statute of limitations of the jurisdiction in which the act was committed. It is essential that the prosecutor be provided with all available information pertaining to a particular child abuse incident to assist him in making this determination in the best interests of all concerned.

Child abuse is a complex phenomenon involving a diversity of etiologic factors and varying degrees of pathology of family interrelationships. Each case must be considered individually in determining the appropriate course of action that best meets the needs of the child, the family and the community. These dispositional decisions can be best made by a combined community team representing legitimate interests in the abused child and his family. At the minimum, it should consist of the child protective agency caseworker, investigating police officer, attending physician, a representative of the prosecuting attorney's office, someone who represents the abused child, and a public or private counsel for the parent. A single course of action should be established for disposition and follow-up of the case to include decisions on the need for petitioning the juvenile/family court for temporary or permanent removal of the child from the family and whether criminal prosecution or family treatment by the child protective agency will be the vehicle of implementation.

The public prosecutor has a great deal of flexibility in disposing of cases, which is too often overlooked when child abuse is involved. He has the power to settle cases informally prior to bringing charges against an offender as well as through the traditional trial process.[18] Based on the merits of a particular case, he may well defer prosecution of the abusive parent and impose conditions of "unofficial probation" for a given period if the offender concurs with such a settlement. To derive the benefits from informal case disposition it is essential that the community team approach to the abusive family be based on a thorough investigation and be well planned and coordinated.

In the occasional case where prosecuting an abusive parent under the criminal statutes is considered to be the appropriate course of action, such a decision should include an understanding that the law enforcement agency acquires full responsibility for the case, the development of evidence and establishment of required elements of proof through standard criminal investigation practices. The child protective agency should fully cooperate in this endeavor. On the other hand, when criminal prosecution is not deemed necessary, active police participation in the case should normally terminate except for providing assistance in juvenile family court proceedings and being alert for further developments with the family. The advantage of two different professional views, instead of one, in either criminal prosecution or juvenile family court proceedings is obvious.

Law enforcement agencies should be informed of all reported child abuse cases within their geographical jurisdictions regardless of whether or not they are serious enough to warrant active police involvement. Forearmed with this information and training, the uniformed patrol officer can remain particularly vigilant for indications of child maltreatment in these families in his area while in the performance of his regular day-to-day duties.

The role of the law enforcement agency in cases of child abuse that has been espoused in the foregoing pages is currently feasible in all geographical areas of the nation, either rural or urban, and in both civilian and military settings. The police must be recognized and accepted as an important and valuable member of every community team to counter the social problem presented by abusive families. It is time that the police review their approach to child abuse and redirect their substantial resources toward meeting this challenge as part of a coordinated team effort. Only through complete cooperation can the potential of all available community resources be achieved in successfully protecting innocent and helpless children from the brutality of their caretakers. Only when this goal has been attained will the concerned public agencies have fulfilled their responsibilities to the children, families and communities they serve.

REFERENCES

1. Swanson, Lynn D.: Role of the police in the protection of children from neglect and abuse. Fed Probation 25:43, March, 1961.
2. Silver, Larry B.: Child abuse syndrome: A review. Med Times 96:816, Aug., 1968.
3. Paulsen, Monrad G.: The legal framework for child protection. Columbia Law Rev 66:680, April, 1966.
4. *Op. cit.*, ref. 2, pp. 814-815.
5. Class, Norris E.: Neglect, social deviance, and community action. Nat Probation and Parole Ass 6:22, Jan., 1960.
6. Myren, Richard A., and Swanson, Lynn D.: Police Work With Children: Perspectives and Principles, U.S. Government Printing Office, Washington (D.C.), 1962, p. 59.
7. Holter, Joan C., and Friedman, Stanford B.: Principles of management in child abuse cases. Amer J Orthopsychiat 38:133, Jan., 1968.
8. *Op. cit.*, ref. 1, p. 44.
9. *Op. cit.*, ref. 2, p. 817.
10. Court, Joan: The battered child. Part I: Historical and diagnostic reflections. Part II: Reflections on treatment. Med Social Work 22:9, April, 1969.
11. Cheney, Kimberly B.: A Suggested Statute and Policy for Child Welfare Protective Services in Connecticut: A Report for the Legislature, May, 1964, p. 84. (N.p. State of Connecticut, 1964.)
12. Paulsen, Morris J., and Blake, Phillip R.: The abused, and battered and maltreated child: A review. Trauma 9:78, Dec., 1967.
13. Task Force on Administration of Justice, The President's Commission in Law Enforcement and Administration of Justice. Task Force Report: The Courts, U.S. Government Printing Office, Washington (D.C.), 1967, pp. 4-13.

17

The District Attorney

ROGER ALLOTT, LL.B.

THE ROLE of the district attorney in child abuse cases is frequently an uncomfortable one. He is caught between the public, clamoring for prosecution of the child abuser, and his own knowledge that a full and vigorous prosecution of the child abuser may neither protect the child from further abuse nor rehabilitate the child abuser.

When a child has died or where the investigation revealed a continued and prolonged period of abuse, thereby causing great injury to the child strongly indicating criminal intent, the district attorney may have no choice but to proceed with a complete criminal trial. With the exception of cases of this nature, a prosecutor has available alternatives to protect the child victim and hopefully rehabilitate the child abuser.

The El Paso County (Colorado) District Attorney's Office, in dealing with a child abuse case, assigns first priority to the protection of the abused child. This concept of protection is a primary consideration during all stages of a case from the initial report to the final conclusion. The priority of ensuring the child's safety and welfare gives the District Attorney's Office a readily available standard on which to base its actions and provides a logical answer when questions arise from the court, the press or the public as to why the district attorney had taken such an action.

This priority is made known to all of the local agencies involved, including the welfare department, sheriff's deputies, police officers, doctors, hospitals and juvenile courts. Having a stated goal from the District Attorney's Office assists all personnel who might be involved in a child abuse case and gives them a frame of reference from which to work while they carry out their various responsibilities.

In order to follow this concept of protection, the district attorney must maintain continuous coordination between the various agencies involved in each case. Frequently the police and welfare agencies may work in opposite directions and fail to exchange information. The district attorney must encourage the free exchange of information, thereby assuring greater cooperation between all concerned. As this cooperation grows, mutual respect for the responsibilities of each agency also develops, and protection of the battered child is much easier to accomplish.

Certain guidelines for law enforcement officers investigating a case of child abuse are necessary. Believing a thorough and impartial investigation of each case to be absolutely necessary, we insist upon prompt reports from the welfare department, hospitals or doctors so that an immediate investigation can be accomplished. Schools and private citizens are also encouraged to make reports.

The basic procedures for this investigation are as follows. An officer, usually in civilian clothes, is asked to:

1. Make a preliminary investigation to determine whether there is any basis for the report on child abuse. This is usually accomplished by talking to the party making the complaint.

2. When the investigating officer is satisfied that there is a basis for the report he will move into the second phase of the investigation. The officer is required to observe the allegedly injured child even if this requires entry without a warrant. The word of the caretaker as to the child's condition must not be considered sufficient.

3. In the event the child has suffered injuries which can be photographed, color pictures are recommended. (Any weapons or objects used to inflict the injuries are to be taken into custody and retained as evidence.)

4. On completion of the investigation, if the officer, using reasonable judgment, feels that the child is endangered in his surroundings, and following the test of the state's statutes, he should forthwith remove the child from the endangering environment and place him in temporary custody of the welfare department or hospital.

This procedure places a heavy responsibility upon the investigator who frequently is young and inexperienced. In spite of this, these officers are most effective in carrying out their responsibilities when given specific guidelines and support. The investigations also provide a method for obtaining immediate protection and necessary medical attention for the battered child. The officers are encouraged to direct their investigation with consideration for the child's welfare rather than to determine who might have been the guilty person.

A complete report is forwarded to the District Attorney's Office and the Child Welfare Department. Rarely is there any disagreement with the officer's action. These reports provide the basis for later prosecution or civil court proceedings if they are necessary to protect an abused child, and frequently guarantee that an infant who is unable to testify in court will have his or her side of the story presented to the court.

When it becomes impossible to remove a child from the endangering environment, the district attorney, where the evidence in his opinion is sufficient to establish probable cause to believe that a crime has been committed, can have the alleged child abuser held for investigation of the criminal offense and thereby protect the child by removing the danger from the environment. This procedure is not recommended although it may be effective in temporarily protecting a battered child when other alternatives open to the district attorney fail.

Once the case has been investigated and the necessary measures are taken to protect the child temporarily, the decision of how to proceed toward a final disposition must be reached. Considerations include the facilities available for treatment of a battering parent or caretaker; the financial resources available for such treatment; the attitude of the battering parent; the character of the beating; previous treatment of the parent; what care and protection can be guaranteed the child during the period of treatment of the parent or caretaker; and possible court supervision which can be imposed. This decision can best be made in conjunction with the Child Welfare Department, which is charged with the ultimate responsibility of the protection of the child. On rare occasion, the district attorney may not agree with the welfare department. This usually occurs when it is felt that the welfare program will not protect the child. If it is impossible to reach an agreement on a therapeutic program, the district attorney can overrule the welfare department and file criminal charges and proceed accordingly.

The filing or potential filing of criminal charges can sometimes be used to encourage abusive parents to obtain needed treatment. Once the treatment program has been started, and the child protected by orders of the juvenile court, the criminal charges can be temporarily deferred until the ultimate goal of treatment is reached, whereupon the charges can be dismissed. The district attorney, with the concurrence of the court and defendant, may defer criminal charges for approximately one year. However, with the present delay in criminal trials, the four to six months wait is usually sufficient to determine if the civil proceeding will be helpful.

In the event a decision is reached to prosecute, there are certain legal entanglements which must be faced. The following comments about some of these entanglements are based on a legal memorandum presented to the members of the Colorado District Attorney's Association. Some of this material may also be of help to welfare attorneys in proceedings to obtain an adjudication that a child has been battered. Even though the material was prepared for Colorado courts it will provide a starting point for research in other jurisdictions.

The corpus delicti is a major hurdle in most child abuse cases since most caretakers will make a self-serving declaration to explain that the injuries to the child happened accidentally. Frequently, the child will be unable to state how the injury occurred. It is well settled in Colorado that a corpus delicti consists of two components: (1) injury and/or death; (2) criminal agency of another as the means. Each of these elements must be established by the prosecution to the jury beyond a reasonable doubt. The court, however, is not the judge of the weight of the evidence. When sufficient evidence has been produced to justify a submission to the jury and support a verdict of guilty, should such a verdict be returned thereon, the requirements of the law have been met. This rule applies to each of the elements of the corpus delicti as it does to the proof of the identity of the accused as the perpetrator; no more, no less. Lowe v. People, 76 Colo 603; 234 P 169 @ 173. Circumstantial evidence is sufficient to establish the corpus delicti in a homicide case if it is such as to prove the essentials thereof to a REASONABLE CERTAINTY. *Downey v. People,* 121 Colo 307, 215 P2d 892 (1950), citing with approval *Bruner v. People,* 113 Colo 194, 156 P2d 111 @ 117 (1945).

Thus, it would appear that even a case based on circumstantial evidence would have a good chance of surviving a motion for a directed verdict if the circumstances are sufficiently strong. In child abuse cases these circumstances may include the findings during the autopsy, x-rays of the long bones of the child, prior severe whippings, exclusive custody and control of the decedent by the accused, and the implausible explanations for the injuries.

The leading Colorado cases are Bishop and Balltrip, briefs of which are presented later in this chapter. The following cases from other jurisdictions in this regard:

People v. Hopper, 302 P2d 94 (Cal 1958). Defendant said child fell from car, but doctors said the injuries were not consistent with this explanation.

Iowa v. Tornquist, 120 NW 2d 483 (Iowa 1963). Child was killed by a blow of some sort and evidence showed prior severe whippings up to two years before death. Held: sufficient to go to jury.

Pettigrew v. Oklahoma, 346 P2d 95 (Okla 1959). The court held that doctor's testimony and autopsy findings were sufficient to show child died by unnatural or violent means.

Corbin v. State, 234 NE 2d 261 (Indiana 1968). The court evidence of autopsy report and prior acts of beating were sufficient to sustain verdict.

Hutchinson v. State, 255 NE 2d 828 (Indiana 1967). Evidence of prior injuries to child and fatal whipping with belt was held sufficient to sustain conviction.

People v. Jacobson, 405 P2d 555 (Cal 1965). The court held a prima facie showing of corpus delicti had been made. "To meet the foundational test the prosecution need not eliminate all inferences tending to show a non-criminal cause of death. Rather, the foundation may be laid by the introduction of evidence which creates a reasonable inference that the death could have been caused by a criminal agency . . . even in the presence of an equally plausible non-criminal explanation of the event." @ 560, 561.

People v. Jones, 9 Cal Rptr 500 (1960). The court said that in prosecution for murder of a three-year-old boy who had been placed in defendant's care by his mother, question of whether death of boy occurred as result of unlawful means was for jury and jury was under no compulsion to believe story of defendant that boy had hurt his head by running into a door jamb.

People v. Brown, 228 NE 2d 495 (Ill 1967). The court held that in child death case that circumstantial evidence need not establish prosecution's case beyond possibility of doubt.

State v. Bodi, 354 P2d 831 (Oregon 1960). Autopsy findings were ample evidence to make out corpus delicti when tied to other evidence in the case.

State v. Silva, 134 A2d 628 (Maine 1957) The court said that jury is entirely justified in giving more weight to probabilities as to causation of traumatic injuries than to mere possibilities, and question of whether injuries were accidental or result of criminal agency was for jury.

Cornell v. State, 105 Co 2d 695 (Ala 1958). The court said that prosecution does not have to prove beyond reasonable doubt that death did not result from an accident, suicide or natural causes, but is required to show only a reasonable probability that a criminal act of another was the cause of death.

State v. Parmenter, 444 P2d 680 (Wash 1968). Conviction was sustained despite defendant's evidence that child habitually fell and evidence of some neighbors that they never saw the child abused.

It is well settled in Colorado that evidence of other crimes or prior transactions are admissible when such evidence tends to establish the particular crime, prove motive, prove intent, prove absence of mistake or accident, prove plan, design or scheme, or prove the identity of the person charged with the commission of the crime on trial. *Schneider v. People*, 118 Colo 543, 199 P2d 873 @ 877 (1948).

In child abuse cases it would appear that evidence of prior abuse such as whippings, abandonment, partiality toward other siblings and other abuse would be admissible.

This would appear to be particularily true in a homicide prosecution to show that the blows were struck with malice. Proof of malice includes the *quo animo* of the defendant, that is the intent, motive or state of mind which led to the fatal blows being struck. Habitual mistreatment of the child of the defendant goes a long way toward convincing the jury that the injuries suffered by the deceased were nonaccidental in nature and tends to show that the caretaker did in fact strike the fatal blows. As to the admissibility of prior acts see the following cases: *Coates v. People*, 106 Colo 483, 106 P2d 354 (1940); *Jaynes v. People*, 44 Colo 535, 99 P 325 (1909); *Berger v. People*, 122 Colo 367, 224, P2d 228 (1950); *Warford v. People*, 43 Colo 107, 96 P 556 (1908); *Clews v. People*, 377 P2d 125 (Colo 1962); *People v. Brown*, 228 NE 2d 495 (Ill 1967); *People v. Lint*, 6 Cal Rptr 95 (Cal 1960); *Clark v. State*, 208

So 2d 637 (Texas 1948); *Commonwealth v. Nelson*, 152 A2d 913 (Pa 1959); *State v. Cauley*, 94 SE 2d 915 (N.C. 1956); *Betts v. State*, 124 SW 424 (Texas 1909).

The test for remoteness of prior acts is whether the evidence offered is so remote in time as to rob it of any probative value. Generally, courts have held that the difference in time between the happening of the event sought to be shown and the act with which the defendant is charged goes to the weight but not admissibility of the evidence. *Berger v. People*, 122 Colo 367, 224 P2d 228 (1950); *Max v. People*, 78 Colo 178, 240 P 697 (1925); *State v. Tornquist*, 120 NW 2d 483 (Iowa 1963).

LEADING CHILD ABUSE CASES

Bishop v. People 439 P2d 342 (Colo 1968)

FACTS

Defendant convicted of second-degree murder of three-year-old stepson based entirely on circumstantial evidence. Evidence showed that the deceased was picked up by the defendant at the grandmother's home in good health without any marks or injuries. Approximately five to six hours later the father called the fire rescue unit which arrived and found the child suffering from severe trauma from which the child died very shortly. The child's physical condition as established by an autopsy was a lacerated liver, transected pancreas, a fractured skull, and bruises on various parts of the child's body. The defendant testified that after leaving the grandmother's house, he and the child had breakfast and took a nap. Upon awakening, the defendant found the child had vomited and had a bowel movement in his pants. Previously that morning he had reprimanded the child by slapping him twice on the buttocks. He claimed that no other punishment had been administered. After finding the child had had a bowel movement in his pants, he placed the child on a toilet seat to clean the child and left the bathroom to get clean clothes. When he returned to the bathroom he found the child on the floor with its head resting against the back of the tub. The child was unconscious. The father said he called the resuscitator and attempted to administer artificial respiration.

POINTS OF INTEREST

1. Malice was required in this case and the defendant's attitude and conduct toward the deceased were both material and relevant for jury determination. An instruction upon an attack of an infant or person of tender years, that malice can be implied from such an attack, was upheld.

2. Defendant argued that the instruction was a correct statement of law (see Balltrip), but that there was absolutely no evidence of any attack upon the child by the defendant. The testimony of the pathologists was that the injuries that the child suffered were consistent with the force of a fist or foot, and that the possibility was extremely remote that such injuries could have been caused by artificial respiration administered by the defendant.

● ● ●

Balltrip v. People, 401 P2d 259, (Colo 1965)

FACTS

Defendant was charged with the death of a three-year-old son of his common-law wife. The defendant had the care and custody of the deceased. At approximately 5:00 P.M., while the wife was at work, neighbors observed the defendant swinging clenched fists at something. At that time a child was heard crying very loudly and people observed the defendant pick up a child and place it on a couch where the witnesses could not see the child, but could then see a fist swinging in the general area where the child had been placed. Shortly thereafter the defendant rushed to the neighbors and stated the child was delirious. The neighbors found the child to be unconscious, and the child later died. Medical testimony at the trial indicated the death was caused by external head injuries to the child. The defendant contended that the child had received head injuries when it fell off a couch and struck his head on a nearby stove.

RULINGS OF THE COURT

1. Murder by one spouse of the other's child is a crime committed by one spouse against the other, and the husband and wife privilege under C.R.S. 153-1-7 does not apply.

2. The court permitted the use of an instruction on implied malice where there is an assault on a child of tender years.

3. The conflicting medical testimony as to how the injuries to the child could have occurred is a jury question as to whether such injuries were caused by blows or falls.

● ● ●

McConnell v. State, 105 So 2d 695 (Ala 1958)

FACTS

Prosecution of mother for first-degree manslaughter of her four-year-old daughter. The mother and father brought the child to the doctor's office at which time she was found unconscious with very obvious brain or spinal column injuries. The child died and an autopsy was performed, revealing several lacerations of the brain which were caused by separate and distinct traumata to the head. The mother stated that she had punished the child many times and would hit her head against a wall, but that she had not done so recently nor during the period immediately before the child had entered the hospital. She stated that the child had fallen off a bed on that date. There was evidence from other witnesses as to whippings that had been administered to the child by the defendant.

RULINGS OF THE COURT

1. Evidence from a neurosurgeon and other medical experts indicating that the injuries causing the death resulted from separate forces applied to the head is prima facie death as a result of a criminal act of another.

2. That in the prosecution of a mother for death of her child the people are entitled to bring out all facts and circumstances leading up to the assult as they tend to show the animus of the mother. The people may show the fact the mother whipped the child on prior occasions, but could not show the details of those events.

● ● ●

State v. Silva, 134 A2d 628 (Maine 1957)

FACTS

The defendant was charged with the death of a 16-month-old stepson who died as a result of injuries. The child's medical history revealed he was extremely neglected by the natural mother for the first three months of his life. He was adopted by the defendant and her husband shortly thereafter. At that time the child suffered from malnourishment and was in the early stages of rickets. These afflictions were corrected with no adverse effects on the bone structure of the child, and no evidence of fractures was found. Two months later, at the age of five months, the child was treated for a cold and the doctor noticed a swelling in the area of the left thigh. He found a complete fracture of the femur which had started to heal. The child was hospitalized. The parents claimed they didn't know how the injury happened, other than to state that the child had been riding in a car which had stopped suddenly and the chair in which the baby was seated tipped over. The child was 16 months old when the doctor saw him again. The child was in a state of shock and died of a severe head injury. According to the parents, the child had fallen accidentally from a high chair. Based on the autopsy, and the previous history when the child was in the hospital, the evidence came forth that the child had suffered from multiple and repeated injuries.

RULINGS OF THE COURT

1. The defendant claimed that the child died as a result of an unfortunate accident or accidents. The court ruled that the jury had in effect said that this was not rational or reasonable to believe and that proper inferences can be drawn from the number of the injuries.

2. The court pointed out that many crimes of this nature are committed in secret and, in such a case, the state must forge a chain of circumstances proving each essential link beyond a reasonable doubt, as in this case where there was no rational alternative except guilt.

3. A jury was entirely justified in giving the more weight to the probabilities as to the causation of nonaccidental traumatic injuries than to mere possibilities.

4. A history of old injuries has probative value in determining whether an accidental causation has been eliminated beyond a reasonable doubt. For a child to have received any one of the serious injuries described above solely as the result of an accident in the course of its comparatively sheltered, circumscribed life would be abnormal. As those abnormal results are multiplied instance upon instance, the likelihood of accidental causation diminishes to the vanishing point.

5. The court found that it was entirely proper for the jury to have evidence as to the relationship between the defendant and the child.

APPENDIX A

EDITORIAL NOTE

The development of reliable and valid methods to identifying potentially abusive parents will be of significant benefit to the early implementation of a meaningful therapeutic program. This study has been underway for three years and the Preliminary Report is presented to assist those who might be interested in this form of research.

The reader should be cautioned: This questionnaire is still in its *developmental stage* and has not yet been completely validated. It *cannot* be used, as yet, for other than research purposes.

The Predictive Questionnaire: A Preliminary Report

Carol Schneider, Ph.D., Ray E. Helfer, M.D., and Carl Pollock, M.D.

For the past three years, efforts have been made to design and validate a questionnaire with the goal of uncovering parents who have the potential to abuse their small children. The ideal questionnaire would be a short, self-administered instrument yielding a score which would clearly identify a person as an abuser or a nonabuser. Unfortunately, the ideal questionnaire will never be available for many reasons. An inherent problem in asking people questions is their tendency to respond with answers which are not necessarily true indicators of their feelings, but which may reflect feelings which are socially desirable. Thus, even though abusers may have specific attitudes which differentiate them from normal, their answers to a paper-and-pencil test may not reflect these attitudes.

Answering an objective attitude questionnaire requires that a conscious awareness of feelings be present. It is possible that many abusers do not know that they have certain resentments or feelings. The complexities of human personality make it probable that a test would find various combinations of feelings or traits in abusers and nonabusers. Instead of a totally homogeneous group, where a score above a certain level would indicate the abusive potential, it is more likely that, if a person has abnormal responses to certain *clusters of questions*, we might say he has the potential for abusing children. If this is true, then a normal person could answer any or many of several questions as would an abuser, but not have the proper combination of answers which would give him an answer profile identifying him as a potential abuser.

This research thus far indicates that known abusers are distinguished from normals, in part, by the extreme variability of their answers to questions in several attitude areas. The crucial areas where combinations involving attitudes of abusers and nonabusers can be differentiated at the present time are: Feelings of loneliness and isolation, expectations for performance of their children, relationships with own parents and spouse, and feelings of anxiety in response to children's behavior.

Rather than reaching the goal of defining a potential abuser by an overall score, the most successful approach will probably lie in first defining a normal person as having *scores which lie within a certain specified range on these crucial attitude areas.* Once the normal profile range is specified, any person's score can be plotted with respect to this profile, and the number of deviations of his scores from normal limits in these crucial areas noted. Any person with perhaps two or more standard deviations from the normal mean will then need a personal screening interview by a trained professional to ascertain the degree to which he presents a danger to his or her children. Thus, we can identify a person as having scores which deviate from normal to the extent that his potential for abusing should be individually assessed. (See Chapter 4 for suggested screening interview techniques.)

The most reasonable goal seems to be to develop a self-administering instrument that identifies all known abusers as having scores outside the normal profiles, and no more than 4 percent (i.e., 2 standard deviations from the mean) of so called normals as potential abusers. Simply identifying which people should receive further screening would be an accomplishment in terms of savings in professional time, protecting small children and identifying those families which need special care.

PRELIMINARY QUESTIONNAIRES

The search for a screening device began by administering two preliminary instruments to 30 known abusers and 30 persons classified as nonabusing normals. One instrument was a semantic differential checklist which required an individual to indicate for various adjective dimensions, such as friendly-unfriendly, on a 7 point scale, point 1 (in this example) representing very friendly and point 7 very unfriendly. With this, we hoped to measure differences between abusers and nonabusers on attitudes toward self.

The other instrument was administered by an interviewer who recorded responses to several questions in the attitude areas of parental expectations of children's behavior, personal feelings of isolation and loneliness, responses to children's behavior, and the past and present relationship of the child's parents to their own parents. Each of the responses to these open-ended questions was scored on a relevant dimension to yield numerically analyzable results. For example, responses to "How were you punished as a child?" were scored a zero for no physical punishment, 1 for mild physical punishment, 2 for moderate and 3 for severe. Such scaling was a subjective judgment on the part of the trained rater. Using the Chi Square Test, those questions which were answered significantly differently by abusers and nonabusers were identified.

In an effort to create a self-administering questionnaire for the next phase of the research, the questions were reworded in a form where the judgments on the part of the person responding would replace the interviewer's subjective views. For example, because known abusers were judged to have described receiving more severe physical punishment as children than nonabusers, the statement, "As a child I received severe physical punishment," was included in the next form of the questionnaire. Persons were then asked to agree or disagree with this statement on a 7 point scale from "strongly agree to strongly disagree." The reader should note that this step is necessary to transform an open-ended response question into a self-administering objective questionnaire item.

Questions which show significant differences between abusers and nonabusers in the interview form may not show these differences in the self-administering form. An interviewer may judge descriptions of punishment to be more or less severe than the abusers themselves judge such punishment. There is no guarantee that the abuser himself will judge the punishment in the same way as an interviewing rater. The researcher must take the risk of encountering such probems in self-administering questionnaires, or else be prepared to expend the necessary personnel for individual interviews where screening is desired. One of the methods used to help resolve such a problem is to ask a duplicate interview question in several different ways in the self-administering questionnaire, in the hopes that at least one way of asking it will produce the desired differentiating response. It is the necessity of doing just this which mitigates against a successful *short* self-administering questionnaire in the initial phases of research devoted to questionnaire development.

This second research effort, then, consisted of designing a self-administering instrument on the basis of the qualitative and quantitative results from the first effort. The attitude areas in which questions were asked were exactly the same as in that first effort. Attention was paid to having several questions in each attitude area so that stable, reliable scores might be obtained in each area. Additional questions were added to the second instrument as more clinical experience was gained.

The major instrument in Study 2 was an 82-item questionnaire, consisting of short statements to which the parent was asked to respond by indicating his or her degree of agreement on a 7 point Likert scale, from "strongly agree to strongly disagree."

In gathering the data, a 30 person nonabusive control group was *matched* with our second known abusive group cf 30 on the basis of parent age, education, socioeconomic status, number of children in the family, and presence in the family of a referent child of the same age as the child who had been abused. This matching was not done in the first study, where secretaries and medical students' wives comprised the nonabusive group. The importance of proper matching of normal and abusing groups must be stressed. Differing expectations of children and attitudes toward child rearing are a function of parent age, education and social class.[1] Because of the failure to consider such variables in the first study, we had little idea whether the significant differences were due to personality differences between abusers and nonabusers, between social classes or if they were due to some other unmatched factor.

RESULTS

Even though no matching was done, the statistical findings from this first study agreed with psychiatric predictions, e.g., the parents who beat their small children reported significantly more severe physical punishment in their own childhood, more anxiety about dealing with their children's problems, more concern about being alone and isolated, more concern with criticism, and higher expectations for performance for their children than did the normal controls. There still remained the suspicion that the psychiatrists had predicted these findings on the basis of comparisons of their abusive patients with the vast majority of their other patients, who are probably socioeconomically and intellectually closer to the medical students' wives than to most of the abusers. If stable differences in the predicted direction between responses of abusers and matched normal controls were found in the second study, then these findings would clearly be unrelated to socioeconomic variables. Such differences would delineate measurable personality characteristics which could be used in defining potential abusers.

On the basis of Chi Square tests in the second study, 32 items showed no potential for discriminating between abusers and nonabusers (p values exceeding .10) and were excluded from further analysis. The remaining 50 responses for the 60 combined abusers and controls were subjected to a cluster analysis using the Tryon-Bailey system.[2] This exceedingly complex system seeks to group into clusters those questions with similar patterns of intercorrelations.

The cluster is a group of related test items. If each subject responds to several items in the same way, i.e., she agrees with all or disagrees with all, these items will form a cluster. Clusters are sought containing items which are related to one another for the entire subject sample, both abusers and matched normals. Having discovered these clusters, legitimate statistical questions can then be asked. If cluster scores on items which are related for the entire subject sample are considered, then will the cluster scores for the abusers be significantly different from the cluster scores for the normals? Since our clusters contain questions which show a consistent, related response pattern for both groups, then any significant differences on cluster scores found between abusers and normals must show that abusers consistently respond in a different direction (e.g., all agree) from the direction in which the normals consistently respond (e.g., all disagree). If one does not combine both normals and abusers for the questionnaire analysis, but instead clusters the abusers alone, the result would be clusters which contain item responses that are consistent and related for abusers only. We would have no idea if normals also answered these questions consistently. Then statistical comparisons of abusers' and normals' cluster scores would run into logical difficulties.

As an example of how this analysis works, let us consider how a hypothesis was tested—that the abuser group has higher expectations for performance from their children than does the matched group of normal controls. First, 10 items having to do with expectations of children were included in the questionnaire. (See Table 1, Cluster 2, for examples of these items.) In the next step, a cluster analysis is used to discover whether the whole population under consideration (abusers and nonabusers) responded to some or all of these items in a consistent way. Perfect consistency in this case would occur if each subject answers all the expectation items in the same way, i.e., there is complete agreement among all subjects answering these 10 items. Such consistently answered items would have high correlations with each other and the computer program would identify these as belonging to a single cluster which could be labeled "expectations," since this was the meaning of the items appearing in the cluster. (Note: The cluster will normally not include *all* 10 expectation items, only those with high intercorrelations.) After forming the first cluster, the analysis continues to examine all possible combinations of other item responses, seeking additional clusters of consistently answered items. The cluster analysis of the second questionnaire yielded four major clusters (see Table 1).

TABLE 1. *Sample Items from Clusters*

CLUSTER 1—ISOLATION AND LONELINESS
  I like myself.
  People are always criticizing me (reflected).°
  I am close to others.
  I am a warm person.

CLUSTER 2—EXPECTATIONS OF CHILDREN
  Children are ready to be toilet trained at one year of age.
  I expect too much of my children (reflected).
  If parents don't expect a lot of their children, they won't be successful.

CLUSTER 3—RELATIONSHIP TO THEIR PARENTS AND CHILDREN
  Most women remain close to their mother after marriage.
  I would describe my relationship to my mother as very close.
  At least one of my children reminds me of someone I don't like (reflected).
  People say one should automatically feel love for their children but it's not that easy (reflected).

CLUSTER 4—UPSET AND ANGRY
  When my baby cries, I often feel like crying.
  People become very upset and angry when they are fed up with their children.
  Children are easily spoiled by others and then give trouble to their parents.
  I am afraid of many things.

  °The term "reflected" indicates that a person agreeing with the other items in this cluster will disagree with the reflected item.

The fact that our questionnaire contains stable clusters of items shows that we have been successful in measuring attitudes in certain areas. However, the important question is, do abusers and nonabusers differ significantly in the ways in which they answer the questions in each cluster? Cluster scores of abusers and nonabusers were compared, using the student t test.

As a group, the abusers saw themselves as significantly less close to others, had higher expectations of their children and had poorer relationships with their own mothers than did the non-abusive matched controls. There was no significant difference in the degree to which these two groups admitted to being made anxious and upset by the behavior of their children. This lack of significance is mainly due to the fact that there were two very disparate types of abusers, one type readily admitting that they were easily upset by their children and the other denying it so strongly that the average of these two types made the overall abusive group average similar to the normal average response. This finding illustrates the difficulty of predicting from significant group differences whether *any given individual* is likely to be an abuser. Statistically significant differences based on group averages tell little about classifying any given individual unless the differences are great and the group variances are small.

Fortunately for our efforts to solve the individual prediction problem, the Tryon-Bailey system has available a component which calculates the score for every individual on each separate cluster. It then groups together those persons who have similar patterns of test item cluster scores. In this step we are forming clusters of *persons,* where each cluster represents a personality type.

The ideal solution would give two clusters of persons or personality types, one containing all the abusers and another containing all the nonabusers. This ideal would occur only if *all* abusers were homogeneous and *all* nonabusers were homogeneous with respect to the attitudes that have been measured. This indeed is not the case, as already has been pointed out.

Both the imperfections of the instrument and the diversity of our subjects' responses are illustrated by the fact that in the second study, five different personality types, instead of the ideal two, were found. Out of the five personality types, two types of nonabusers and three types of abusers appeared. One type of nonabuser appeared to have certain neurotic problems of a kind which might need treatment but would not classify him as a potential abuser. The other appeared to be what we would call a "well-adjusted" nonabuser, i.e., "normal" personality type.

The three types of abusers appeared to be: A pure type which fits exactly the prediction which psychiatrists have made from their studies, and two types who deny that they have abuser attitudes in *some but not all* of the crucial prediction areas.

This finding seems to indicate that if enough questions are asked in enough areas, an abuser will give a sufficiently abnormal pattern of responses to be identified. This second questionnaire did not do a sufficiently good job of identifying known abusers. The resulting scores misidentified two abusers (7 percent) as neurotic type nonabusers and six nonabusers (20 percent) as "denying" abusers. This is a higher percentage of failure to properly identify individuals than is acceptable. It is significant that no abuser had a normal nonabuser profile and no nonabuser had a pure type abuser profile.

SPECULATIONS ON CONTINUED RESEARCH

As the search for a valid and reliable prediction instrument continues, certain speculations might be made about the progress that appears to be on the horizon.

Figure 1 shows the type of profile chart which might be developed and used to identify a given individual as a potential abuser. Average cluster scores on each of our

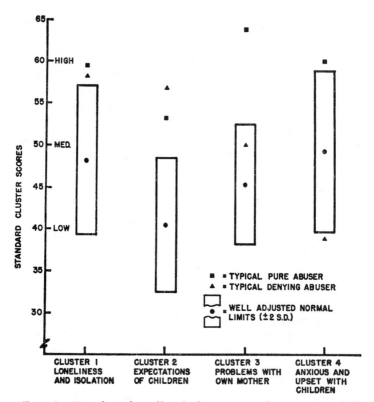

Fig. 1. Hypothetical profile of cluster scores discriminating child abusers from normals, showing average item cluster scores for three personality types.

four clusters for our well-adjusted normal group are given. The unbroken lines surrounding each cluster score define the area in which 96 percent of the normal scores (2 standard deviations) on this cluster fall. Also plotted are hypothetical cluster scores which a typical pure abuser* and a typical denying abuser might have if they answered our question-

*For graphing purposes, the "typical pure abuser" would have the mean score on each cluster actually found in Study 2 for this personality type.

naire. As can be seen from the graph, the typical pure abuser has all four of his cluster scores outside normal limits, and the typical denying abuser has three of his scores outside these limits. Comparing any person's score profile to the normal profile and its reasonable limits (i.e., 2 standard deviations from the mean) would show if this person's cluster scores were outside the normal limits. One might then say that the occurrence of 2 or more deviant scores would mean this parent or future parent should have a more intensive screening interview.

It should be emphasized that, at present, this graph is only a hypothetical picture of how the profiles for a normal type and an abusive type might differ, based upon what is still an experimental questionnaire, one which is still too likely to misidentify an individual.

Early in 1971, a third study was begun on another revision of the questionnaire. The new instrument contains 74 items and uses the same scale of 7 points from "strongly agree" to "strongly disagree." Based on the results of the second questionnaire, all the items which clustered in the analysis have been retained, and new questions have been added in areas which did not form cluster. These additions were based on promising Chi-Square results and further clinical experience. Nondiscriminating items were eliminated, although some efforts were made to change the wording of items which, on the basis of face validity, ought to discriminate between the groups. Following Study 3, a validation study on this finalized form of the questionnaire will be conducted. Attitude areas included in the questionnaire for Study 3 which may differentiate abusers from nonabusers are: Feelings of isolation, reaction to criticism, feelings toward the spouse, parental treatment, expectations of children, attitudes toward punishment, and feelings of being nervous, upset and potentially losing control of behavior. Only further data analyses will indicate if we have been successful in this extraordinarily difficult task of constructing a valid and reliable questionnaire which will be useful in identifying parents who have the potential to abuse their small children.

REFERENCES

1. Sears, Robert, Maccoby, E., and Levin, H.: Patterns of Child Rearing. New York, Harper, 1957.
2. Tryon, R. C., and Bailey, D. E.: Cluster Analysis. New York, McGraw Hill, 1970.

APPENDIX B

EDITORIAL NOTE

The development of a "Center for the Study of Abused and Neglected Children" has been the dream of many. Whether or not this will ever become a reality will depend upon the generosity of a federal agency or some philanthropic individual or group.

The Center is described here in some detail in the hope that this will stimulate someone or some group to implement the idea and develop a better understanding of the total abnormal rearing process, thereby helping more abused and neglected children and their families.

The Center for the Study of Abused and Neglected Children

RAY E. HELFER, M.D.

THE AMOUNT of knowledge that is currently available to assist in the development of methods to either prevent or treat the problems of abnormal rearing of children is indeed small. The work that has been done to date in this area is little compared to what must be accomplished in the future. Only through intensive investigation and research of the presenting symptoms (i.e., physical abuse, neglect, emotional "battering" etc.) of the abnormal rearing spectrum, can we progress forward with our limited but increasing understanding.

The pressing needs for service placed upon the child welfare agencies in the country demand that their major effort and responsibility continue to be to serve those families in need, in the best manner available.* The need for service must not cloud a need for better understanding that's equally as great. The support and development of research into the basic causes of these abnormal rearing processes, and innovative therapeutic methods of dealing with them, must continue. The current, somewhat archaic (and certainly overtaxed) methods of delivering "service" can no longer be expected to meet the demands.

With this commitment a group of well-known experts in the problems of child abuse and neglect met in Denver in

*Currently some large metropolitan areas (N.Y.C.) have over 300 cases of suspected abuse reported per million population. Chicago can only service 40 percent to 50 percent of those families who are reported.

March of 1969.* The specific task to which the group addressed itself was: *To develop the criteria and recommendations for the establishment of Centers for the study of abused and neglected children in large metropolitan areas.* The desire of the participants was to develop specific recommendations which would assist any group or agency in the densely populated areas in establishing a Center which dealt specifically with the problems of these children and their families.

DEFINITION AND SCOPE OF THE CENTER

For the purpose of this discussion the following definition of child abuse and neglect was developed: *The neglected or abused child is any child whose health and development are impaired or endangered for reasons of physical assault or a failure to provide adequate care and protection.*

The overall objective of any program, which has as its goal the study of abused and neglected children, would be to develop methods and gain understanding which in some way would decrease the incidence of child abuse and neglect within the specific geographic area in which the program was located.

Several more specific objectives might include:

1. To improve upon the methods of early identification of the abused and neglected child.

2. To develop treatment programs which would strengthen the family unit from which these children come and to develop criteria to identify those families who can best be strengthened.

3. To promote improved community attitudes toward the handling of these children and their families.

4. To provide a method of developing coordinated community services.

*This seminar was sponsored, in part, by the Children's Bureau, Grant No. Project 218.

5. To assist in the improvement of physicians' and other professionals' attitudes in regard to child abuse.

6. To develop an ongoing research and evaluation program which will evaluate current and innovative ways of caring for the abused and neglected child as well as developing and evaluating innovative methods of providing care.

7. To assist the community in developing appropriate legislative and other governmental supportive action.

8. To develop training programs in every phase of providing services to abused and neglected children.

SERVICES PROVIDED TO THE COMMUNITY AND FAMILIES

The primary responsibility of such a Center is in the area of education, demonstration and research. The staff has, however, an obligation to maintain a high degree of expertise which can only be fostered through providing some degree of ongoing service to a limited number of cases. The Center should provide, or have ready access to, the following services for these cases:

1. Medical and psychiatric diagnosis.
2. Social evaluation of the home and family.
3. Legal counsel for children, parents and staff.
4. Therapeutic intervention including:
   a. Medical care for the child and his parents.
   b. Psychiatric consultations for the total family if needed.
   c. Social services including case work, group work and other services that may be needed, such as day care, homemakers, foster homes, etc.
   d. Early court involvement where indicated.
5. Long-range follow-up programs.
6. Provision for the early protection of the abused child.
7. A method by which families are kept appraised of the current status of the case.

Providing expert consultative services on a 24-hour basis to the professionals within a specific community is of primary importance in the functioning of a Center of this type. These consultations can be handled by phone, by direct personal contact, or in small groups. The professional community should feel free to request assistance at any time.

In addition to providing service to individually selected patients, the Center would accept referrals from courts, social agencies within the community and law enforcement departments. The referrals would be a two-way arrangement in that the Center would also use these community facilities in working out appropriate disposition for specific cases. The Center should serve as a liaison between agencies where this seems to be appropriate.

Finally, the Center must develop methods to encourage early referral of suspected or potential cases of child abuse or neglect to the appropriate agency. Among the people who should be especially encouraged to make referrals are physicians, nurses, school personnel, hospital administrators, court officials, social workers and, most important, the spouse of a child abuser, and the child's grandparents.

DEVELOPMENT OF TRAINING PROGRAMS

The Center would establish specialized training programs for community professionals to assist them with the problems of caring for abused and neglected children. These training programs would be geared to the individual interests and backgrounds and could be run as short-term seminars, in-service programs or extended fellowships. These professionals might include the following:

1. Police
2. Social agencies
3. States attorneys
4. Physicians
5. Private attorneys
6. Judges
7. Nurses

8. Local and state health department personnel
9. School personnel
10. Press, TV and radio personnel
11. Lay groups
12. Specialized lay therapists

RESEARCH AND EVALUATION

Members of any group considering the development of such a Center will find it helpful to ask themselves this question: "Assuming that we are funded for a three year program, what must we *do* in that period of time to demonstrate to the funding organization that the Center has accomplished its objectives?" For this evaluation to be meaningful, the emphasis must be placed on the word *DO*. Subjective feelings of success will not produce refunding or new Centers in other areas. Objective research and criteria of success will.

The Center for the Study of Abused and Neglected Children should be expected to accomplish some of the following:

1. Decrease the death rate due to child abuse and neglect within the defined geographic area.

2. Decrease the recurrence rate within the same area.

3. Demonstrate improved facilities for the immediate protection of a child when indicated.

4. Develop a long-range program for measuring the emotional status of the abused child.

5. Demonstrate an increase in the number of reports received by the appropriate agency, especially reports of early or suspected cases.

6. Demonstrate an improved communication between appropriate agencies.

7. Stimulate the creation of new community resources where indicated.

8. Measure changes in community and professional attitudes toward:

    a. The Center.

    b. The problems of child abuse and neglect.

    c. The acceptance of the abusive parent.

9. Measure what demographic and cultural factors contribute to child abuse and neglect in the area.

10. Show that existing community agencies have increased their services (and operating budgets) for children.

11. Demonstrate an increased interest and involvement on the part of lay groups, the press, radio and TV.

12. Measure the degree of awareness of the program in the community (e.g., do they know the program exists, do they know how to refer a case, etc.?).

13. Develop and test criteria for determining when children should be removed from or returned to the home.

14. Develop innovative therapy programs and measure their effectiveness.

15. Develop and test new methods of early case finding and prediction of potential abusers.

16. Compare results of care provided to children handled by the Center with those handled outside the Center.

17. Demonstrate an ability to locate and give progress reports on all cases in which the Center was involved over a long-range period.

18. Provide a 24-hour consultation service for professionals within the community.

19. Develop improved and strengthened family life in specific cases by showing:

    a. Decreased police involvement with the family.

    b. Decreased court involvement with the family.

    c. Improved job record by father.

    d. Improved school attendance by children.

    e. Improved school performance by children.

    f. Realistic budget management.

g. Increased attention to the health of both children and parents.

h. Better family planning.

i. More involvement of family with others about them.

20. Record a cost accounting of services rendered and research performed.

21. Show that existing and/or new community services are able and willing to gradually take over and pay for the services previously studied or provided by the Center.

22. Demonstrate that the product is "salable" to federal and/or state funding agencies.

23. Demonstrate that needed legislative changes have been made.

24. Record an increase in times that the courts have accepted the recommendations of the staff of the Center and community agencies on specific cases.

25. Measure the beneficial or harmful effects of separating a child from his family, and determine which method of handling cases is to be recommended.

26. Establish criteria for training of therapists.

27. Record an increased interest in these training programs.

28. Show that the "graduates" are using their knowledge in a manner for which they were trained.

29. Investigate the effect of punitive sanctions imposed upon parents who abuse their children.

STAFFING AND ORGANIZATION OF THE CENTER

The disciplines that must be included in the development of the Center for the Study of Abused and Neglected Children come from a variety of professional backgrounds. These might include administrators, pediatricians, psychiatrists, social workers, public health nurses, attorneys, law enforcement personnel, psychologists, and research and training specialists. No one discipline can provide the expertise necessary for the comprehensive services that are required.

The administrative structure, however, must be based upon the firm foundation of an existing medical center or health facility. The primary purpose of performing both research and training demands that the Center be placed within, or be closely affiliated with, a university based program. The need for strong "back-up" support can only be realized in this setting. Figure 1 depicts the recommended table of organization.

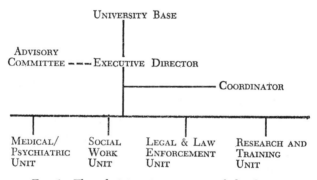

Fig. 1. The administrative structure of the Center.

The relationship of the Center to a specific community can best be depicted in the diagram provided in Figure 2. There should be close communication between all the responsible community facilities. This would be the primary responsibility of the executive director. The Center should be physically located in either a hospital, medical center, or an appropriate clinic. The reason for putting the Center in a health care facility is that the initial problems of abused and neglected children require highly integrated medical services.

FUNDING

Total operational costs can not be given because they are dependent on so many variables—size of Center, number of

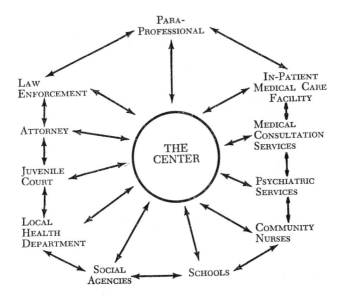

Fig. 2. The Center and the community.

staff on Center payroll versus community agency payroll, degree of service and/or research it is to perform, and so on. It certainly would be feasible for a community to begin with a full- or part-time coordinator, part-time pediatrician and psychiatrist, and a social worker, with a total budget around $10,000 to $15,000 a year. On the other hand, a large Center may be contemplated with a budget as high as $250,000 per year. Local needs and funds must be the determining factors.

The funding of such a program must be of primary concern to the Center's advisory committee. Private foundations and federal, state, and local funding agencies must be approached. Even though multiple funding may provide administrative problems, this should be given serious consideration. Table 1 lists several possible sources of funding that a group or community may wish to explore.

TABLE 1. *Possible Sources of Funding*

FEDERAL

1. Maternal and Infant Care Programs (HEW)
2. Office of Economic Opportunity
3. National Institute of Mental Health (several divisions)
4. Social Security Administration
5. Vocational Rehabilitation (HEW)
6. Housing & Urban Development (Model cities)
7. Department of Labor
8. Office of Early Childhood Development (HEW)

SHORT TERM FUNDING

1. Private foundations
2. United Hospital Fund
3. Individual donor
4. Service organizations (Rotary, Lions, Kiwanis Clubs)
5. Business corporations
6. Unions

FINANCIAL CAMPAIGNS

1. Mass media (TV, telethon, etc.)
2. Rock concerts
3. Show business benefit
4. Professional fund raiser
5. Dances
6. Community organizations
7. Street fair
8. Art exhibits
9. Political clubs
10. Professional organizations

* This material was developed at the Harrison House Child Abuse Symposium subcommittee report by Dr. Theo Solomon.

CONCLUSIONS

The problems of child abuse and neglect require a multidisciplinary approach in any attempt at solution. Failure to assist these children and their families results in multiple social, physical and emotional ills of all those involved. Unless interrupted in some way, the cycle of child abuse and neglect is endless. With few exceptions, children who survive this form of rearing develop into parents who rear their children as they were reared.

Not only must this cycle be interrupted for the individual child, but new and practical ways must be found which are capable of helping the tens of thousands of children who are abused or neglected each year. The development of Centers for the Study of Child Abuse and Neglect in large metropolitan areas is proposed as one inroad into this constantly increasing problem. The Centers seem, to the participants in the Denver seminar, to be both a feasible and practical approach.

ACKNOWLEDGMENT

The writer must be considered merely as the recorder and compiler of the thoughts and contributions of every participant in the seminar. This document represents the composite efforts of every individual. It is rare to find individuals representing so many disciplines who can work together as a unified group as did these truly knowledgeable and dedicated professionals. Those who will benefit the most from their work will indeed be grateful.

The participants in this seminar were:

> James S. Apthorp, M.D.
> Pediatric Trauma Coordinator
> Los Angeles Children's Hospital
> California

> The Honorable James Delaney
> Juvenile Judge
> 17th Judicial District Court
> Brighton, Colorado

> Mrs. Kay Drews
> Former Child Abuse Coordinator
> University of Colorado Medical Center
> Denver

Miss Elizabeth Elmer
Former Director
Infant Accident Study
Children's Hospital
Pittsburgh, Pennsylvania

Chris J. Flammang
Police Science
University of Tennessee
Nashville

Ray E. Helfer, M.D.
Associate Professor
Department of Human Development
College of Human Medicine
Michigan State University
East Lansing

C. Henry Kempe, M.D.
Chairman, Department of Pediatrics
University of Colorado Medical Center
Denver

Glen Shelton Key, Director
Department of Social Work
Children's Chicago Memorial Hospital
Illinois

Miss Kathryn Koehler
Regional Medical Social Consultant
Children's Bureau
Denver, Colorado

Earl R. Peters, M. D.
Chief, Pediatric Services
Naval Hospital
San Diego, California

The Honorable Justine W. Polier
Judge, Family Court
New York City

Brandt Steele, M.D.
Department of Psychiatry
University of Colorado Medical Center
Denver

William Sylvester White
Presiding Judge
Juvenile Court of Cook County
Chicago, Illinois

Sam S. Wood
Detective, Police Department
Denver, Colorado

Bibliography

This selected bibliography is made available through the co-operation of the Children's Bureau, Medlars Survey, and the personal files of many individuals. The editors will be grateful for additional books and articles, especially those of an international value, which might be brought to our attention by readers outside the United States.

1. Material Published by the American Humane Association

Becker, Thomas T.: Child Protective Services and the Law, 24 p.
Bishop, Julia Ann, et al.: An Intensive Casework Project in Child Protective Services, 34 p.
Christy, Duane W., et al.: Innovative Approaches in Child Protective Services, 24 p.
Cohen, Morton I., et al.: Neglecting Parents, 28 p.
Cooke, Lena, et al.: Round the Clock Coverage in Child Protective Services, 20 p.
De Francis, Vincent: The Fundamentals of Child Protection, 71 p.; Child Protective Services—A National Survey, 32 p.; Protecting the Child Victim of Sex Crimes Committed by Adults, 230 p.; Child Abuse Legislation in the 1970's, 134 p.; Special Skills in Child Protective Services, 16 p.
Merrill, Edgar J., et al.: Protecting the Battered Child, 30 p.
Mulford, Robert M., et al.: Protective—Preventive Services—Are They Synonymous, 24 p.
Penner, Lewis G., et al.: The Protective Services Center, 20 p.
Philbrick, Elizabeth: Treating Parental Pathology, 18 p.
Tormes, Yvonne M.: Child Victims of Incest, 40 p.
Wald, Max: Protective Services and Emotional Neglect, 20 p.

2. The Child

Dalton, Katharina: Children's hospital admissions and mother's menstruation, British Med J 2:27, 1970.
Elmer, Elizabeth, and Gregg, G. S.: Developmental characteristics of abused children, Pediatrics 40:596-602, 1967.
Green, A. H., et al.: Reactions to the threatened loss of a child: A vulnerable child syndrome, Pediatrics 34:58-66, 1964.
Helfer, Ray E.: A plan for protection, Child Welfare 49:486-494, 1970.
Kushnick, Theodore, Pretrucha, D. M., Kushnick, J. B.: Syndrome of the abandoned small child, Clin Pediat (Phila) 9:356-361, 1970.
Milowe, Irvin D., and Lourie, Reginald S.: The child's role in the battered child syndrome, J Pediat 65:1079-1081, 1964.

Winick, Myron: Malnutrition and brain development, J Pediat 74:667-679, 1969.

Young, Leontine R.: Wednesday's Children: A Study of Child Neglect and Abuse. New York, McGraw-Hill, 1964 (195 pp.).

3. Community Agencies

Birch and Belmont: The problem of comparing home rearing vs. foster-home rearing in defective children, Pediatrics 28:956, 1961.

Brieland, D.: Protective services and child abuse, Soc Service Rev 40: 369-377, 1966.

Davoren, Elizabeth: The role of the social worker, in Helfer, R. E., and Kempe, C. H., eds.: The Battered Child, Chicago, Univ of Chic Press, 1968.

Delsordo, James D.: Protective casework for abused children, Children 10:213-218, 1963.

Foresman, Louise: Homemaker service in neglect and abuse: I. Strengthening family life, Children 12:23-25, 1965.

Kempe, C. H.: Some problems encountered by welfare departments in the management of the battered child syndrome, in Helfer, R. E., and Kempe, C. H., eds.: The Battered Child, Chicago, Univ of Chic Press, 1968.

Miller, M. B.: Community action and child abuse, Nurs Outlook 17:44-46, 1969.

Silver, Larry B., Dublin, C. C., Lourie, R. S.: Community agencies: Actions, non-actions and interactions in cases of child abuse, Soc Casework, in press.

Stringer, Elizabeth A.: Homemaker service in neglect and abuse: II. A tool for case evaluation, Children 12:26-29, 1965.

4. The Doctor/Dentist

DeWees, P. E.: The role of the family doctor in the social problem of child abuse: Comments on new legislation affecting the legal immunity of physicians, North Carolina Med J 27:385-388, 1966.

Finberg, Laurence: A pediatrician's view of the abused child, Child Welfare 44:41-43, Jan., 1965.

Helfer, R. E.: The responsibility and role of the physician, in Helfer, R. E., and Kempe, C. H., eds.: The Battered Child, Chicago, Univ of Chic Press, 1968.

Joyner, E. N.: M.D. responsibility for the protection of the battered child, New York J Med 27:59-61, 1971.

Lux, B.: A dentist's eye-view of delinquency, Dent News 6:7, 1969.

Shaw, Anthony: The surgeon and the battered child. Surg Gynec Obstet 119:355, 1964.

5. Follow-up Studies

Johnson, Betty, and Morse, Harold A.: Injured children and their parents, Children 15:147-152, 1968.

Morse, Carol W., Sahler, O. J. Z., Friedman, S. B.: A three-year follow-up study of abused and neglected children, Amer J Dis Child *120*: 439-446, 1970.

Terr, Lenore C., and Watson, Andrew: The battered child rebrutalized: Ten cases of medical-legal confusion, Amer J Psychiat *124*:1432-1439, 1968.

6. General Reviews

Allen, Hugh D., *et al.*: The battered child syndrome, Minn Med: *I. Medical Aspects* 51:(12)1793-1799, Dec. 1968; *II. Social and Psychiatric Aspects* 52:155-156, Jan., 1969; *III. Legal Aspects* 52:345-347, 1969; *IV. Summary* 52:539-540, 1969.

Bain, Katherine, *et al.*: Child abuse and injury, Milit Med *130*:747-762, 1965.

Birrell, R. G., *et al.*: The "maltreatment syndrome" in children, Med J Aust 2:1134-1138, 1966.

Elmer, Elizabeth, *et al.*: Children in Jeopardy: A Study of Abused Minors and Their Families. Pittsburgh, Univ of Pittsburgh Press, 1967.

Erwin, Donald T.: The battered child syndrome, Medicoleg Bull *130*:1-10, 1964.

Fleming, G. M.: Cruelty to children, Brit Med J 2:421-422, 1967.

Fontana, Vincent J.: The Maltreated Child: The Maltreatment Syndrome in Children, ed 2, Springfield (Ill.), Thomas, 1971.

————: The maltreatment syndrome in children, Hosp Med, March, 1971, p. 7.

Gluckman, L. K.: Cruelty to children, New Zeal Med J 67:155-159, 1968.

Gregg, G. S., and Elmer, E.: Infant injuries: Accident or abuse, Pediatrics *44*:434-439, 1969.

Heins, Marilyn: Child abuse—analysis of a current epidemic, Mich Med *68*:887-892, Sept., 1969.

Helfer, Ray E., and Kempe, C. Henry, eds.: The Battered Child, Chicago, Univ of Chic Press, 1968.

Helfer, Ray E., and Pollock, Carl: The battered child syndrome, Advances Pediat *15*:9-27, 1968.

Isaacs, Susanna, and Lond, M. B.: Physical ill-treatment of children, Lancet *1*:37-39, 1968.

Joyner, Edmund N., III: The battered child, New York J Med *26*: 383-385, 1970.

Kempe, C. H.: Pediatric implications of the battered baby syndrome, Arch Dis Child *46*:28, 1971.

Kempe, C. Henry, *et al.*: The battered child syndrome, JAMA *181*:17-24, 1962.

Nomura, F. M.: The battered child "syndrome," a review, Hawaii Med J *25*:387-394, 1966.

Paulson, Morris J., and Blake, Phillip: The abused, battered, and maltreated child: A review, Trauma 9:3, 1967.

Silver, Larry B.: Child abuse syndrome: A review, Med Times 96:
    803-820, 1968.
Simons, B., Downs, E. F., and Hurster, M. M.: Child abuse:
    Epidemiologic study of medically reported cases, New York
    J Med 66:2783-2788, 1966.
Smith, Austin E.: The beaten child, Hygeia 22:386, 1944.
Storey, Bruce: The battered child, Med J Aust 2:789-791, 1964.
Zalba, S. R.: The abused child, Soc Work: I. A Survey of the
    Problems 11:3-16, 1966; II. A Typology for Classification
    and Treatment 12:70-79, 1967.

7. History of Child Abuse

Allen, Anne, and Morton, Arthur: This Is Your Child: The Story
    of the National Society for the Prevention of Cruelty to
    Children. London, Routledge and K. Paul, Ltd., 1961.
Radbill, S. X.: A history of child abuse and infanticide, in Helfer,
    R. E., and Kempe. C. H., eds.: The Battered Child, Chicago,
    Univ of Chic Press, 1968.

8. The Hospital

Birrell, R. G., and Birrell, J. H. W.: The maltreatment syndrome in
    children: A hospital survey, Med J Aust 2:1023-1029, 1968.
Elmer, Elizabeth: Abused young children seen in hospitals, Soc
    Work 5:98-102, 1960.
Holter, Joan C., and Friedman, Stanford: Early case finding in
    the emergency department, Pediatrics 42:128-138, 1968.
Kempe, C. Henry: The battered child and the hospital, Hosp
    Practice, Oct., 1969, p. 44.
Rowe, Daniel S., et al.: A hospital program for the detection and
    registration of abused and neglected children, New Eng J Med
    282:950-952, 1970.

9. Law/Police/Registry

Cheney, Kimberly B.: Safeguarding legal rights in providing pro-
    tective services, Children 13:86-92, 1966.
Curran, W. J.: The revolution in American criminal law: Its
    significance for psychiatric diagnosis and treatment, Amer J
    Public Health 58:2209-2216, 1968.
De Francis, Vincent: The battered child—A role for the juvenile
    court, the legislature and the child welfare agency, Juvenile
    Court Judges J 14:2, 1963.
Driscoll, Paul: Child Abuse Legal Aspects of the Physician's Duty,
    Trial and Tort Trends of 1967, p. 395.
Flammang, Christopher: The Police and the Underprotected Child,
    Springfield (Ill.), Thomas, 1971.
Franklin, Lee R.: An exception to use of the physician-patient
    privilege in child abuse cases, Univ of Detroit Law J 42:88-
    94, 1964.

Gregg, Grace S.: Physician, child-abuse reporting laws, and injured child; psychosocial anatomy of childhood trauma, Clin Pediat (Phila) 7:720-725, 1968.

Ireland, W. H.: A registry on child abuse, Children 13:113-115, 1966.

McCoid, Allan H.: The battered child and other assaults upon the family, Minn Law Rev 50:1-58, 1965.

Myren, Richard A., and Swanson, Lynn D.: Police Work with Children, Children's Bureau, Welfare Administration, U.S. Department of HEW, Government Printing Office, Washington, D.C., 1962.

Paull, D., Laurena, R. J., and Schimel, B.: A new approach to reporting child abuse, Hospitals 41:62-64, 1967.

Paulsen, Monrad G., Parker, Graham, Adelman, Lynn: Child abuse reporting laws—some legislative history, George Washington Law Rev 34:482-506, 1966.

Paulsen, Monrad G.: The law and abused children, in Helfer, R. E., and Kempe, C. H., eds.: The Battered Child, Chicago, Univ of Chic Press, 1968.

————: Legal protections against child abuse, Children 13:42-48, 1966.

————: The legal framework for child protection, Columbia Law Rev 66: 679-717, 1966.

————: Child abuse reporting laws: The shape of the legislation, Columbia Law Rev 67:1-49, 1967.

Reinhart, John B., et al.: The abused child: Mandatory reporting legislation, JAMA 188:358-362, 1964.

Russell, D. H.: Law, medicine and minors—IV, New Eng J Med 279:31-32, 1968.

Silver, Larry B., Barton, W., and Dublin, C. C.: Child abuse laws—are they enough? JAMA 199:65-68, 1967.

Simons, Betty, et al.: Child Abuse: A Perspective on Legislation in Five Middle-Atlantic States, and a Survey of Reported Cases in New York City, Columbia University School of Public Health and Administrative Medicine, New York, February, 1966.

Swanson, Lynn D.: Role of the police in the protection of children from neglect and abuse, Fed Probation 25:43-48, 1961.

10. The Nurse

Fulk, Delores Lensby: The battered child, Nurs Forum 3:10-26, 1964.

Golub, S.: The battered child: What the nurse can do. RN 31:42 45 Passim, 1968.

Hiller, R. B.: The Battered child—a health visitor's point of view, Nurs Times 65:1265-1266, 1969.

Hopkins, Joan: The nurse and the abused child, Nurs Clinics of North America, vol. 5, Dec., 1970.

Johnson, M.: Symposium: The nursing responsibilities in the care of the battered child, Clin Proc Child Hosp DC 24:352-353, 1968.

11. Pathology

Adelson, L.: Slaughter of the innocents—a study of forty-six homicides in which the victims were children, New Eng J Med 264:1345-1349, 1961.

Myers, S. A.: The child slayer. A 25-year survey of homicides involving preadolescent victims. Arch Gen Psychiat (Chicago) 17:211-213, 1967.

Myers, Steven A.: Maternal filicide, Amer J Dis Child 120:534, 1970.

Weston J. T.: The pathology of child abuse, in Helfer, R. E., and Kempe, C. H., eds.: The Battered Child, Chicago, Univ of Chic Press, 1968.

12. Psychodynamics

Cohen, M. I., et al.: Psychologic aspects of the maltreatment syndrome of childhood, J Pediat 69:279, 1966.

Doxiadis, Spyros: Mothering and Frederick II, Clin Pediat (Phila) 9:565, 1970.

Elmer, Elizabeth: Fifty Family Study: A Study of Abused and Neglected Children and Their Families. University of Pittsburgh School of Medicine, Pittsburgh, Pennsylvania, June. 1965.

Flynn, William R.: Frontier justice: A contribution to the theory of child battery. Amer J Psychiat 127:375-379, 1970.

Haward, L. R.: Some psychological aspects of pregnancy. Midwives Chronicle 83:199-200, 1969.

Jenkins, Richard L.: The psychopathic or antisocial personality. J Nerv Ment Dis 131:318-334, 1960.

Melnick, B., and Hurley, H. B., Jr.: Distinctive personality attributes of child-abusing mothers. J Consult Clin Psychol 33:746-749, 1969.

Morris, Marian G., and Gould, Robert W.: Role reversal: A necessary concept in dealing with the "battered child syndrome." Amer J Orthopsychiat 33:298-299, 1963.

Reinhart, J. B., and Elmer, E.: Love of children—a myth. Clin Pediat (Phila) 7:703-705, 1968.

Resnick, P. J.: Child murder by parents: A psychiatric review of filicide. Amer J Psychiat 126:325-334, 1969.

Silver, Larry B.: The psychological aspects of the battered child and his parents. Clin Proc Child Hosp DC 24:355-364, 1968.

Silver, Larry B., Dublin, C. C., Lourie, R. S.: Does violence breed violence. Contributions from a study of the child abuse syndrome. Amer J Psychiat 126:404-407, 1969.

Steele, B. F.: Parental abuse of infants and small children, in Anthony E. J., and Benedik, T., eds.: Parenthood: Its Psychology and Psychopathology, Boston, Little, 1970.

Steele, B. F., and Pollock, C. B.: A psychiatric study of parents who abuse infants and small children, *in* Helfer, R. E., and Kempe, C. H., eds.: The Battered Child, Chicago, Univ of Chic Press, 1968.

Wasserman, Sidney: The abused parent of the abused child. Children *14*:175-179, 1967.

13. Radiology

Baker, D. H., and Berdon, W. E.: Special trauma problems in children. Radiol Clin N Amer 4:289-305, 1966.

Barmeyer, G. H., Anderson, L. R., and Cox, W. B.: Traumatic periostitis in young children, J Pediat 38:184-190, 1951.

Caffey, John: Multiple fractures in the long bones of infants suffering from chronic subdural hematoma. Amer J Roentgen *56*: 163-173, 1946.

————: Traumatic lesions in growing bones other than fractures and dislocations—clinical and radiological features; The MacKenzie Davidson Memorial Lecture. Brit J Radiol *30*:225-238, 1957.

Griffiths, D. L., and Moynihan, F. J.: Multiple epiphysial injuries in babies (battered baby syndrome). Brit Med J 4:1558-1561, 1963.

Gwinn, John L., Lewin, Kenneth W., and Peterson, Herbert G.: Roentgenographic manifestations of unsuspected trauma in infancy. JAMA *176*:926-929, 1961.

Kringe, H. N.: The abused child complex and its characteristic x-ray findings. South African Med J *40*:490-493, 1966.

Rowe, N. L.: Fractures of the facial skeleton in children. J Oral Surg *26*:505-515, 1968.

Shopfner, Charles E.: Periosteal bone growth in normal infants. Amer J Roentgen 97:154-163, 1966.

Silverman, F. N.: The roentgen manifestations of unrecognized skeletal trauma in infants. Amer J Roentgen 69:413-427, 1953.

————: Radiologic aspects of the battered child syndrome, *in* Helfer, R. E., and Kempe, C. H., eds.: The Battered Child, Chicago, Univ of Chic Press, 1968.

14. The School

Gil, David G.: What schools can do about child abuse. Amer Educ 5:2-4, 1969.

Murdock, George C.: The abused child and the school system. Amer J Public Health *60*:105-109, 1970.

15. Signs and Symptoms

Bakwin, Harry: Multiple skeletal lesions in young children due to trauma. J Pediat *49*:7-16, 1956.

Bhattacharya, A. K.: Multiple fractures. Bull Calcutta Sch Trop Med *14*:111-112, 1966.

Caffey, John: Significance of the history in the diagnosis of traumatic injury to children. J Pediat *67*:1008-1014, 1965.

Dine, Mark S.: Tranquilizer poisoning: An example of child abuse.
    Pediatrics 36:782-785, 1965.
Eisenstein, Elliot M., Delta, Basil G., and Clifford, John H.:
    Jejunal hematoma: An unusual manifestation of the battered
    child syndrome. Clin Pediat (Phila) 4:436-440, 1965.
Elmer, Elizabeth: Identification of abused children. Children 10:
    180-184, 1963.
Friedman, Morris: Traumatic periostitis in infants and children.
    JAMA 166:1840-1845, 1958.
Gillespie, R. W.: The battered child syndrome: Thermal and
    caustic manifestations. J Trauma 5:523-524, 1965.
Green, Arthur H.: Self-destructive behavior in physically abused
    schizophrenic children. Arch Gen Psychiat (Chicago) 19:
    171-179, 1968.
Gregg, G. S., and Elmer, E.: Infant injuries: Accident or abuse?
    Pediatrics 44:434-439, 1969.
Hamlin, Hannibal: Subgaleal hematoma caused by hair-pull
    (Letter). JAMA 204:339, 1968.
Hawkes, C. D.: Craniocerebral trauma in infancy and childhood.
    Clin Neurosurg 11:66-75, 1964.
Kiffney, G. T.: The eye of the battered child. Arch Ophthal
    (Chicago) 72:231, 1964.
Kim, Taek, Jenkins, Melvin E.: Pseudocyst of the pancreas as a
    manifestation of the battered child syndrome. Report of a
    case. Med Ann DC 36:664-666, 1967.
Koel, B. S.: Failure to thrive and fatal injury as a continuum.
    Amer J Dis Child 118:565-567, 1969.
Kunstadter, R. H., et al.: The battered child and the celiac syn-
    drome. Illinois Med J 132:267-272, 1967.
McCort, James, et al.: Visceral injuries in battered children.
    Radiology 82:424-428, 1964.
McHenry, Thomas, Girdany, Bertram R., and Elmer, Elizabeth:
    Unsuspected trauma with multiple skeletal injuries during
    infancy and childhood. Pediatrics 31:903-908, 1963.
Moyles, P. D.: Subdural effusions in infants. Canad Med Ass J
    100:231-234, 1969.
Nelson, G. D., and Paletta, F. X.: Burns in children. Surg Gynec
    Obstet 128:518-522, 1969.
Pickel, S., Anderson, C., and Holliday, M. A.: Thirsting and hyper-
    natremic dehydration—a form of child abuse. Pediatrics 45:
    54-59, 1970.
Polomeque, F. E., et al.: "Battered child" syndrome: Unusual
    dermatological manifestation. Arch Derm (Chicago) 90:326-
    327, 1964.
Silver, Larry B., Dublin, C. C., and Lourie, R. S.: Child abuse
    syndrome: The "gray areas" in establishing a diagnosis.
    Pediatrics 44:594-600, 1969.
Simpson, J. S.: Self-mutilation by 13-year-old girl. Pediatrics 45:
    1008, 1970.

Sussman, S. J.: Skin manifestations of the battered-child syndrome. J Pediat 72:99, 1968.

Swischuk, L. E.: Spine and spinal cord trauma in the battered child syndrome. Radiology 92:733-738, 1969.

Tank, E. S., Eraklis, A. J., and Gross, R. E.: Blunt abdominal trauma in infancy and childhood. J Trauma 8:439-448, 1968.

Teng, Ching Tseng, Singleton, Edward B., and Daeschner, C. W., Jr.: Skeletal injuries of the battered child. Amer J Orthop Surg 6:202-207, 1964.

Till, K.: Subdural haematoma and effusion in infancy. Brit Med J 3:804, 1968.

Touloukian, R. J.: Abdominal visceral injuries in battered children. Pediatrics 42:642-646, 1968.

Wison, J. C., Jr.: Fractures and dislocations in childhood. Pediat Clin N Amer 14:659-682, 1967.

Woolley, Paul V., Jr., and Evans, W. A., Jr.: Significance of skeletal lesions in infants resembling those of traumatic origin. JAMA 158:539-543, 1955.

16. Treatment/Prevention

Boardman, Helen E.: A project to rescue children from inflicted injuries. Soc Work 7:43-51, 1962.

Feinstein, Howard N., et al.: Group therapy for mothers with infanticidal impulses. Amer J Psychiat 120:882-886, 1964.

Holter, J. C., et al.: Principles of management in child abuse cases. Amer J. Orthopsychiat 38:127-136, 1968.

Housden, Leslie George: The Prevention of Cruelty to Children. New York, Philosophical Library, Inc., 1955, 406 pp.

Jacobziner, Harold: Rescuing the battered child. Amer J Nurs 64: 92-97, 1964.

Jenkins, Richard L.: Interrupting the family cycle of violence. J Iowa Med Soc 70:85, 1970.

Pollock, C. B.: Early case finding as a means of prevention of child abuse, in Helfer, Ray E., and Kempe, C. Henry, eds.: The Battered Child, Chicago, Univ of Chic Press, 1968.

Rall, Mary E.: The Casework Process in Work with the Child and the Family in the Child's Own Home. National Conference of Social Work, Casework Papers, 1954, pp. 31-43, 1955.

Schulman, I. L.: On the management of the irate parent. J Pediat 77:338-340, 1970.

Shaw, Anthony: How to help the battered child. RISS 6:71-104, 1963.

Index

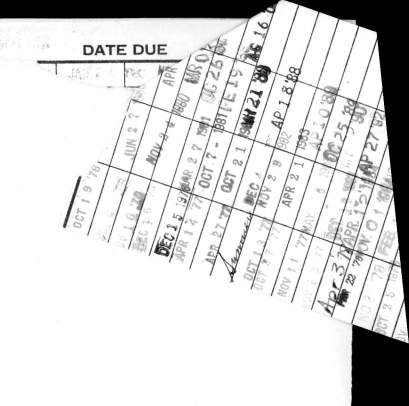